# HOLLYWOOD AUTEUR

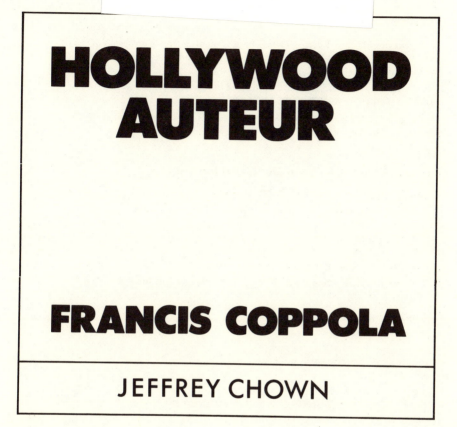

# HOLLYWOOD AUTEUR

## FRANCIS COPPOLA

### JEFFREY CHOWN

PRAEGER

New York
Westport, Connecticut
London

**Copyright Acknowledgments**

Excerpts from Marjorie Rosen, "Francis Ford Coppola," *Film Comment*, Vol. 10 (July/August, 1974), pp. 43–49 reprinted with permission. Copyright © 1974 by the Film Society of Lincoln Center.

Quotes from Francis Ford Coppola reproduced by Special Permission of *PLAYBOY* Magazine. Copyright © 1975 by PLAYBOY.

Quotes from David Thomson and Lucy Gray, "Idols of the King," *Film Comment*, (September/October, 1983), pp. 64–75. Reprinted with permission.

**Library of Congress Cataloging-in-Publication Data**

Chown, Jeffrey.
    Hollywood auteur : Francis Coppola / Jeffrey Chown.
      p.     cm.
    Bibliography: p.
    Includes index.
    ISBN 0–275–92910–8 (alk. paper)
    1. Coppola, Francis Ford, 1939–   —Criticism and interpretation.
I. Title.

PN1998.3.C67C48   1988
791.43'0233'0924—dc19                     87–30535

Copyright © 1988 by Jeffrey Chown

Library of Congress Catalog Card Number: 87–30535
ISBN: 0–275–92910–8

First published in 1988

Praeger Publishers, One Madison Avenue, New York, NY 10010
A division of Greenwood Press, Inc.

Printed in the United States of America

∞

The paper used in this book complies with the Permanent Paper Standard issued by the National Information Standards Organization (Z39.48—1984).

10  9  8  7  6  5  4  3  2  1

# Contents

# Acknowledgments

First and foremost, I would like to thank my family for their patience during the long process of writing this book, my wife Stephanie, and my children Patrick and Brianna.

A number of people read and commented on my manuscript through its many stages of evolution. In particular, I would like to thank Gerald Mast, Herbert Eagle, and Diane Kirkpatrick for their close attention and constructive criticism. Additionally, Frank Beaver, William Alexander, Daniel Fleming, Diane Carson, Farrel Corcoran, Martha Cooper, Robert Self, James Monaco, Anthony LaRocca, Jr., and Alison Bricken provided helpful advice on specific aspects of the writing. Many of my students at Northern Illinois University read portions and gave feedback; in particular I would like to thank Matt Grey, Rima Wright, and Torrey Lott. It seems as if I have used a legion of typists and word processing personnel: thank you to Gloria Bennish, Janet Chown, Julie Swatzell, Debbie Riggs, Crystal, Amber and Helen Satterlee especially. I'd also like to thank two grandmothers for their northwoods hideaways, where I completed several chapters: Hazel Krempel and Sada Blain. Important friends who empathized with me were: Joanna Rapf, Steve Hu, John Kelly, Robert Miller, Arthur Doederlein, Robert Denton, Lois Self, Mary Corcoran, and of course my many relatives. Institutionally, I would like to thank the Northern Illinois University and University of Michigan libraries for space and support services, and the Library of Congress Motion Picture Division for its viewing facilities.

# 1
## *What's in a Name?*

### Introduction

Francis Coppola's profound impact on contemporary American film has been multi-faceted. Notably, he directed some of the most critically acclaimed and influential films of the 1970s: *The Godfather* (1972), *The Conversation* (1974), *Godfather II* (1974), and *Apocalypse Now* (1979). With the exception of *The Conversation*, these were large scale commercial successes as well. However, the last several years have seen his notoriety as a producer/mogul/gambler eclipse his reputation as a director. His self-styled brand of brinksmanship, evident in his personal financing of *Apocalypse Now* and *One from the Heart* and his ownership and loss of the Hollywood General Studios, has made him a media celebrity of the first order. At the same time, Coppola was instrumental, with less flamboyancy and media-hype, in shepherding original American talents such as George Lucas, John Milius, Carroll Ballard, and Walter Murch into prominence; in making Abel Gance's *Napoleon* an American film event of 1981; and in fostering in the United States the work of such foreign directors as Wim Wenders, Jean-Luc Godard, Hans-Jurgen Syberberg, and Akira Kurosawa. Nor can Coppola's exemplary work as a screenwriter be disregarded. His conception of the title character in *Patton* (1970) brought two halves of a split society together in movie theatres to marvel at the relevance of a World War II general to the turmoil of the Vietnam era; his original screenplay for *The Conversation* was a timely examination of the surveillance community so prominent in the Watergate scandal. Along with all this creative work and patronage, Coppola has also set his sights on heralding the new video technology that he promises will revolutionize traditional Hollywood production methods.

Perhaps more pervasive and significant is the example Coppola has set in epitomizing the film director as superstar: the view that it is film directors, rather than novelists, journalists, or politicians, who have the firmest grip on the pulse of America's consciousness with an art form that can enthrall, mesmerize, inform, and influence the mass audience in a manner no other medium can approach. The reasons for Coppola's preeminence in what Diane Jacobs has called the "Hollywood Renaissance," or the rise of a generation of film school-trained directors, are not easily pinpointed. Although at one time Coppola's *The Godfather* stood as the all-time box office champion, other films—especially those of George Lucas and Steven Spielberg—have since surpassed that record. Other directors have demonstrated more technical mastery, and lesser known directors may have treated more profound subject matter than has Coppola. What makes Coppola stand out, however, is a keen and at times tragic sense of potential unachieved in the American cinema, the failure of both the system and its practitioners. Throughout his career, even as he has been a spokesperson for less restricted creativity in Hollywood films, his own films have grappled with the challenge of creating something original and unformulaic, sometimes successfully, sometimes unsuccessfully. In a statement that typifies his long-standing adversarial position toward his Hollywood employers, a young Coppola said: "You can't just shake your fist at the establishment and put them down for not giving you a chance. You have to beat them down and take money from them . . . you have to set your sights and be unscrupulous—in an intelligent way. You have to practice what might be called a 'creative compromise.' "[1]

That brand of "creative compromise," and, of course, the journalists' attention to it, had by 1974 vaulted Coppola's star to full ascendancy. The phenomenal financial success of *The Godfather* in 1972 upset the orderly profit curve of the multinational Gulf & Western, owner of Paramount. Coppola followed this success with a one-two combination in 1974: *The Conversation*, a decidedly noncommercial "personal" film, and *Godfather II*, a sequel that nonetheless took chances. Critics responded favorably to Coppola's apparent ability to combine commercial success with artistic depth, hoping that he was the young messiah that would lead Hollywood out of the creative doldrums of the 1960s. Pauline Kael, writing about *Godfather II*, articulated some of the high expectations then accruing to Coppola: "The sensibility at work in this film is that of a major artist. We're not used to it: how many screen artists get the chance to work in the epic form, and who has been able to seize the power to compose a modern American epic. And who else, when he got the chance and the power, would have proceeded with the absolute conviction that he'd make the film the way it should be made? In movies, that's the inner voice of the authentic hero."[2]

Coppola's lustre as the "hero," as the leader of the film school generation then taking over Hollywood, has since been tarnished. The same Kael, in a not atypical review of *One from the Heart* (1982), called him a confectionary artist, who had been consumed by technology. Whether there is subjectivity in critics' response to Coppola the man is, of course, difficult to speculate. However, youth has given way to middle age and Coppola's personal brashness, abrasiveness, and tenacity are not endearing qualities in a bearded millionaire whose celebrity is no longer fresh. He has steadfastly refused to give the public a clone of the immensely entertaining *The Godfather*, whereas his friend and colleague George Lucas had no compunction about rehashing the *Star Wars* formula twice. For whatever reason, Coppola is no longer seen as the filmmaking arm of the counterculture, a problematic perception in the first place. The 1980s media have been almost gleeful in depicting him as a mad, eccentric mogul, who gambles millions on self-indulgent fantasies.[3] Coppola's very real accomplishments and laudable ambitions have been obscured. Amateur psychoanalysis of the director's personal motivations has pushed into the background an appreciation of one of the most interesting canons of film in the last 15 years, and moved to the foreground an obsession with the melodrama of the director's personal life.

However, the aim of this study is not to reclaim the "authentic hero" Kael spoke of in 1974, the visionary artist who now seems lost. Searching for a hero sometimes characterizes the worst excesses of the *auteur* theory. Instead, suffice it to say here that viewing Coppola as the patron saint of modern cinema obscures the very important insights into the process of filmmaking in America today that a more systematic view of Coppola's career yields. In his earlier career especially, he at times embodied some of the worst things about American film: opportunism, conventionality, studied ignorance of troubling social issues, and superficiality. This study will attempt a more balanced, objective view of Coppola's considerable originality and accomplishments by attending to his failures of vision as well as his successes. Coppola's career provides a way of thinking about Hollywood: both about how its product could be better and what its limitations to the present have been. Necessarily, much attention will center around Coppola's juggling of ends versus means; as many artistic compromises litter the road to films combining epic form with distinct vision such as *The Godfather, Godfather II, Apocalypse Now*, and *Cotton Club*, or to films with unmistakable originality such as *The Rain People, The Conversation, One from the Heart*, and *Rumble Fish*.

The compromises that made possible this remarkable body of films spring from a combination of special abilities that transcend the traditional role of film director, at least as defined in the studio era. Coppola has a producer's business acumen, a salesman's ability to pre-sell his products, a marketing expert's knack for publicity, and an executive's verve for infighting; but he was able to combine those talents with his well established screenwriting ability, rapport with and understanding of actors, and considerable technical knowledge. This unique combination is not universally admired, however. David Thomson, writing about the shifting power relationships in modern Hollywood seen in the rise of the director and the fall of the producer, muses: "The artists have gained ground by acquiring the manners and language of the traders."[4] In general, Thomson worries, the new directors are adolescent in their artistic and creative imagination, but overly sophisticated in their business prowess. Creativity, personal experience, and maturity are stunted: "On the West coast of America, pictures are still a business, and no one can survive there without devoting his energies to the acquisition of power."[5]

Perhaps because these same Hollywood power struggles are so inherently dramatic, in the early chapters of this study we find that the stories behind how Coppola got to make his early films—such as *Dementia 13*, *You're a Big Boy Now*, or *Finian's Rainbow*—are really more compelling in their demonstration of his business prowess, personal ambition, and technical knowledge than are the stories behind the rather unremarkable films themselves. Those same traits are, of course, essential to the *opportunity* to exercise artistic vision in the later masterworks. It is possible to search these early films in the manner of literary analysis for echoes of themes that preoccupy the director's later masterworks, but that would distort their essence: Coppola's early films were pawns in an ongoing chess game, expended for creative autonomy. An honest study of any Hollywood director, and Coppola especially, cannot extricate the business from the art without distortion; both must be considered together. Coppola's career illuminates the dilemma of any artist working in the Hollywood context.

Besides the financial sophistication demanded by the new Hollywood, there is the need to understand the form and mechanics of film, perhaps at the expense of understanding its subject matter, which has contributed to James Monaco's worry about "a generation of cinematic technotwirps":

It's now clear that the film-student generation—Bogdanovich, Friedkin, Lucas, Spielberg, DePalma, Scorsese, and others—had learned everything about film, and nothing about life. The result has been a cinema that is formally extraordinarily sophisticated at the same time that it is intellectually preadolescent.[6]

Coppola's name is conspicuously absent from Monaco's list. Monaco, in 1979, was sensitive to Coppola's aspirations and optimistic about Coppola's potential, dubbing him "a leader" and pronouncing: "If Coppola can find a way to turn the rewards that occasionally accrue to directors in the new freelance Hollywood system into real power and freedom, he will revolutionize the industry."[7] Sadly, that revolution has yet to come about. Although Coppola may only be at the midpoint of his career at this writing, in interviews he laments being born before his time, being an artist more suited to the vision required for the on-coming video revolution. Perhaps one of his most publicly embarrassing moments came at an Academy Awards ceremony when he declared that video technology would make the industrial revolution seem like a small town tryout and then was jeered by the Hollywood audience. His "dream" projects are indicative of these ambitions: *Megalopolis*, a study of 24 hours in New York overlaid against Catiline Rome, and *Elective Affinities*, a quartet of films based on the structure of Goethe's novel of the same name, but in substance dealing with Japan's historic relationship with the United States. Coppola envisioned the latter project as the first film shot entirely in state-of-the-art video. However, work on these "dreams" is dependent on the successful resolution of Coppola's current business woes, especially his multi-million dollar debt to Chase Manhattan Bank.[8] The creative freedom Coppola at times enjoys, even the "final cut" he now receives contractually, is more relative than it would appear.

Presently, Coppola is an artist preoccupied with both his and his generation's failings. Even as he works to pay back enormous debts, he is intent on challenging himself, experimenting, and taking risks, seemingly in a studied effort to prepare himself for some future magnum opus. Part of this preparation involves an ongoing political education and search for a personal orientation to the political/thematic sides of his films. Often films such as *Patton* or *Apocalypse Now* seem to straddle carefully the ideological fence between right and left, hawk and dove. Perhaps this position is less Machiavelian than it would seem, as in interviews Coppola seems troubled about his own self-definition. For instance, in 1974:

I've thought about this. I've never been very sophisticated politically—I've been too busy trying to make it—so now I sit back and think, "What's my opinion about this? Am I a Communist? Am I a Fascist? What am I?" And I started to make some rules about things I won't do in films anymore, and one of them is that I will never again make a violent film. I'm of the opinion that whatever you put in a movie just floats around for a long time, and if that's the case, why not make a positive film.[9]

In the same year, Coppola commented to *Playboy*: "Politically, no one knows what I am, including me."[10] These statements in themselves, however, define a position. For any serious consideration of the ideology of modern American film, "I've been too busy trying to make it" should ring in the ears. The demands for business sophistication in the practice of modern American filmmaking, noted by Thomson earlier, and the critics' perception of an essential shallowness in modern American film are not unrelated phenomena. The ideology of Hollywood has never depended on its proponents being self-aware of their function within the system. Still, the honesty that leads Coppola to the above self-confessed ambivalence does not rule out the possibility that a more ideologically sophisticated artist will emerge from the already commercially and technically sophisticated one. Coppola's self-imposed taboo on violence now reads ironically because it came on the eve of his involvement with *Apocalypse Now*. However, in the chapter on that film, we will indeed see that Coppola the individual progressed both politically and in his orientation to the depiction of violence during that film's long production process. It would seem apathy or naiveté gave way to an honest indeterminacy.

Coppola's self-questioning is also a manifestation of an intellectual curiosity and hunger for knowledge that prevents his view of the world from stagnating. His films become a series of personal challenges to whether he can formulate a perspective toward new subject matter, be it such diverse subjects as the Oklahoma teenage experience, jazz-age Harlem, or a kabuki view of Las Vegas, the grist of recent films. Critics have reacted negatively to such thematic leap-frogging, and words such as "shallow," "facile," or "self-indulgent" often crop up in the less-admiring reviews. The ticket-buying public has also become confused by the implications of "A film by Francis Coppola"; it doesn't always mean Italian weddings and gangland violence. The apparatus designed to identify films for people to pay to consume is not easily served by Coppola's brand of self-exploration.

But one of the unique facets of Coppola as an individual director is the prodigious and compulsive research he has done on the subject matter of his films, for example, the Mafia, Batista's Cuba, Vietnam, Las Vegas, Oklahoma teenagers, or jazz-age Harlem nightclubs. At times he has employed a staff of researchers and librarians working with state-of-the-art, computer-based information systems, and he routinely conducts extensive interviews with experts in the subject area of prospective films. This care and attention to factual background produced the list of "200 Things" Coppola brought to *Apocalypse Now*,[11] a selection of facts, opinions, circumstances, and other details about the Vietnam War that Coppola incorporated into the film to create its sense of realism, even with its surreal style, and its integrity, whether or not one agrees with the ultimate conclusions of the film. Modern big-budget films have taken on the quality of events; we expect a finality from them, but perhaps a film like *Apocalypse Now* is more important for the informed, disturbing questions it raises than for the polemical answers it avoids.

Coppola approaches the content of his films conscientiously, but often the content's narrative frame proves frustrating to him. His problems editing *Godfather II* and finding an ending for the narrative of *Apocalypse Now* were much publicized. He and William Kennedy reportedly went through forty drafts on *The Cotton Club* and were still tinkering with the plot as production began. Whether such practice is perfectionism, or simply frustration with creative deficiencies is difficult to say. But Coppola wrote an article for *The Washington Post* about his alienation from current Hollywood narrative filmmaking and mused:

It is true—I am more interested in technology than I am in content. This, in some circles, is the same as admitting that one is a child molester and likes it. The truth is that I am interested in a content that I cannot get at. I yearn to be able to move into a world where story and content is available to me; where my ideas connect into a pattern that could be identified as story. But I truly cannot get there. And I find it equally impossible, though I have tried, to recycle the old stories of the past as most movies do today.[12]

Perhaps Coppola's frustration is manifested in a central ambivalence toward his narrative protagonists that threatens to become modernist. Natalie of *The Rain People*, Harry Caul of *The Conversation*, Michael Corleone of *Godfather II*, Willard of *Apocalypse Now*, Hank and Frannie of *One from the Heart*, and recently, Dixie Dwyer of *The Cotton Club* are all characters with mannerisms and quirks that make them less than attractive. Classical Hollywood narratives' reliance on audience identification with the protagonist, the star persona, is breaking down with these characters. This is no better demonstrated than when *Apocalypse Now*'s Willard cold-bloodedly murders a woman halfway into the film. Empathy with the protagonist becomes problematic thereafter. Coppola recently confessed to greatly admiring *Koyaanisqatsi*, a feature-length avant garde film that he had a hand in distributing, which fell far outside the boundaries of the narrative tradition. During the brief heyday of his Zoetrope Studio, Coppola sponsored work by such narrative iconoclasts as Wim Wenders, Jean-Luc Godard, and Hans-Jurgen Syberberg. Coppola is perhaps not temperamentally suited to the films the Hollywood system would like him to make. He uses multi-million dollar films to explore areas of personal curiosity, often to financially ruinous results. He flirts with modernism and the avant garde. He flaunts his adamant refusal to make a *Godfather III*. Yet through it all he is not about to abandon the Hollywood system of filmmaking and scale back his productions to the level of, for instance, John Sayles' early low-budget features.

The tension between Coppola's personal imagination and aesthetics and the strictures of the narrative forms in which he works is often the most fascinating, and sometimes frustrating, dialectic of his career. Ultimately, Hollywood co-opts his apparent rebellion by making it seem as if there is room for Coppola's brand of "creative compromise," when in fact *Megalopolis* and *Elective Affinities* remain pipedreams (as does Stanley Kubrick's *Napolean*). *One from the Heart* has joined *Heaven's Gate* as cautionary fables about what directors should not do, a perverse illustration of William Blake's aphorism that "the road of excess leads to the palace of wisdom." Perhaps Coppola in his "failures" reinforces the Hollywood system more than in his financial successes.

In discussing Coppola's paradoxical role in the Hollywood system, we should not overlook his individual filmic sensibility, his affinity for visual irony and visual expressivity. In his intuitive grasp of the montage possibilities of juxtaposing Michael's executions with his attendance at the religious ceremony in *The Godfather*, or the vivid depiction of a psychedelic war in *Apocalypse Now*, or his employment of jazzy cutting rhythms and cinema verité in *You're a Big Boy Now*, or the simple conception of Patton standing in front of a giant American flag, Coppola is an outstanding visual film artist with unusual talent.

What Coppola's Hollywood career seems to demonstrate, however, is that his perceived independence, power, and reknown are now necessarily dependent on the ability to generate original stories and compelling visual images. He had an enormous commercial success with *The Godfather*, which allows him a measure of relative freedom in the Hollywood context, but his continuing importance and notoriety revolves around his basically adversarial disposition toward the medium known as Hollywood film. He has never fully capitulated to the system that at one point gave him tremendous financial rewards. From *You're a Big Boy Now* onward, Coppola has provided a role model for Hollywood artist/directors interested in gaining more control of their art, a role model teaching the lessons of temporary compromises for future goals, of weighing ends against means, of flamboyancy as a weapon, of reckless gambles for high stakes. Such tactics exact a personal cost. His hired-hand status on *The Cotton Club* was a case in point, as he won the right to final cut on the $47 million film through a bitter court fight with Robert Evans and the financial backers. This is not to suggest that final cut equals creative autonomy, but it is a measure of relative freedom. In this medium, realizing one's creative vision to any degree relies on talents and personal initiative that go beyond one's skill as a director or visual artist.

Thus, the following analyses of Coppola's films will have the dual perspective of assessing both the aesthetic/thematic value of his work, proceeding from his filmic sensibility, and also the production processes that shape that work and reveal so much about today's Hollywood filmmaking context. Coppola's filmmaking career is a microcosm of the larger dialectic of art and commerce in the Hollywood system. The following section will explain the methodology this study uses to address that dialectic.

## The Auteur Theory

One of the most helpful tools in organizing film history and understanding the art of film has been the *auteur* theory. It has been a controversial critical tool and may even be somewhat out of fashion of late. Even as this study considers Coppola's career and what it illuminates about the inner dynamics of Hollywood, it will also scrutinize the applicability of the auteur theory in the Hollywood context. First let us briefly review the term's evolution.

Although Eisenstein's essay "Dickens, Griffith, and the Film Today," published in 1944, is an *auteur* analysis, and much was written about individual film directors pre–1950, the term "auteur theory" came into use in the French journal *Cahiers du Cinema* in the 1950s. Francois Truffaut originally termed it "les politiques des auteurs," and the Americanization "auteur theory" obscures the fact that it is more an approach, or "attitude" as Andrew Sarris put it, than a theory.[13] Whether in critical practice or in theory, the *auteur* is thought of as the single dominant personality behind a work of film art, a creative personality whose imprint should be discernible throughout the body of his or her films. An actor, a producer, or a screenwriter could in theory be an auteur, but in practice the dominant critical bias has been in favor of the director. This bias has caused many heated objections to the auteur approach in the past thirty years, particularly from screenwriters who felt their own importance in the filmmaking process was slighted and that the director was merely an interpreter of their original vision. This specific objection is alleviated to a certain extent with Coppola, however, because he works in some capacity as a screenwriter on all his films. (It is interesting to note that until *One from the Heart*, Coppola's two worst films at the box office were the two based on his own original screenplays, written as a "challenge" to himself; *The Rain People* and *The Conversation*; the rest are adaptations and collaborations.) Still, the criterion of whether a director was active in the scripting process was never prominent in the auteur debate.

Perhaps a more fundamental objection to the auteur theory came from more recent critics who felt it overemphasized the individual at the expense of understanding the system. The auteurists shared the view that even within a highly collaborative, technical, expensive medium such as feature filmmaking, there *should* be gifted, hypersensitive, hyperexpressive individuals who could translate their inner thoughts, drives, experience, and feelings into artistic statements through sheer force of personal will. This "great man" conception of the film experience was decidedly Romantic. John Caughie speculated that this bias was a regressive step because it came "precisely at the moment at which romanticism was becoming less secure in other branches of criticism, and in a medium in which an aesthetic of individual self-expression seemed less appropriate."[14]

In terms of Coppola's career, the Romantic conception of the auteur as an individualistic artist seeking personal expression through an artistic medium is made ludicrous when we consider the following images: In *Apocalypse Now*, Coppola sifting through a parade of influences including Joseph Conrad, John Milius, and Sir James Frazer, and then determining his ending by scrutinizing audience questionnaires and computer printouts. Or, in *The Godfather*, Coppola collaborating with Mario Puzo in fashioning a script and then at the last minute calling in Robert Towne for "script doctoring." Or *You're a Big Boy Now*, wherein he shamelessly pirated narrative ideas from David Benedictus's novel, while in no way attempting to embrace the vision of the book. There is a certain absurdity to saying *any* Hollywood film is a John Ford film, or a Frank Capra film, or a Milos Forman film. The best studies of these directors pay full attention to the catalytic function of the director in relation to his many collaborators. In the many decisions a film director makes day in, day out, we can, with close attention, locate a sensibility; but we should be careful about ascribing the sort of originality and vision that we might to a Romantic poet. If we examine a body of work with the title "Francis Coppola films," we need to keep the implications of that signification in mind. Strict, formalist analysis of the films themselves as "Francis Coppola films" is misleading in terms of how the signified individual, Francis Coppola, functions as a creative agent in those texts.

Some of the other criticisms leveled at the auteur theory and its practice over the last three decades revolved around the motivations and unexamined assumptions of its major practitioners. Did the auteurists gravitate toward the flamboyant stylists whose formal excesses were easier to notice? Did the auteurists, particularly the French, write about the artistic personalities they wished to become? Perhaps the most unsettling challenge to the auteurist project came out of literary studies, in particular Roland Barthes' essay "The Death of the Author." Barthes suggested that historically, critics had created canons of texts to be examined out of their own need for self-aggrandizement. When a text is chosen that needs an explicator it increases the need for and therefore the power of the critics: "Historically, the reign of the Author has also been that of the Critic."[15]

All of which should make someone writing a book about Francis Coppola introspective. Most of Coppola's films do not scream out for explication. *The Godfather* or *The Cotton Club*, as with most Hollywood big-budget films, can be appreciated quite well without a critic leading us toward "deeper meanings." I question any notion that there is a hidden "personality" at work in Coppola's films that needs ferreting out for our added pleasure. What *is* fascinating about Coppola's work and worth further exploration are matters somewhat extrinsic to his texts and bound up in the concepts of Hollywood careerism or professionalism. For instance, if one is ideologically committed to change in the practice of Hollywood feature filmmaking, it used to be tempting to see Coppola as an iconoclastic hero, an idealistic whiz kid from UCLA, who waged war with the Philistines of the Hollywood corporate establishment in a battle for creative autonomy, whose career constituted an ongoing melodrama of commerce struggling with art. In the last ten years another fable has emerged wherein Coppola is a mad, eccentric genius, whose financial excesses are reminiscent of von Stroheim. A variation is that his ego has run amuck and that he is in need of a comeuppance. Such conflict and drama pervades the journalistic writing on Coppola; an article on his career in *Newsweek* was written as a pseudo-screenplay treatment of his life as a motion picture.[16]

Perhaps at this juncture it is appropriate to drop the pretense of third-person objectivity and admit my own fears of being perceived as a Coppola partisan when coming to the defense of the unpopular *One from the Heart* and *Rumble Fish* in Chapter 8. These are two films I feel were dreadfully misjudged by American critics because of just the sort of biases as I have discussed above. There is the worry that we develop identification, empathy, or antipathy for various film directors much as we might for any fictional character they created, that film authors have become quasi-deities for the knowledgeable much in the same fashion as movie "stars" have functioned traditionally for the general audience. Pauline Kael in the 1960s intuitively honed in on the underlying pleasure aspect of the auteurist project when she smirked that some of the auteurists in their preference for male action directors (Ray, Hawks, Fuller, Ford) were merely intellectually justifying their adolescent fantasies.[17] However, whatever truth that intuition held does not remove the fact that the seriousness of the auteurist's enterprise broke the ground for the semiotic, structuralist, marxist, feminist, and psychoanalytic approaches of the 1970s, approaches that have aided immeasurably our understanding of film. Although after the theoretical breakthroughs of the 1970s, it is difficult to go back to the suppositions and methodologies of 1960s' auteurism.

In the 1980s, the need to attain respectability for film studies is not as pressing as the question of *how* to study film. The hagiography of great directors now becomes a testing ground for new critical theories redefining the canon. For instance, in her feminist/psychoanalytic essay, "Visual Pleasure and Narrative Cinema," Laura Mulvey announced she hoped to destroy the cinephile's pleasure associated with some of the canon's misogynist directors.[18] The original auteurists' canon has become the laboratory for competing or complementing ideologies such as feminism, psychoanalysis, semiotics, structuralism, or marxism.

All of these critical approaches should more or less have an impact on a consideration of Francis Coppola's career. However, the one approach toward Coppola's films that seems to have dominated critical writing on Coppola has been the materialist approach. Considering American film as a product, and Francis Coppola as one of the leading producers, was the concern of five important books in this field (he receives chapters in all five): Diane Jacob's *Hollywood Renaissance* (1977), Michael Pye and Lynda Myles's *The Movie Brats* (1979), James Monaco's *American Film Now* (1979), Robert Kolker's *A Cinema of Loneliness* (1980), and David Thomson's *Overexposures: The Crisis in American Filmmaking* (1981).[19] These books form an interesting chronological continuum from optimism to pessimism about the state of modern American film. Jacob's book, first on the scene and written in a journalistic discovery-of-a-new-trend style, sees a new Renaissance of talent, creativity, and vision in contemporary Hollywood film. Pye and Myles follow with a marxist economic approach that yields a sober view of children of suburban American initiating a takeover and revolution in the American film industry. Monaco fuses the economic sophistication of Pye and Myles to the journalistic range of Jacobs and is somewhat dazzling in his wealth of information; Monaco portrays a generally dire but not hopeless situation wherein film art struggles under corporate domination. Kolker's study, the most academic and literary of this group, depicts five representative American auteurs (Arthur Penn, Stanley Kubrick, Coppola, Martin Scorsese, and Robert Altman) as talented artists with inescapable ideological weaknesses. Finally, David Thomson in an allusive style uniquely his own, delineates American film as a depressing, but fascinating cultural wasteland. He sees Coppola as typical of the failed potential of an art form tragically compromised by its business structure.

The weight of these five studies, however, suggests that if the auteur is an "effect of the writing," as some of the auteur-structuralists suggested, then it is a vital effect. In journalistic, nonacademic writing about film, the auteur has never been more prominent. A preoccupation with deals, power, and finance has emerged with the director at center stage. *Variety*'s reports on film grosses have become a regular feature in newspapers, often with the director's name attached. As James Goodwin notes in his appropriately titled essay "The Author is Dead, Long Live the Author": "The auteur in American cinema, from being a workhorse harnessed to the studio system (at least in the minds of some auteurist critics), has become a celebrity and selling point in the marketing of motion pictures."[20] This preoccupation with money, power, and celebrity caters well to the interests of a materialistic society, bringing to mind the sportswriters who complain about a public more fascinated with baseball players' salaries than batting averages. But it may be that this preoccupation with money has a demystifying function that in the final analysis is not at odds with the theoretical work of intellectuals such as Michel Foucault, who posed the author as a subject in need of a new critical orientation.[21]

Still, even if we rhetorically reduce Coppola from a creative artist to a "complex and variable function" in the discourse of Hollywood film, the fact remains that his recent films exhibit appreciable differences from the mainstream of the discourse. Surely from the materialist vantage point, the practice of identifying auteurs, even in the worst excesses of idolatry, was always a means of product differentiation, of seeking out excellence. However subjective that notion of excellence was, it was a consumer guide. The root of the critical backlash toward auteurism of the last few years has been in the reaction to the mystification that auteurists attached to the power of the creative individual. This, it is felt, obscured the way in which that individual functioned within the Hollywood production system. For auteurism to retain currency at this juncture, that function must be demystified. Formerly we thought that a privileged meaning came from art that could be called "truth," and that a critic's lifework could easily be spent in the pursuit of that concept. Now it seems that "truth" lies in the understanding of art's function as a commodity in a larger system of social discourses. This requires more self-awareness of the function of criticism in the creation of "auteurs," and new attention to the methodology of auteur analysis.[22]

In terms of this book as a discourse about an individual subject, Francis Coppola, this orientation has immediate methodological implications. Were I attempting to illuminate the great themes of a major artist by finding their seeds in earlier work by the author, an extensive examination of Coppola's first screenwriting efforts would be in order. In the fashion of literary analysis such a study would examine Coppola's 1963 work on *Is Paris Burning* and 1964 work on *Patton* for keys that explain Coppola's view of man in warfare in *Apocalypse Now*. It would examine the view of women and marriage in Italian culture represented by Coppola's uncredited script of *My Last Duchess*, which later became *Arriverderci Baby* (1966, Ken Hughes). It would contrast Coppola's adaptation of E. Y. Harburg's *Finian's Rainbow* and its concern with white oppression of blacks with Coppola's later *The Cotton Club*. However, such models of analysis are inappropriate because of the inordinate weight they put on thematic content, distorting the way in which an artist such as Francis Coppola operates in the discourse known as Hollywood feature film. Such models proceed from the inappropriate view that a Hollywood artist carefully refines a world view until it matures in later masterworks.

To the contrary, what was really being refined throughout Coppola's early career was his sensibility about how to operate within the norms of the Hollywood production system. Thematic concerns are largely irrelevant. The early screenwriting experiences that compellingly illuminate Coppola's later successes are the anecdotal tales of how he found work: Coppola's lying to Roger Corman about his ability to speak Russian and then writing subtitles for Russian science fiction films (pre-dating Woody Allen's *What's up Tiger Lily?*); Coppola writing the screenplay for *Pilma Pilma* on a caffeine high the night before his military draft physical and then winning the prestigious Samuel Goldwyn competition with the results; Coppola writing the script for *Dementia 13* in three nights after selling it to Corman on the basis of one scene of sex and violence; or Coppola acting as "script doctor" for about forty scripts in several years at Warner Brothers/ Seven Arts. Such anecdotes are not very important for verifying or validating authorial intention, but they illuminate a context in which the author works and continues to work.

Ignorance of this context leads to inflated claims for the artist's vision and virtuosity. A by no means unusual example of this inflation is found in the earlier mentioned *Hollywood Renaissance* by Diane Jacobs, in which she compares the characters of Robert Altman to the characters of Francis Coppola:

Coppola's characters possess an illusion of the control so conspicuously missing from Altman's universe, but guilt and/or violence are destined to thwart them. Michael Corleone constructs a complex business network founded on the inevitability of violence, and it is this violence that weds his otherwise "normal" ambitions to their fetid means. As in Hitchcock's (and Shakespeare's) cosmos, order, specious though its moral implications, must win out in the end; and Michael Corleone, like Bruno of *Strangers on a Train* and Macbeth, must suffer.[23]

Mario Puzo, no doubt, would become livid at the assertion that Michael Corleone is a "Coppola character." Though unstated, Jacobs probably works on the assumption that a director/screenwriter can shape a character from an original novel into quite another creation in a film, which is true to a certain extent with *The Godfather*. However, the aspects of Michael Corleone she refers to, the "normal ambitions" becoming corrupted by the business network he constructs (actually inherits), were certainly in the original novel and cannot be referred to accurately as a Coppola creation. Coppola himself is quite candid about not wanting this sort of ascription: "But you must always remember that I came into this whole thing as a hired director. I did not write the book; at first I didn't even like it. I am not interested in the Mafia. I do not like violence in films. I did the whole thing to get out of a big financial predicament. I look joyously forward to the day when they no longer put (*The Godfather*) in parentheses after my name."[24] Such candor has a way of leveling romantic auteurist claims about *The Godfather* as a personal expression of Coppola the man. Still, *The Godfather* is not *The Brotherhood*, a weak Mafia film alleged to have been fashioned out of Puzo's original manuscript when Paramount first bought the rights. Coppola injected a certain sensibility into the project.

Evidence of the creative decisions Coppola made during the production is not available by simply looking at the text; too many other creative agents were at play. Production accounts and interviews with the creative personnel must be considered; otherwise writing about the auteur becomes, as Robert Towne scornfully described it, "like trying to describe what happened at an orgy when you weren't there."[25] These reminiscences should not be the sole tool, as memory and ego can wreak havoc with "the facts." In addition, we should scrutinize the final film text versus the novels, original screenplays, journalistic pieces, or other sources that gave birth to the project. This should not be done on the model of literary "adaptation" studies, which seek, to determine whether the film text approximates or honors the original literary text; rather it should simply use the original source as a tool to discern the creative process. The ultimate experience of a film, as compared with an earlier printed work, is so radically different that we should not make too much of the connection; looking at the two together should merely be used to understand the choices made.

The final methodological consideration would be genre. Dudley Andrew has observed: "Genre is a shorthand for convention, for the industrial prototype every director is given by the producer. It is commonplace now to suggest that the values internal to any film result from the particular ratio it exhibits between convention and invention, between the requirements of genre and the ingenuity and world view of an auteur working with that genre."[26] Andrew argues that this definition should be at odds with a materialist analysis because: "After all, unlike most consumer items, the value of each film depends largely on its perceived distinctiveness."[27] It is quite apparent that Coppola and his contemporaries (Lucas, Spielberg, Scorsese, etc.) review past films like academicians. This has led many critics to charge that these directors merely re-cycle the cinematic past. However, genre theory has clearly established that genre only maintains its viability by constant mutation; redundancy destroys its power to convey new information.[28] Thus directors such as Coppola are obliged in maintaining a career to provide the "distinctiveness" that Andrew identified. To isolate Coppola's own particular sensibility, we need to view his work against the genres in which he works, and he, unlike most directors of the studio era, works in many: art film, gangster film, war film, musical, thriller, teen film, and various sub-genres.

In following the above methodological steps, it may seem that the individual Coppola texts are de-emphasized as the be-all, end-all objective of this inquiry. Often it will seem I attend more to matters peripheral to the texts than to the texts themselves. This is no accident, nor is it a simple concession to the celebrity power of Coppola (perhaps it is a "complex" concession). My contention is that the thematic/stylistic textual preoccupation of traditional auteur studies has distorted the way in which we understand director cinema. Only a few of us attend a film by a given director with the intention of discerning specific stylistic or thematic allusions to the director's other work, especially such allusions as are the grist of usual auteur analysis. We instead attend films by specific directors expecting a certain orientation to film. That orientation does involve, to some extent, questions of textual consistency. But the auteur theory needs to encompass other questions as well. In Francis Coppola's case, one of those other questions involves how the phrase "a film by Francis Coppola" has become a selling point, both by Coppola himself as a professional seeking to differentiate his product from the next professional, as well as by the corporations that profit by this system. These materialist questions and artistic, textual questions need not be mutually exclusive. In fact, the greatest insight should come when they are considered in tandem.[29]

## NOTES

1. Fred Baker and Ross Firestone, *Movie People* (New York: Douglas, 1972), p. 64.

2. Pauline Kael, *Reeling* (Boston: Little, Brown and Co., 1976), p. 402. The original review appeared in *The New Yorker*, December 23, 1974.

3. For example, "The Movie Man Who Plays God," by Aaron Latham, in *Life*, 4, no. 8 (August 1981), 61–74.

4. David Thomson, *Overexposures: The Crisis in American Filmmaking* (New York: Morrow, 1981), 65.

5. Thomson, p. 59.

6. James Monaco, *American Film Now* (New York: Oxford University Press, 1979), 51.

7. Monaco, p. 328.

8. The figures on this debt vary tremendously, depending on what source one reads. In October of 1986 Coppola told Gene Siskel: "At the worst (after *One from the Heart*) I was $50 million in debt. My home was part of the collateral, and I suppose I could have taken the easy way out and declared bankruptcy. But I wasn't brought up that way. So [thanks in part to cassette revenues] I worked my way back as a professional journeyman director to where I currently owe only $5 million." "Celluloid Godfather," *Chicago Tribune*, October 5, 1986, Section 13, p. 4.

9. Hal Aigner and Michael Goodwin, "The Bearded Immigrant from Tinsel Town," *City Magazine* (San Francisco), June 12–25, 1974, p. 40.

10. William Murray, "Interview: Francis Ford Coppola," *Playboy*, July 1975, p. 68.

11. G. Roy Levin, "Francis Coppola Discusses *Apocalypse Now*," *Millimeter*, 7, no. 10 (October 1979), 194.

12. Francis Ford Coppola, "The Director on Content Versus Technology," *Washington Post*, August 29, 1982, p. 3D.

13. See Francois Truffaut, "A Certain Tendency of the French Cinema," in *Movies and Methods*, Bill Nichols, ed. (Berkeley: University of California Press, 1976), 224–237.

John Caughie challenged Andrew Sarris's translation of "la politique des auteurs" into the "auteur theory" in "Teaching Through Authorship," *Screen Education*, 17 (Winter 1975/76), p. 5, pointing out that the original *Cahiers'* use of the term indicated a stance against traditional notions of aesthetic value in the French cinema at that time. Although Sarris has acknowledged that the "auteur theory" is more an attitude than a theory, Caughie pointed out it is "an insistence which he might himself admit indicates his interest as being the distribution of directors along a hierarchial scale of value, rather than the more theoretically based investigation of how precisely the director produces meaning within the film."

14. John Caughie, *Theories in Authorship* (Boston: Routledge and Kegan Paul, 1981), 11.

15. Roland Barthes, "The Death of the Author," in *Image/Music/Text* (New York: Hill and Wang, 1977), 147.

16. David Ansen, "Coppola's Apocalypse Again," *Newsweek*, February 16, 1981, pp. 79–80.

17. See her essay "Circles and Squares," in *Film Theory and Criticism*, Gerald Mast and Marshall Cohen, eds. (New York: Oxford Press, 1979), 666–79.

18. Laura Mulvey, "Visual Pleasure and Narrative Cinema," *Screen*, 16, no. 3 (Autumn 1975), 6–18.

19. Diane Jacobs, *Hollywood Renaissance* (New York: Delta, 1977); Michael Pye and Lynda Myles, *The Movie Brats* (New York: Holt, Rinehart, and Winston, 1979); James Monaco, *American Film Now* (New York: Oxford, 1979); Robert Kolker, *A*

*Cinema of Loneliness* (New York: Oxford Press, 1980); and David Thomson, *Overexposures: The Crisis in American Filmmaking*, (New York: William Morrow, 1981).

20. Goodwin, *Quarterly Review of Film Studies* (Spring 1984), 116.

21. Michel Foucault, "What is an Author?" from Caughie's *Theories of Authorship*, p. 290.

22. In an excellent article on the subject, Stephen Crofts writes: "The concept of the author-name facilitates the rethinking of critical reputations. In film-critical discourses, the author-name remains the principal mode of classifying films. It is instrumental in establishing critical reputations, maintaining them, killing them, resurrecting them. But it does not operate autonomously. Such reputations are a function also of some congruence between, on the one hand, the ideological configurations around the film(s) at the moment of its production, and on the other, the ideological configurations of the critical endeavor which, from time to time, constructs its fictions from the film(s), text(s) which will of course offer resistances to some readings, but which cannot *impose* any reading. To justify authorship by appealing to the quality of the directors it throws up is to say no more than that ideological formations do not change overnight." "Authorship and Hollywood," *Wide Angle*, 5, no. 3 (1983), 20.

23. Jacobs, p. 108.

24. Francis Ford Coppola, "Nothing is a Sure Thing," *City Magazine* (San Francisco), 7, no. 54 (December 11, 1974), 38.

25. John Brady, *The Craft of the Screenwriter* (New York: Simon and Schuster, 1981), 427.

26. Dudley Andrew, *Concepts in Film Theory* (New York: Oxford, 1984), 116.

27. Andrew, p. 117.

28. See: Herbert Eagle, "Film Genre/Genre Film: Mutual Implications," in *Film: Historical-Theoretical Speculations*, Ben Lawton and Janet Staiger, eds. (Pleasantville, NY: Redgrave, 1977).

29. John Caughie wrote: "The danger of the literary analogy implicit in the terminology of *auterusim* has always been that it places consideration of film outside consideration of its conditions of production, treating the intentionality and individuality of literary production, and the industrial and popular basis of film production as if they were one and the same thing." In: "Teaching through Authorship," *Screen Education*, 17 (Winter 1975/76), 5.

# 2

# *Learning to Crawl*

## *You're a Big Boy Now*

One of the more fascinating details about *You're a Big Boy Now* is that Coppola submitted the $800,000 feature film as his master's thesis at UCLA in Cinema Studies. Every subsequent account of the film mentions the detail, but none pauses to ask why Coppola felt compelled to do such a thing. His formal classwork must have ended about 1962 when he won the school's Samuel Goldwyn award for his screenplay *Pilma, Pilma*. Between his undergraduate degree from Hofstra in 1960 and the shooting of *Big Boy*, he had gained experience working in various capacities: as a soft-core pornographic film director; as a jack-of-all-trades for Roger Corman, including the writing and directing of the low-budget horror film *Dementia 13* (1963); as a top screenwriter for Seven Arts, doing scripts for *Is Paris Burning?* (1965), *This Property is Condemned* (1966), and for other uncredited work on projects such as *Reflections in a Golden Eye* (1967); and finally as a screenwriter on the then unproduced *Patton* (1970). With a career so firmly launched, why would Coppola bother to complete the M. A. requirements? As future employment insurance? As a publicity stunt? As an ostentatious gesture toward former classmates or teachers? Perhaps only Coppola knows the answer for certain, but the unusual thing about *You're a Big Boy Now* is that it seems a hybrid of an imaginative student film and a polished Hollywood film. If film school should serve the purpose of preparing one for a career in the industry as well as developing a free imagination, then perhaps *Big Boy* is the most appropriate M. A. thesis ever submitted.

What is the nature of student film production versus Hollywood film production? A few suggestions: if the students are working in a fictional narrative mode, quite often they are forced by monetary and time constraints to use unprepared or "live" locations for shooting. A chase scene might be shot on a city street, with bystanders quite unaware that a film is being made. Were the same piece of footage to be shot in a typical Hollywood film, an army of technicians would check the lighting conditions and sound quality, build sophisticated camera tracks and cordon the area so that no passersby interfered with the action (extras acting "naturally" would replace the bystanders of the student film). In the process some of the spontaneous and realistic quality of the action would be lost, but the voyeuristic fantasy that we are watching reality from an undetected perspective would be preserved.

Thinking more of documentary production, Siegfried Kracauer wrote of the inherent cinematic properties of a city street when filmed from an unnoticed camera position: "The street in the extended sense of the word is not only the arena of fleeting impression and chance encounters, but a place where the flow of life is bound to assert itself."[1] As to the stylistic ramifications of such content, Kracauer observed: "This affinity for the adventitious again implies that the medium does not favor pictures which seem forced into an obvious compositional pattern."[2] In the typical Hollywood street scene there is no "flow of life." Instead we find familiar compositional patterns and rehearsed actions—the unexpected can cause production delays and loss of money. A student film, on the other hand, exhibits a certain freedom and carelessness with respect to such concerns. If an unsuspecting passerby happens to trip one of the chase participants, fine, it looks more realistic. Thus virtue is made of necessity.

Kracauer was writing in 1960. Much of his approach has affinities with cinema verité, a theory of film that went back to the work and writings of Dziga Vertov, but was to reach its widest exposure just after Kracauer in the 1960s, when technological advances and ideological currents contributed to its greatest flowering. In a retrospective look at the movement, a critic commented: "Cinema verité is a practical working method based upon a faith in unmanipulated reality, a refusal to tamper with life as it presents itself."[3] This refusal meant that practitioners did not use actors, did not attempt to control the environment, did not use a script, did not use musical soundtracks, did not use large crews that would call attention to themselves, and so forth. It was possible to borrow some of the techniques of cinema verité, as Hollywood did with the handheld camera, live sound, and location filming, but the basic philosophy of observing rather than controlling reality is at odds with fictional narrative filmmaking. Still, toward the end of the 1960s a number of films broke down this distinction: *Medium Cool* (1969), which mixed live footage of the 1968 riots at the Democratic convention in Chicago with a fictional narrative, and the non-Hollywood, more experimental *David Holtzman's Diary* (1971) and *No Lies* (1971), which were sham cinema verité.

As film schools in the 1960s were a hotbed of cinema verité activity, Coppola must have had a thorough exposure at UCLA, and it is not surprising that Coppola's first major Hollywood film, *You're a Big Boy Now*, leans often toward the virtues of the spontaneous, haphazard student film and toward cinema verité, although at the same time it has the production values and tighter narrative structure of the professional Hollywood film. There are a number of street scenes that are shot clandestinely with an improvisational quality. The penultimate scene, a chase through Macy's, was shot at the actual, unprepared location with real people reacting to the zany behavior of the actors. Coppola's comments on the making of the film indicate a closeness both to the philosophy and technology of cinema verité:

As far as I am concerned, film has gone from the hands of the technician to the hands of the artist. For example, we shot a number of scenes at night without any lights, using Eastman Kodak color film 5251, a fantastic film that will give you anything you want. We didn't force the film. We didn't use reversal Ektachrome. We just rode around in the back of a convertible, pointing the camera where we wanted. We were warned that our footage would come out black, but all of it developed beautifully. The old line technicians baby the film. They work under the theory that you are supposed to create an artificial environment and then control it. But you can never create an artificial environment as beautiful as natural life— and you no longer have to try to do so.[4]

The technique of riding in the back of a convertible while shooting footage of an unprepared location is quintessentially cinema verité. However, that Coppola pointed the camera at an actor being used in a larger narrative than the scene being shot made the film a hybrid. We find the traditional 90-minute Hollywood narrative film infused with a new sensibility—an imagination honed by a film school curriculum with a curiousity about the medium itself and how it could be manipulated. Add to this a certain level of technical expertise developed by Coppola's hands-on experience as a jack-of-all-trades for Roger Corman on the industry's fringe and his subsequent house-writer experience at Seven Arts, and we have someone both knowledgeable of the form and prepared to push it. As we shall see, Coppola was most conventional in this early exercise when it came to narrative structure, but was more innovative where the cinematographic aspects of the production process were concerned. Consequently, *You're a Big Boy Now* showed a flashy surface of visual innovation that immediately commanded attention. Not surprisingly, the film attracted critical praise, led by a rave review and prediction of a new artistic talent by Joseph Morgenstern of *Newsweek*, who observed: "Not since Welles was a boy wonder or Kubrick a kid has any young American made a film as original, spunky or just plain funny as this one."[5] However, before discussing the film itself, we should remember that talent and creativity are not the sole determinants of who receives $800,000 to make a film for Hollywood. The story of how Coppola maneuvered himself into the director's position for this film is more revealing of the entrepreneurial drive and aggressiveness central to his notoriety today than the actual text of the film, which in retrospect makes Morgenstern's rave seem a bit hyperbolic.

While Coppola was with Gore Vidal in Paris working for Seven Arts on the screenplay for *Is Paris Burning?*, he also stayed up nights working on the initial script for *You're a Big Boy Now*. In interviews[6] Coppola has referred to this extracurricular activity as "sanity therapy," without elaborating on why he needed such therapy. One can surmise that Coppola felt more involved with his own screenplay about a young fellow living in New York and working at the library where Coppola himself had worked than with being a junior partner with Gore Vidal on a bloated war epic, which was later to prove an embarassment. "Personal experience" scripts of the variety Coppola was writing are rejected daily in Hollywood, where the most marketable scripts are genre pieces for older, bankable stars. Coppola, however, devised and executed a scheme for directing this script that reminds one of the machinations of Don Corleone.

One of the first steps was Coppola's discovery of the British novel *You're a Big Boy Now* by David Benedictus. That author's debut novel, *The Fourth of June*, a black humor satire of British boarding schools, had attracted favorable notices from highbrow reviewers. The second novel, *Big Boy*, did not do as well critically and was certainly not a best seller. The novel was influenced by, but at the same time kept a wry, modernist distance from, the works of the British "Angry Young Men," making it an unlikely prospect for Hollywood adaptation. Seeing similarities between Benedictus' story and his own developing ideas, Coppola personally paid $1,000 for the movie rights to the novel against $10,000 on completion of a film, with the intention of fashioning a screenplay out of Benedictus' novel. The catch was that as a hired employee of Seven Arts anything Coppola wrote technically belonged to that company. However, as the owner of the film rights to the novel, Coppola had the final say over whether the script was made into a film. Describing a method that would characterize many of his subsequent projects, Coppola later reported the course of events as follows:

The way we worked was the way I work now, which is, I don't ask anybody if I can make a movie. I present them with the fact that I am going to make a movie, and if they're wise they'll get in on it. In this world of motion pictures, very few can resist getting in on something if it looks like it's going. And that's how I did *Big Boy*. We got the package together—we were going to make a movie, we were shelling out our own money and using credit cards and what have you. We said we were already making it, that it was almost too late to get in. So Warner Brothers/ Seven Arts said, "Well, we might as well make this movie."[7]

In another interview, Coppola related: "I told the company, 'I own the book on which the screenplay is based. Consequently, I own half, and you own half—so let's get together.' "[8]

Coppola accepted an $8,000 director's fee on the film, although he had previously been paid $50,000 to write the screenplay for *Patton* in early 1966 and had allegedly turned down another screenplay offer for $75,000. (While most people's wages are a matter of privacy, with Coppola, as with so many other celebrities, they are part of the ongoing myth.) The film originally was going to be a $250,000 "quickie," but Coppola finagled the budget up to close to $1 million, partly by persuading name performers such as Geraldine Page, Julie Harris, Rip Torn, and Michael Dunn to take small parts in the film. The studio forbade him to shoot in New York because of the expensive production costs, but he personally convinced Mayor John Lindsay to intervene and cut the red tape as well as secure the New York Public Library as a film location for the first time in that institution's history. A press agent described Coppola's pre-production meetings with the studio executives as follows: "You should have seen it. Typical conference-table session, with all these stuffy executives sitting around offering the moon to this funny-looking guy with a beard in blue jeans."[9] Just 27 years old at the time, Coppola's gambler's sensibility, his drive, his ambition, and his vision were solidly in place. But if the business acumen was well developed by this point in his career, what of his artistic growth?

Perhaps the best place to start an examination of this question is with the screenplay that he had adapted from the original novel by David Benedictus. The final film adaptation shows few major deviations from the narrative chain-of-events established by Benedictus. However Coppola, in choosing to adapt *You're a Big Boy Now* for the screen, felt no particular allegiance to the vision of middle-class Britain that dominated the novel. In fact, he transposed the action from London to New York and changed the occupation of Bernard, the protagonist, from shoe clerk to librarian's assistant. He later remarked: "I wanted to film it in Europe, but Seven Arts wasn't interested in a $20,000 movie shot there in black and white with a handheld camera and unknown actors, so they made me come home."[10] Coppola's overarching concern was with visual style, editing, texture. When it came to narrative areas, Coppola was a bit like Nietzsche's looting soldier, taking what he wanted and could use from the novel, but in no way attempting to embrace its vision. The novel is a black comedy satire in the Evelyn Waugh tradition, whereas the film, although also comic, is more a celebration of youth coming into experience than a satire of it. The film owes more stylistically to the "youth films" of the 1960s (especially the 1964 Richard Lester-directed *Hard Day's Night*), than to the work of the Angry Young Men. Benedictus visited the set and remarked about the adaptation to Rex Reed: "Now instead of being scarred for life by this sadistic Barbara Darling, the young hero will get a nice girl in the end. Still, I think there

have been fewer concessions to public taste than in most American films."
Reed does not indicate whether there was irony in the comments, but then
again Benedictus did not regard this work as a masterpiece in need of
protection. Decrying Hollywood artistic opportunism was already becoming passé by this point in time.

Because the film is one of the least seen of the Coppola canon and also
to give an idea of the adaptation Coppola did, I will trace the basic narratives
of the film and novel concurrently. The "big boy" of the title in both cases
is Bernard Chanticleer, a rather naive, bumbling youth (19 in the film, 22
in the novel), breaking the strings to his mother's apron and finding out
about women. In the novel Bernard is a shoe clerk working at an outlet
that his father runs near London. Coppola transposed Bernard, making him
a library worker at the New York Public Library, where his father is the
Director of Incunabula. In both cases Bernard has a friend, Raef Delgrado,
a would-be poet who tries to lead Bernard down a decadent path. Raef is
fond of cutting kites free at their apogee to give them a symbolic liberation.
In the novel, Raef specializes in selling customers shoes they do not need.
As a librarian in the film, Raef gives his co-workers various drugs with
which to "turn on." In both works, Bernard's parents decide to set their
son up in an apartment in the city with a landlady named Miss Thing, a
spinster who is to report to his mother any encounters Bernard has with
members of the opposite sex. Bernard, as one would expect, encounters:
first, Amy Prentiss (a co-worker) and then, more dramatically, Barbara
Darling, a vampish actress who alternates between mothering Bernard and
castrating him. In both novel and film, Bernard's affair with Barbara is a
failure, and she ends up with Raef. In both, Bernard also discovers his father
is a lecher, and in a fit of despondency over the entire situation, Bernard
steals something from his father's office—in the novel, a special shoe horn,
in the film a Gutenberg bible. Bernard is arrested and Amy bails him out.
Benedictus sardonically ends his novel with Amy being run over by a bus
and Bernard going to visit Barbara three years later to find her a mother
and as unobtainable as Lolita at the end of Nabokov's novel. The movie,
quite to the contrary, ends with Amy and Bernard romping through New
York and then through a pretzel factory to the sounds of "The Lovin'
Spoonful," an up-beat 1960s' rock group, singing: "Go on and take a bow,
'cause you're a big boy now."

When Coppola was in the British Isles shooting *Dementia 13* for Roger
Corman, the producer continually sent him telegrams imploring "More sex
and violence"; Coppola showed good commercial sense and for the most
part complied. (Someone did come in later and shot an extra gore scene.)
No such explicit dictum was at work in the adaptation of *You're a Big Boy
Now*. Perhaps a more artistic dictum, "More visual dynamics," was behind
Coppola's conception and approach to the film. The film is saturated with
attempts at visual excitement: fast cutting, natural environments, dynamic

camera movement, manufactured action scenes, and cinema verité treatment of the actual milieu. However, it is rarely a case of visuals attempting a translation of the more interior workings of the novel. It is rather cinematic techniques for their own sake. Coppola claims that his conception of the film began with the vision of library employees roller skating among the stacks. Hence, the film started with an image before the narrative or the themes were defined. But, indeed, it is a striking image and in few films have libraries been made so visually interesting. The scenes in the library abound with ostentatious tracking and dolly shots, which suggest a flamboyant student filmmaker let loose with sophisticated Hollywood equipment. Subdued or "seamless" Hollywood camera style is not in evidence. Coppola told Morgenstern: "This one has more baloney in it than I'd like. My style's more subtle than that. But I went for flashy stuff because it's commercially sound for a first picture of your own."[11]

Throughout the film Coppola showed more interest in visual flights than in details of narrative motivation. When Bernard received a letter from Barbara, Coppola represents his response with an extended series of shots of Bernard joyously roller skating to work. Along the way Bernard plays hopscotch with a young boy, kisses a baby, and accidentally rips the carriage; one shot, in the manner of a Buster Keaton film, shows him going one way past an intersection and then reversing himself with a truck chasing him. However, it seems to be a great deal of energy expended in establishing Bernard's response to a woman with whom he is eventually incompatible. Similarly, after Bernard is tricked into taking drugs by Raef during some kite flying, Bernard chases the kite all over Central Park, interrupting baseball games and family portraits along the way, and finally falling into a pond. We would think there would be some narrative resolution to Bernard's drug taking: for instance, he is caught by an authority figure, he devises revenge on Raef, his consciousness is raised, or some such denouement. However, Coppola was more interested in visual excitement; narrative causality is moot.

After Bernard steals the Bible at the library, he is chased to Macy's. Coppola's description of how the culmination of that chase was filmed indicated his intention to produce a cinematically striking sequence by borrowing cinema verité techniques at the expense of a carefully planned narrative:

I wanted to see what would happen when this madness hit Macy's at eleven in the morning with no one outside the film having the slightest idea what was going on. When I presented the scene to the people in the production, they said, "Well, we'll have to put the juniors (baby spots) over here and five wires over here and the extras over here—and obviously we can't afford to do all that." So I got to try it the way I originally wanted. We got three cameras and started to shoot the scene in natural light—an uncontrolled mixture of sunlight, fluorescent light, and incandescent light. Then, without anyone knowing about it, Peter and his pursuers began running through the store. It was terrific. It started a riot. Little old ladies were having heart attacks. One guy grabbed Peter and started a fight with him—which Peter won. Some kids started ripping Peter's clothes off him. My only regret is that we didn't have thirty cameras to get everything down on film. (1970 note: it didn't look as good on film as it did being there.)[12]

These remarks typify Coppola's daring, his determination to get something other than standard Hollywood fare, his unimpressed attitude toward old-line Hollywood technicians, as well as a film student's delight in the medium and what can be created with it—all contributing to the hybrid quality of the film.[13]

On the other hand, in contrast to his experimental attitude toward the filming process, Coppola, when dealing with issues raised by the narrative, and when not neglectful, seemed very conscious of obeying traditional Hollywood notions about what would be commercial. This is demonstrated most notably in the change Coppola made in the ending. Benedictus ended the novel with Amy dying and Bernard settling down to a boring life: "Finally he became an apprentice, at a criminal weekly wage, to a small private firm of quantity surveyors, who would have preferred a shopbreaker to a shoplifter, as showing more attack and initiative, but who anyway used Bernard as a tea-boy-cum-charwoman, in which capacity initiative and aggression were not *sine quis non*."[14] Having throughout established the narrator as exhibiting a comic aloofness with respect to the characters, Benedictus could appropriately close the novel this way; there is no identification with the characters, so nothing cathartic is required. The ending fits with the anti-narrative and self-reflexive tendencies of a modernist novel; it thoroughly violates any expectations the reader might have of a classically romantic ending.

Instead of Benedictus's intellectual distance in describing Bernard's predicament in being arrested, Coppola went for an action oriented spectacle in the slapstick chase scene in Macy's department store. There is some distancing in the employment of this silent movie convention, but the greater concern seemed to be that Hollywood narrative demands an exciting climax. Following this, in both the novel and the film, Amy bails Bernard out of jail. However, as against a typical happy ending, the novel goes on to describe Bernard's difficulties with contraception and with Amy's mother, and ends sardonically with Amy's death. The film, on the other hand, climaxes with Bernard and Amy romping joyously in a pretzel factory, a true Hollywood happy ending.

While modernist approaches to film were being explored at this time in the work of Resnais, Godard, Losey, and other feature film directors, Coppola's more immediate concern seemed to be the film's popular success. Any commentary the film might have suggested on the nature of man's experience of art was secondary to whether the film succeeded in simply pleasing the audience and paying off the studio's investment, which in the end would determine whether any further experimentation in film would be allowed Coppola. The modernist elements that do turn up in the style of the film are merely a pose. Certainly Coppola knew which way the wind blew in calling attention to himself, getting his project made and noticed, and ensuring that his career continued.

In one particular example, Coppola's avoidance of class issues raised by the novel seems very deliberate. In the novel, Bernard had a habit of looking at signs, initials, or writing on wall and free associating. Coppola employed this in the adaptation and *Time* magazine commented on "the wackiest free-association camera work since Richard Lester made the Beatles work *A Hard Day's Night*." At one point in the film, Bernard sees some graffiti saying "Niggers go home." Bernard free associates: "Home is where the heart is, Niggers go where your heart is, my heart is in the highlands," and then a subjective fantasy shot shows a Black bag-piper leading children through a pastoral setting. Benedictus used this scene for a different effect. In the novel the slogan is written by the British National Party, a rightwing white-supremist party. Bernard muses about it for a while and then out of sympathy for the underdog decides to write a message of his own. Unfortunately, as he picks up a piece of chalk, a large, menacing black male appears and, thinking Bernard the original graffiti writer, chases him away. Coppola, quite aware of American sensitivities about the race question, eschewed the punch line to this scene. On the one hand, this exemplifies a certain cowardice characteristic of American films when dealing with controversial issues. On the other hand, Benedictus's original scene embodied a darkly comedic mode that would have jarred with the totality of Coppola's film.

Coppola does pepper the film with his own social commentary, but it is much weaker than Benedictus's version. Raef, the would-be poet, is very much a contemporary 1967 character, who tries to turn Bernard on to various drug experiences. (The novel came out in 1963.) Barbara moonlights as a go-go dancer in a 1960s disco. One can feel the much-heralded generation gap in the relationship between Bernard and his father. I. H. Chanticleer constantly talks down to his son and makes Bernard hold an umbrella over him as he practices his golf putting in the rain. However, despite the topical references one would never guess from the film that the Vietnam War was going on, and that the same Central Park that Bernard gambols through was the scene of much anti-war activity. The film flirts with topicality but never embraces it.

In sum, Coppola's use of Benedictus' novel was very pragmatic. Coppola exhibited no reverence for the integrity of another artist's vision. The novel was a pawn in Coppola's larger struggle with the Hollywood establishment. (It is likewise doubtful that Benedictus expected great things when he sold the movie rights for a mere $1,000 option.)

## Youth Film

The author of the only full-length English-language study of Coppola, Robert K. Johnson, was an enthusiastic defender of the film.[15] Johnson found a certain poignancy in the midst of the comedy and suggested that on second viewing the film had more to offer than *The Graduate*, another film about youth coming into experience in the 1960s that was far more successful at the box office. Another reaction to the alleged poignancy of *Big Boy* was offered by Robert Kolker in his *A Cinema of Loneliness*:

*You're a Big Boy Now* is so representative of a moment in the history of recent cinema that it is now almost unwatchable. The "youth film," started by Richard Lester with *A Hard Day's Night* and *Help* (the roots of which go back to the rock and roll and beach-party films of the fifties), climaxing with *The Graduate* and *Easy Rider*, and then dying swiftly with a string of films from MGM at the turn of the seventies, was part of a strange, touching, and cynical period for Hollywood.[16]

Kolker, in his analysis, went on to dismiss content discussion, and focused solely on the editing style of the film, speculating on how much influence the editor, Aram Avakian, had on the eventual look of the film. Kolker pointed out similarities in style in Arthur Penn's *Mickey One*, also edited by Avakian, and noted that both films are atypical of their respective director's style. As was mentioned earlier, Coppola felt the film's style was "flashier" than his personal sensibility, and it seems likely there was a strong collaboration between Avakian and Coppola in creating an American extension of the techniques that Truffaut and Godard explored in *Shoot the Piano Player, Breathless*, or *Jules and Jim*. Much of the vitality and energy of the film results from the same techniques of jump-cutting and disjunctive editing first experimented with by the French.

Kolker mentioned that this period in American film was "touching and cynical," which would initially seem a contradiction. Indeed, as we have seen, there is a cynical edge to Coppola's adaptation strategies. Even to one not aware of the adaptation process, a cynical quality emerges from the trendiness of the film's style, as some of the contemporary reviewers commented. But a case can be made for the "touching" qualities of the film as well. The youth film as a genre represented a symbolic liberation from the straitjacket style and substance of Hollywood films in the 1950s and early 1960s when a dearth of imagination and vitality made films in the manner of *Cleopatra* seem like dinosaurs compared to the films emerging from Europe. The rawness of films in the "youth film" cycle was part of their charm; they were returning to concerns closer to our imaginative home, reflections of a world around us rather than the farfetched grandiosity of bible epics, big budget musicals, or other overdone genre pieces. If the filmmakers were desperate to make any kind of film, some of the audience was desperate to see something a bit rebellious. What makes the youth films "unwatchable" today, as Kolker suggested, is partly the apprenticeship status of the people who originally made them, and perhaps our own jaded sensibility about youth films as the result of watching too many carefully packaged "teenpics" of the last ten years. When the youth films were good, which wasn't often enough, they rose above the artificially imposed formulas of what Hollywood executives thought the youth of America wanted to see. *You're a Big Boy Now* is ultimately much more visually imaginative than the standard "youth film."

Examples of the "flashiness" of the cutting style and its debts to the *Nouvelle Vague* are found in the scenes in which Bernard is in front of his mirror shaving and brushing his teeth. The action could be shown in a single take, but Coppola and Avakian intentionally distort it with a series of quick jump cuts. Bob Fosse uses a similar technique and positioning in *All That Jazz*, when Roy Scheider comments: "It's showtime!" The dysjunctive editing is frequently employed in other segments of the film and suggests a sense of excitement and independence in Bernard, even in his mundane actions, correlating with the emotions he must be feeling on moving from his family's home to the big city. The overwhelming weight of the "flashy" editing is on this aspect of Bernard's life. We have long segments of his running through Central Park, rollerskating down city streets, wandering around 42nd Street, and at the end frolicking with Amy in a pretzel factory. From the visuals and editing we might infer that life is one big lark for Bernard. However, from the motivations in the main narrative line, another picture emerges. Bernard's fondest desire is to meet the actress Barbara Darling. After he meets her, however, she proves to be a vamp who seduces him, causes him sexual impotence, and then sneers at his frustration as she runs off with his best friend. Bernard's parents and landlady are extremely insensitive toward Bernard with no resolution of this tension in the plot itself. Amy chases Bernard throughout the movie and he eventually ends up with her, but we never feel he was that passionate about her to begin with, since Barbara was much more the driving force in his life. At one point Raef tells Bernard that "Pain is part of freedom," a line Coppola added in his adaptation. In the editing and the visual style there is a good deal of freedom, but no sustained visual correlative to the pain, alienation, and loneliness that is also a part of Bernard's newfound freedom. The visual experience of Bernard's highs would be intensified if we felt his lows as well, but that apparently did not fit into the scheme of "flashiness."

Still, despite its lack of balance, *You're a Big Boy Now*, much like *The Godfather*, has an impressive visual density. Even at this early point in his career, it is apparent that Coppola had an extremely fecund imagination for dreaming up "bits" to enliven the narrative. As illustration, we might consider an extended sequence dealing with Bernard's relationship with Amy.

The Bernard/Amy sequence begins as Bernard wanders around 42nd Street sex shops. The music, visuals, and acting suggest a wonderment on Bernard's part—a suburban boy making his first personal acquaintance with the big city. The scene has a cinema verité quality (recall Coppola's comments above about using fast film at unprepared locations). Bernard ventures into one of the pornography parlors and guiltily decides to try some of the peep shows. One is a series of flash cards harking back to the origins of motion pictures. The next is a more technically sophisticated peep show resembling a movieola. Bernard, in slapstick fashion, gets his tie caught in a sprocket while watching a beckoning siren, and is in danger of being choked to death. In a stroke of serendipity, but not believability, Amy appears, pulls out scissors, and rescues Bernard by severing his tie. As a metaphor for the larger concerns of the narrative, Amy's symbolic rescue is a bit forced, but not without a certain innocent charm, despite the potential castration metaphor. At other points in the film Coppola shows an incipient talent for slapstick to which he has never returned: the best of the sequences is when Bernard cannot turn off a milk machine in a snack bar and piles up a pyramid of glasses of milk while Amy tries to complain about his father's lechery—the frustration with the milk machine an effective correlative to his difficulty in comprehending his father, and perhaps symbolically his mother as well.

Following the 42nd Street scene, Coppola proceeds with a montage of "young love" visuals: whimsical music accompanies short cuts as Bernard and Amy talk to each other in adjoining phone booths, watch New York street musicians, view each other on a television street monitor, and so forth. Most of this sequence uses non-synchronous sound, emphasizing the environment as a catalyst in their discovery of each other. The scene ends ominously with Bernard inadvertently and insensitively insulting Amy as her bus door clangs shut. But another date has been arranged, and in the next scene of this sequence, Bernard and Amy go to a very raucous discotheque. In the novel Benedictus had a similar scene wherein Bernard and Amy go to a jazz club; Bernard ineptly loses Amy in the crowd and leaves without her. Coppola had other intentions in the film. In the conception of the scene, he makes the disco a visual and auditory overload. The walls have huge rear screen projections of the more explicit violent scenes of Coppola's *Dementia 13*, which Johnson found a "pointless private joke," but nonetheless seem in keeping with the tone of the disco. Bernard tries to talk to Amy over the din by rolling a menu into a megaphone. The music stops as he is still shouting, his comic embarrassment underlining his estrangement from this milieu. Amy tries to entice Bernard to dance, but suddenly Barbara Darling appears as a go-go dancer. The editing and visuals intensify as the shots jump quickly from psychedelics of Barbara dancing, a correlative to the intense subjective hold she has on Bernard, to shots of Bernard staring raptly, to Amy sizing up the situation and trying to distract Bernard by suggesting they adjourn to his place. The editing matches the pounding pace of the music, as at one point Amy shouts "What about me?" and the "me" is intercut twice more in staccato fashion. Amy drags Bernard out of the disco and onto Times Square, the billboard surreally flashing Bernard's thoughts about Barbara and suggesting a certain solipsism in his view of the world at the moment. The finale of the sequence is the thwarting of Amy's plans to seduce Bernard. In a slapstick flourish, Miss Thing's pet rooster attacks them as they attempt to enter his room; in the ensuing melee Miss Thing falls down the stairs and breaks her arm.[17]

This sequence was described at some length because it suggests the visual creativity Coppola brought to the film, his sense for streamlining the narrative, his predisposition for visually dynamic situations, and his active and often successful search for objective correlatives to the interior workings of character psychology and narrative. The sequence, if anything, is lively. It may not be permeated with great insight into the infatuations of youth, but it is certainly not sugar-coated sentimentality either.

There are other scenes scattered throughout the narrative that have real power and are executed deftly. While the film played up to the "Now generation," it was not without an occasional critique of the new ethics that were evolving in 1967. This is exemplified particularly in the scene in which Bernard is moving in with Barbara. More and more men and women were living together without marriage during this era of "Free Love," "the Pill," and the protest against the established values concomitant with the Vietnam War. Coppola views such arrangements with a satiric eye not present in Benedictus' version of this scene by having Bernard place his belongings inappropriately all over Barbara's eccentrically decorated apartment as he moves in with her on the spur of the moment. We are happy Bernard has gotten what he desired so desperately, but nervous about his thoughtless violation of Barbara's space. She has been saccharine up to this point, but when she returns to find a silly picture of Bernard's mother with locks of hair affixed to the frame, she savagely asks Bernard, "Who are you?" At once we feel Bernard's hopes dashed, but we also understand that the old ethics of courtship and romance, repressive as they might have been, protected fragile souls from dilemmas like this. To emphasize the point, and perhaps grant a small measure of revenge for Bernard, Coppola has Barbara ask Raef the same question when he moves in with her and tries to assume intimacy. This was a departure from the novel's rather passive attitude about new ethics and was Coppola's own wry comment on contemporary mores.

The Bernard/Barbara sequence also illustrates Coppola's meticulous staging of the indoor scenes of *You're a Big Boy Now*. Scenes were carefully rehearsed several weeks before the production began and videotaped, a fairly revolutionary process at the time, 1967. Coppola's reputation as an actor's director came later in his career, but even as a fledgling director, he felt strongly about working intensely with actors in advance of shooting to create characters that went beyond the screenplay. Coppola's propensity for giving the characters life beyond what we immediately see on the screen, a "method acting" device, produced a surprisingly realistic quality even when juxtaposed with the antirealist slapstick antics of much of the film. It is the same tension we find when the realistic New York locations and mise-en-scene are used in combination with anti-realist editing style.

Perhaps because of these stylistic tensions, the film went the route of pre-*Annie Hall* Woody Allen films—loved in California and New York, but shunned in the hinterlands. Reportedly, it only recovered its costs on the subsequent television sale.

The critical response was very mixed: there were those who were wildly enthusiastic about the stylistic elements of the film. Others found the narrative hackneyed and superficial. Richard Schickel wrote the most condemning review:

> Mr. Coppola is a young man standing in front of a distorting mirror, trying on both the old and new intellectual clothing of his culture while trying out, at the same time, the imperfectly observed manners and gestures of the adult world. Somehow he has managed to convince himself that the occasionally bizarre combinations that sometimes result from this activity are, taken together, a creative act, and not just self-indulgence.
>
> It makes one very tired, as self-admiring brattiness always does. Worse it makes one fearful. If the film is, by some mischance, a success, the imitations of it are going to form the most unbearable cycle since the Gidget pictures.[18]

The film was not the success that Schickel feared, nor did it really inspire a cycle of films: the ensuing "youth films" were much more topical and lacked *Big Boy's* sense of humor and visual style (e. g., *Getting Straight*, 1970; *Drive He Said*, 1971; *The Strawberry Statement*, 1970).

Some of the hostility might proceed, we could speculate, from reaction to the brashness of Coppola's interviews of that period, for instance his audacity in declaring in *Newsweek*: "I pattern my life on Hitler. . . . He didn't just take over the country. He worked his way into existing fabric first."[19] Three months before the premiere, an article appeared in which Coppola declared: "I can make $100,000 a year as a script writer. If the movie's a bomb it won't destroy my reputation as a director because I don't have any" and "I'm turning out the most expensive underground movie ever made."[20] Such colorful quotes have a way of making Coppola's success seem very individualistic. Lynda Myles and Michael Pye build a case that Coppola's freedom on this film had much to do with the free-wheeling nature of Seven Arts, which had not had time to develop stiff, conservative policies like other major studios, and also with Phil Feldman's partnership with Coppola in producing the film, after Coppola's initiative.[21] These sort of details do not make colorful, journalistic copy. Still, in his subsequent career, Coppola's ability to generate colorful copy has much to do with his ability to get his projects off the ground.

In retrospect, it is ironic that Coppola, so interested in experimenting with cinema verité techniques and uncontrolled locations in a fictional mode with *You're a Big Boy Now*, would fifteen years later make *One from the Heart*, a film that budgeted $4 million for an artificial set and in which the director attempted to exercise total control over every element. Often Coppola seems a filmmaker in search of a style.

To those interested in the development of Coppola the director, *You're a Big Boy Now* is an interesting film; there is certainly enough going on in the film to command one's attention. On its own as a cinematic entity, however, it did not ensure that Coppola would get future film projects, rather it was Coppola's ability to call attention to himself, to make himself interesting to the *Newsweek* journalists and at the same time to the movie moguls who eagerly scan this press for some new trend that may escape them. The moguls do not mind someone declaring that he would overthrow them in the manner of Hitler if it means that he would bring some people to the ticket window along the way. With *Big Boy* the young director had found notoriety. Coppola's career was off and, like Bernard in the park, running.

### Finian's Rainbow

One of the funniest and most effective moments in Coppola's *Finian's Rainbow* (1968), judging from audience response, is the scene in which Howard (Al Freeman)—a black scientist, now a servant—serves a Bromo-Seltzer to the bigoted Senator Billboard Rawkins (Keenan Wynn). In order to keep his tobacco research financed, Howard must take a butler's job in which he is expressly required to do an exaggerated "Stepin' Fetchit" routine in serving his employer, Rawkins, who likes his blacks to act in a particularly servile fashion. Rawkins, however, becomes a victim of his own bigotry. After a confrontation with a black geologist, Rawkins wants his Bromo in a hurry. Howard, obeying orders, shuffles and walks as if on a treadmill, never quite getting to the increasingly distressed Senator. We are delighted by the farcical turnabout; for once the idea of keeping blacks in their place boomerangs on the bigot.

One is tempted to draw a metaphor here for the young Coppola at this early stage in his career. We saw how with *You're a Big Boy Now* Coppola conducted a brazen publicity campaign centered around his plans for a more personalized form of filmmaking. Was this 29-year-old film school "whiz kid" swallowing a bit of pride, like Howard, and serving a Bromo of pre-

packaged Hollywood musical to the Warner Brothers/Seven Arts establishment with some future payoff in mind? And in light of Coppola's later
disowning of *Finian's*[22] and the relative box office and critical failure of the
film, did the seemingly correct delivery of the metaphorical Bromo also
comically boomerang on the management's desires? Such metaphors are
always seductive, but closer examination will show Coppola's interaction
with the film to be more complex and problematic. *Finian's* has all the
contradictions of Coppola's later big-budget commercial epics: the constricting conventions of a Hollywood studio genre piece versus Coppola's
more stylistically experimental personal sensibility, good "liberal" intentions toward the thematic content hampered by a certain political naiveté,
and the juxtaposition of Coppola's announced intentions versus the sum
total of his practice. Viewed in the context of Coppola's career rather than
as a text in itself, *Finian's Rainbow* is a fascinating film. However, as a text
itself, this sprawling adaptation of a twenty-year-old Broadway musical
about racial bigotry and leprechauns leaves much to be desired.

Gerald Mast articulated a discrepancy between Coppola's big commercial
epics (*Finian's Rainbow, The Godfather, Godfather II, Apocalypse Now*) and
his "smaller, more offbeat style pieces" (*You're a Big Boy Now, The Rain
People,* and *The Conversation*). Mast reasoned: "The big projects allow Coppola to exercise his craft, particularly his abilities as a script writer; they
also provide him with the money to make the films he wants to make and
to run his own American Zoetrope studio in San Francisco."[23] This is true
with *Finian's*, insofar as Warners was so happy with the rushes that they
gave Coppola carte blanche and $800,000 to go on the road with the sub-
sequent *The Rain People*. However, as we'll see, Coppola was not in any
particular financial bind following *You're a Big Boy Now*. His reasons for
taking on *Finian's Rainbow* were idiosyncratic and undercut some of the
careerist proclamations about a new kind of filmmaking he had made in
connection with *You're a Big Boy Now*. Coppola took a few deep sips from
that Bromo he was delivering.

Perhaps soured on some of the deal-making squabbles connected with
*Big Boy*, Coppola in 1967 resolved to write a personal film, an original
screenplay on a subject then and later of great interest to him, surveillance
in modern society. Years later, he reflected on how he was diverted to
*Finian's Rainbow*:

You see, after *You're a Big Boy Now*, I made a resolution—I was not going to make
that mistake of having a promising first film and going straight into a big Hollywood
clunker. And I went and got a small office and started to write the movie I'm doing
now, *The Conversation*. I wrote the first three pages. Then I got a phone call from
a guy who asked if I knew anyone who would do *Finian's Rainbow*. I thought about
it and gave him suggestions and hung up. The next day he called back and said,
"What about you?"[24]

This could be one of the pivotal moments in Coppola's career. He was not working with a deadline for *The Conversation* script (as he later would be with *The Great Gatsby* or the revisions of *Apocalypse Now*), and self-discipline and concentration are necessary to complete such a project. As anyone who has labored under such conditions knows, distractions present themselves; indeed, one looks for them as a psychological release from the task at hand. Coppola was tempted by the proverbial devil in the guise of a big budget, star-studded musical with a fat director's fee. He strayed from his own project, a screenplay much in keeping with his proclamations about "new" film, and did not return to it for six years. In accepting the offer to do *Finian's*, Coppola recalled the stage version as having been a warm, happy experience in his childhood. He himself had written and produced a musical comedy, *A Delicate Touch*, in college. Tempted by the idea of staging some of the famous songs from Burton Lane and E. Y. Harburg, Coppola thought it might be a good exercise to work on such an adaptation, and, perhaps the key to the decision, it was something that might impress his father, a man who had labored for several years in musical comedy without achieving much acclaim.[25]

Besides personal idiosyncrasies, there is the cultural/historical context for Coppola's participation with *Finian's Rainbow*. Pye and Myles, in their book *The Movie Brats*, argue that the opportunities given the young directors who eventually became the "new" Hollywood came in the context of Hollywood studio executives' growing desperation in a search for a means of insuring their investment. The problems of rising production and distribution costs, the challenge of television, and the widening generation gap brought on by the Vietnam-era counterculture had put the studios in financial jeopardy. The Hollywood film industry was searching for a packaging formula, an alchemy that would guarantee the financial success of a major project against these risks. In the case of *Finian's*, someone got a bright idea: trot out a twenty-year-old hit musical whose integrationist message had initially been a bit too liberal for the conservative Hollywood establishment to gamble on (particularly with the HUAC hearings right around the corner); get an established, venerable Hollywood persona like Fred Astaire to give the act class; and just so as not to alienate totally that segment that might view Astaire as an "old fogey," bring in a pretty, British pop singer named Petula Clark, who had been topping the charts for several years with youth-oriented songs like "Downtown." The final ingredient, and perhaps the catalyst to the whole formula, was a young director with a Richard Lester touch, who would shake up the old conventions with a youthful zing, but who was not about to drift pretentiously into the avant garde. Hence, came the phone call to Coppola, the young upstart who had received good press on *You're a Big Boy Now*.

Later when the footage was in, Warners was convinced it had the alchemy and budgeted a $2,000,000 advertising campaign, allegedly its biggest campaign until that point, for a film that had cost only $3,500,000 to make. *Variety* reported how the campaign would be handled:

Theme of the effort will consist of four main points, two concrete—the music and the cast, and two abstract—the "happiness factor" of a fun family film and the "now factor" spotlighting its social themes (Negroes in the South).

Per last named, W7 plans the first "calculated exposure" of a pic to the underground and protest press. Special screenings for such papers plus college students will be skedded, and the opposite end of the spectrum will also be hit—football fans. In return for full-page ads in every National Football League and American Football League program, music from Finian's will be played at half-time at every NFL and AFL game.[26]

That the marketing people thought that college students and the protest press would go for this film with the right "push" suggests just how wide the generation gap was in 1968. To understand this remarkable myopia, however, another historical context should be fleshed out: that of 1947 and the premiere of the original hit play.

### The Original Play

Usually a play with 750 performances on Broadway will be adapted into a film within a few years. However, *Finian's* was considered a "hot potato" in Hollywood circles because of its focus on racial bigotry and because of the fact that it was the first Broadway show in years to have a racially mixed cast.[27] The original authors of the play also wanted unusual controls and $1,000,000 for the rights, which contributed to the twenty-year delay. Even so, *Gentlemen's Agreement* was considered daring in 1947, and a good role for a black in Hollywood was as a servant in a Southern melodrama like *Gone with the Wind* (1939). *Home of the Brave* came along in 1949, as Hollywood liberals such as Stanley Kramer and Otto Preminger began to get watered-down messages across.

The original idea for *Finian's* came to E. Y. Harburg, the lyricist of "Over the Rainbow," as he was mulling over two different ideas for a play—one a fanciful story about a fellow who steals a pot-of-gold from a leprechaun, and the other a social commentary story (resembling *Black Like Me*) about a Southern senator who is racially transformed. Harburg decided to combine the two plots in what a drama critic later dubbed a "shot-gun marriage."[28] It produced a fantasy/realism hybrid.

Consider *Finian's* plot: Before the action of the play begins, the Irishman Finian has stolen a pot-of-gold from leprechauns and has come to America to bury it near Ft. Knox, because he rather quaintly believes that the rich soil of a rich nation will make the gold "grow" into a larger hoard. In the vicinity of Fort Knox, Finian meets up with the sharecroppers of Rainbow Valley, who are about to be squeezed out of their property by Billboard

Rawkins, a bigoted Southern Senator who wants to keep them ignorant and poor by preventing the construction of a dam to generate electricity in their area. (This is not long after the TVA became an issue.) Finian nonchalantly prevents Rawkins' takeover by paying the back taxes on the land with his last dollars. The sharecroppers are interracial, so Rawkins attempts to get the land by drafting a law that prohibits black and white co-habitation on farmland. Meanwhile, Finian's daughter Sharon is romantically involved with Woody Mahoney, the brother of Susan the Silent (the benevolent landowner for whom the sharecroppers work). Sharon becomes angry about Rawkins's law and, as she accidentally stands over the hidden pot-of-gold, wishes the Senator to be black—which, of course, occurs. Thus the main tension of the ending revolves around whether Sharon will be burned as a witch for the aforementioned deed. The police arrest her as she and Woody attempt to be married. During these proceedings, we have also been introduced to Og, a leprechaun who has trailed Finian to America to recover the pot-of-gold and also fallen in love with Susan the Silent. When Og finds the magical gold, there are only two wishes left. One is used to give Susan the Silent a voice and the other is used to restore Rawkins' Caucasian appearance. Og turns into a mortal, although not unhappily, as he is united with Susan. Rawkins changes his personality for the better. Woody and Sharon marry, and Finian leaves to seek metaphorically "another rainbow." This is a musical, and interwoven throughout is a parallel contrast of fairy-tale romance and social commentary in the musical text. On the one hand we have the light love songs: "If This Isn't Love," "That Old Devil Moon," and so on. On the other we have wry songs of social satire reminiscent of Kurt Weill's *Threepenny Opera*: "When the Idle Poor Become the Idle Rich," "Necessity," and "That Great Come and Get It Day."

By 1968 the boundaries between what could and couldn't be done had changed from those under which Harburg operated in 1947. In order to maintain a roughly equivalent balance between the bite of the social commentary and the harmony of the romantic fantasy, an adaptor would have to make changes accordingly. Several hours before the world premiere of *Finian's Rainbow*, in an interview with Joseph Gelmis, Coppola offered the following estimation of what his position in adapting the play had been:

I knew there were pitfalls. If I did it faithfully it was going to look like a twenty-two-year-old show. So I tried to make it faithful and yet make it acceptable for contemporary audiences. I think I always knew that the show, critically, was going to be received ungenerously. A lot of liberal people were going to feel it was old pap, because of its dated civil rights stance. And they were going to say, "Oh, the real *Finian's Rainbow* we remember was wonderful." If they were to look at the material today, they might not love it so much. And the conservatives were going to say it was a lot of liberal nonsense. I knew I was going to get it from both ends. And it sort of hurt my feelings.[29]

Whether Coppola's analysis is correct or not, it disclosed a certain lack of vision and an alienation from the project on the part of the filmmaker. He did not feel affinity with the liberals, nor with the conservatives; he did not advocate a middle ground; in short he did not develop a position. Instead Coppola worried about what people who had seen the play on Broadway would think, probably a very small part of the audience the film would potentially reach, and only made cosmetic changes. However, when one approaches a project that is intrinsically issue-oriented, one needs a clear grasp and perspective on these issues, as well as a handle on the audience addressed. That the film did not achieve that perspective is reflected in Renata Adler's comments in the *New York Times* that the film had "quick updatings of Negro personalities to match what people who have lived in Beverly Hills too long must imagine modern black sensibilities are."[30] Coppola had not lived in Beverly Hills, but there were problems with the updatings of the black characters, as will be discussed below.

Before Coppola joined the project, Warner Brothers anticipated the possibility that *Finian's* could be too antiquated for 1968 audiences. Coppola explained: "They had readapted it and made it about a hippie from San Francisco, and all kinds of things."[31] Knowing the play, one initially shudders a bit at this idea—a hippie in Rainbow Valley? Juxtaposed with the magic of leprechaun and warm old fashioned songs like "How are things in Gloccamora?" One can easily sympathize with Coppola's desire to return as closely as possible to the original play. However, before we dismiss that displaced hippie, a transient phenomenon of the 1960s rudely barging in on a timeless world of fantasy, let us consider Harburg's description of Woody in the play script:

Woody, in the navy-blue garb of a merchant seaman, is back from fighting fascism and fleas in the South Pacific and is no pushover for people who like to push other people around.[32]

Furthermore, Woody is a labor organizer. Was this character any less topical in the 1940s than a hippie from San Francisco would be in the 1960s? What transcended the rather formulaic use of type in the play was the good-natured ribbing that Harburg gave the man-of-his-time. Much like Garry Trudeau with *Doonesbury*, Harburg made this anti-establishment labor organizer preferable to the establishment in a nondogmatic fashion—human foibles were allowed. The same sensibility could have been applied to the 1960s' hippie from San Francisco; the main problem with such a substitution is that dramatically a hippie in a red-neck, Southern rural area would call for tensions and conflicts that Harburg's play as written could not provide; an equivalent wit would have to be found. As it happened, Coppola did tamper with the Woody character, but in ways that in retrospect seem even more puzzling than the possibility of making him a hippie from San Francisco.

The 1940s' idea of an optimistic returning veteran was dated in 1968 and the film seemed set in the present. But one would think that the original union organizer status would not have been anachronistic in the politically aware 1960s' climate when labor organizers and folksingers in the mold of Woody Guthrie were being lionized by the counterculture. Quite surprisingly, in the film version Coppola changed Woody to a *tobacco salesman!* Not a word is uttered about labor organizing. Coppola integrated Woody into a vision of a New South, where blacks and whites work together and use new technological research to improve their lot.

Although the original play had a racially mixed cast, the principal roles were all white. Susan Mahoney was a benevolent landowner and the majority of the black characters were her sharecroppers, apparently happily working on her land. Howard, the black character with the most lines in the play, was a student at Tuskeegee Institute. He, as was mentioned earlier, appeared in the vignette in which he serves the Bromo to Senator Rawkins. Other than that scene, which did not affect the narrative flow, Howard had no other function in the play; one wonders if Harburg wrote the scene with the idea that it might have to be deleted later. Blacks were allowed a certain level of dignity—the Stepin' Fetchit shuffling darkie stereotype was not in evidence in the play—but from a modern vantage point the treatment of racism in the original play has to be seen as patronizing, however well intentioned it was in its own time.

Coppola took the black character Howard and gave him more prominence in the plot. No longer were the blacks sharecroppers, as in the original play, but in a subtle bit of euphemism, which ambiguously reflected the "hippie" alternative, they were now members of the "Rainbow Valley Tobacco Cooperative." Howard became their research scientist working on a new mentholated tobacco. Coppola transformed Harburg's labor organizer Woody into a salesman/fund raiser for Howard's research efforts, and apparently his close friend. Thus, while Coppola had discarded the original play's rather underdeveloped idea of a labor organizer seeking to better the lot of the poor, he had substituted an optimistic vision of a new South, blacks and whites working together with good old American ingenuity and technology to better their existence. Harburg ended his story with the capitalists Shears and Robust being unrealistically tricked into writing a check to the landowners for worthless mineral rights. Coppola instead ended in more cinematic style with a spectacle, a fire in the laboratory that causes Howard's previously smokeless tobacco to smoke. (The strategy is similar to the chase finale he supplied for *You're a Big Boy Now*.) This scientific miracle is not explained, but we infer that prosperity for the Cooperative will now ensue. Not surprisingly, the filmmaker who would later sink thousands of dollars into buying state-of-the-art film equipment and would try to revolutionize film editing with video playback systems, at this early stage showed an interest in glorifying science, technology, and innovation as the great saviors of our time, quite able to solve social problems through their advances.

However, the upgrading of Howard's intellectual capabilities and importance to the community in the adaptation does not relieve Coppola of the charge that the film is patronizing to blacks. In a film that derives much of its appeal from its romance, Howard is given no romantic interest, and he has no musical number to resolve any sort of tension within the narrative. Thus we cannot think of him as a major character, and we still have a story about the problems of blacks with no major black characters.

The film had been cast when Coppola arrived on the project, which certainly restricted the extent of the revisions he could make in the screenplay. However, if we might speculate about the decisions made in the adaptation, one change that may have made the film more topical and interesting to the 1968 audience would have been to follow literally Sharon's example with Rawkins: to change Woody into a believable black character. Then instead of the rather facile and unconvincing device of building tension through Sharon's being prosecuted as a witch, the more topical theme of miscegenation could easily have given the narrative a drive. Such a transformation need not have altered the play's light touch. *Guess Who's Coming to Dinner?* a few years earlier explored miscegenation as a metaphor for the way whites and blacks co-exist in America. The above second guessing is merely a hypothetical illustration of Coppola's failure to make the sort of major revamping that would have been necessary for the film to be more appealing to contemporary audiences, if that can be supposed to have been an aim of the adaptation. His decision to remain, more or less, faithful to the original play doomed his efforts to failure. As it stands, it is difficult to accept the film's plea for dignity for blacks when it does not dignify any of its black characters with a full-scale characterization.

Coppola's other minor fiddling with the original play script is also in line with the general lack of relevance to modern audiences. For instance, on two occasions when the sharecroppers are in conflict with the authorities, Howard commands the group to "Sit" in direct reference to one of the most widely employed Civil Rights strategies, the "sit-in." In neither case does the sitting-in produce any results; in the second instance Howard is shown being carried away with an impotent look on his face. As a means of up-dating the play, the device was rather ill-conceived and pointless.

Although Coppola's next film, *The Rain People*, was to be viewed by some as a women's picture before its time, there are some slightly misogynistic nuances to a few of the changes Coppola made in *Finian's*. Just prior to Woody and Sharon's "Old Devil Moon" duet, Harburg originally had Woody explaining to Sharon that there was a valley legend about people falling in love on moonlit nights when the moon was not in view. Woody claims just before the song that he made up the legend. In the film version, Coppola substituted an interchange in which Woody tells Sharon that there are werewolves about and that if she does not grab the nearest, handsomest fellow, these werewolves will get her. Apparently taken in, Sharon complies; Woody, as in the original, tells her he made up the legend and they begin the song. Coppola's treatment of the scene is harmless enough, but still works on a notion that men are stronger than women and need to protect them (and, in this case, seduce them). At another point, the sharecroppers discard their old belongings and in a two-second cut we see a black sharecropper tossing his struggling wife on the same scrapheap. Finally, although admittedly the leprechaun Og treats Susan the Silent's love rather cavalierly in Harburg's original play—he tells her joyously "When I'm not near the girl I love, I love the girl I'm near"—Coppola in no way mitigates this; in fact, in the staging he has Og drop Susan roughly on the ground when he stops to talk to Finian.

The discussion of *You're a Big Boy Now* elaborated the distinctions between "film school" filmmaking and Hollywood filmmaking. Despite the dominance of Hollywood norms in *Finian's*, there is one short passage in the film that seems to hark back to Coppola's student filmmaking roots. In the play we are told that Woody is coming on a train (off-stage). The film predictably showed this bit of cinematic action. Coppola began the short travelling segment with jump cuts of Woody with his guitar in various poses at different parts of the train—on top of it, in front of it, and so forth. Coppola ended the little segment with the camera rushing down the aisle of the train in exaggerated fast motion three times, apparently toward Woody, who appears in a blur. The intention of the style of the segment was probably to suggest Woody as an out-of-the-ordinary hero who would save the day for the beleaguered Coop, something never borne out in the plot. The frenetic, unusual camera movement, however, looks very much like something one could see at a student film festival and it is surprising that a Hollywood film editor left it in the film. (Perhaps George Lucas, who was a student intern on the film and formed his first partnership with Coppola, had something to do with this momentary departure from traditional Hollywood style.)

Coppola used a sense of spatial disorientation at the very beginning of the film, as the credits were rolling, much more effectively. He employed a montage of Sharon and Finian wandering around famous American landmarks: the Golden Gate Bridge, the Statue of Liberty, Glacier National Park, and so on. Coppola explained later that he was attempting to give a mythic status to Finian's voyage to America. However, the imagery nicely ties in with the original play's examination of the American dream by evoking symbols of that dream. One should add that this device suspiciously echoes the opening panorama of the Swiss Alps in *The Sound of Music*, only in a less lyrical fashion.

Where Coppola had his greatest successes in the film, and where we can see flashes of the genius that will inform his later films, is in the cinematic style of the film, the opening up of a theatre-bound play into an exciting visual experience in the open air. Most notably this occurs in the editing process. With *Big Boy*, Coppola distinguished himself by using a Richard Lester style, a disdain for match-cutting in sequences where characters seemed to run aimlessly but frenetically to the beat of contemporary music in a cinematic "objective correlative" to the mood of the 1960s generation. It was intended that Coppola would "jazz up" *Finian's* by applying this same style to the old Burton Lane/Fred Saidy score. And that he did, with, in my opinion, more success and ingenuity than displayed in *Big Boy*. Typical of this style is the staging of "When the Idle Poor Become the Idle Rich." The singing of the song is continuous, but the exact spatial location of Fred Astaire as the singer may change every ten seconds. In one shot he will be playing chess with a farmer, in another giving empty packages to attractive farm-girls, in another dancing up the side of a barn. The abandonment of invisible editing or match-cutting in this fashion relies on the assumption shared with the audience that we know this is not objective reality, that people do not sing in the street with group approval. Yet we welcome this transcendence of reality; the jump cutting acts as a crescendo to the boisterous quality of the sentiment expressed in the song. Such a cutting style would fail in a quiet, intimate duet between two lovers, but when applied to the task of preventing large groups of people from becoming cumbersome, the device is extremely effective and a harbinger of music video style in the 1980s.

Equally effective in the staging of the musical numbers is Coppola's eye for giving each number a distinct visual flair. As he described his efforts:

I wanted to do the musical numbers. I dreamed up the way the numbers were going to be done. I said, "Grandish," I'll shoot it on a hill and have Petula Clark hanging white bed sheets. And "If This Isn't Love" will be done with children's games. And "On That Great Come And Get It Day" they're going to throw away all their old furniture in big piles. And for every number I had an idea. I figured it out. And I wanted to.[33]

Coppola initially did not appreciate the degree to which he successfully used the studio and backlot of Warners. In several early interviews he lamented the fact that the studio did not allow him to shoot on location in Kentucky. (Later, Coppola's browbeating the studio into financing location shooting in Sicily on *The Godfather* figured crucially in that film's success.) Nonetheless, one of the charms of *Finian's* is its inspired utilization of the available studio sets, again demonstrating Coppola's ability to thrive on compromise. A counterpoint is established between the indoor artificial greenery of the set and the Burbank backlot locations. The indoor set emanates a dark bluish green color in its artificial vegetation, not realistic looking, but pleasant. It is used for all the romantic scenes, the night scenes, and the leprechaun magic scenes. The outdoor set, the Warner's backlot, is more realistic looking; we have horizons, blue skies, and more space. In this setting the scenes of social commentary occur, as do the satiric songs about class struggle, and the interactions between the sharecroppers and the agents of Senator Rawkins. Form, as embodied in the mise-en-scene, is here appropriate to content, as defined by the events occurring. Interesting demonstrations of the harmony between the mise-en-scene and the narrative occur in the two scenes where continuous actions begin in one setting and end in the other.

Coppola later changed his mind about the desirability of location shooting on *Finian's*. After the film had been released in the United States, he went to the English premiere, and John Russell Taylor quoted him in England as observing: "The film had to be made almost entirely on the backlot at Burbank and I think in a way that was right. It helps one to avoid the irrelevant picturesque and to control exactly the out-of-this-world effect wanted."[34]

In the final image of the film, Fred Astaire, off to another rainbow, walks down a hill to a highway where, strangely enough, a red Volkswagen is driving by. The attentive viewer is jolted as if a leprechaun had walked into the Godfather's office. A violation has occurred, and were this not an image that appears as people are putting on their coats to leave, it would have been a serious mistake. It seems as if the community with which we have become associated throughout the course of this film should have vanished like the one in *Brigadoon*; red Volkswagens are alien objects. One is tempted to speculate that Coppola was well aware of this incongruity's implications and was making a self-referential comment on the mise-en-scene's function in a musical's fantasy.

The success of the mise-en-scene in *Finian's* may have been an important factor in Coppola's later decisions to try to resuscitate the old-time studio style of making films—in particular, in his next musical, *One from the Heart* (1982). Coppola, instead of going to Las Vegas and risking complications and distractions (as had occurred in the jungles of *Apocalypse Now*), spent millions of dollars building a set to simulate Las Vegas and to allow filming under controlled studio conditions.

However, despite Coppola's professed fondness for the collegiality of the artistic community in the studio era, he did not get along well with one of that era's greatest successes, Fred Astaire's personal choreographer, Hermes Pan. The Astaire/Pan collaborations of the 1930s and 1940s were legendary for the rigor of their preparation—often two months rehearsal for scenes taking several minutes in the final film. Although Coppola rehearsed the dramatic portions of *Finian's* extensively before production, his improvisatory approach to the musical elements led to a clash with Pan that resulted in Pan leaving the film and years later commenting:

A director who was a real pain when we were working on *Finian's Rainbow* was Francis Ford Coppola. He may have been great on *The Godfather*, but he knew very little about dancing and musicals. He would interfere with my work and even with Fred's. Fred is such a gentleman he wanted to try to please, but Coppola and Joe Landon, the producer, actually told me, "Try not to make Astaire be like Astaire." I said, "Who do you want him to be like?" "We want him to be Finian." I said, "He's Astaire, and nobody's going to forget that." "No, we don't want Astaire, we want Finian." "Well, you're not going to get Finian," I told him, "you're going to get Astaire." That would never have happened with Louis B. Mayer because they were too aware of what the public wanted. You see, these schoolboys who studied at UCLA think they're geniuses, but there is a lot they don't understand.[35]

The improvisatory, rapid-fire production approach Coppola adopted toward the musical elements irked Pan, but had much to do with the miraculously low, $3.5 million budget, for a film with the feel of a big-budget spectacle. An anecdote should illuminate this: at one point in the production, lead dancer Barbara Hancock's feet were burned so badly on a hot studio floor that she could not dance for a week. Instead of waiting and wasting the week, Coppola took the rest of the cast outdoors and improvised and filmed some of the big production numbers.

When Coppola brought in this same improvisatory footage, the Warners executives loved it and were so tantalized with thoughts of a box office blockbuster that they blew the film up to 70mm for a roadshow-style distribution, a move that later distressed many because it chopped off Astaire's famous feet in one sequence. The executives gave Coppola carte blanche on his next film, *The Rain People*, while *Finian's* was still in post-production, and they agreed to finance George Lucas's *THX–1138* and a program of other young filmmakers' films on Coppola's endorsement. The executives knew the old-time musical style of *Top Hat* was irrecoverable, given the present mode of production, but they wrongly surmised that Coppola's frantic "youth film" style was the logical replacement. Audiences and most critics were not enamored with this new style musical, although it is difficult to estimate how much the unsatisfactory Civil Rights stance discussed above had to do with the disfavor.

Coppola had finished shooting *The Rain People* by the world premiere of *Finian's Rainbow* (October 9, 1968); in light of the reaction to *Finian's*, this was fortunate indeed. Renata Adler's aforementioned review in the *New York Times* was the most vitriolic; she commented: "The cast is full of children who act as artificially and insincerely as the whole enterprise, directed by Francis Ford Coppola, would suggest."[36] She went on to suggest that the producers were "hoping only to sell it to television as a family musical and get it over with." Perhaps it was this very family orientation in a time of *Bonnie and Clyde* (1967) and *The Wild Bunch* (1968) that made some of the other negative reviews pull punches. Pauline Kael, for instance, criticized the movie but remarked: "Still, compared with, say, *Doctor Doolittle* or *Half a Sixpence*, this big, clean, family musical isn't so bad."[37] Even in a generally favorable review by Arthur Knight this rejoinder seemed almost obligatory: "For the sad fact is that too much has happened in the intervening time; the ugly face of racism has come too close for anyone today to regard Finian's goodhearted, lighthearted magic as even a palliative to the problem."[38]

Perhaps the British were not as sensitive about the race issue as their American counterparts, if one can judge by the extremely favorable review by Tom Milne in *Sight and Sound*. The review was written at the height of the discovery of American studio genre pieces by serious film scholars, and Milne saw *Finian's* as a deserving heir to the artistry of the classic musical:

As Godard once remarked of *The Pajama Game*, they are not dancing because they are dancers, but because they feel the need to; and *Finian's Rainbow* is above all a demonstration of the naturalness of the musical as a means of expression, with barely an interior visible throughout the entire film, with dancers pounding rough grass and muddy earth instead of carefully prepared surfaces, and singers actually experiencing the emotions they celebrate.[39]

Milne was particularly admiring of the movement and editing style which was discussed earlier, and spent considerable time detailing how the musical sequences were woven together. At one point he remarked:

The whole sequence has that effortless choreographic flow and overall rhythm that hasn't been seen in the cinema since *Summer Holiday* and *Silk Stockings*—and allows one to hope that Coppola can and will take over the Mamoulian mantle.[40]

In the ensuing years, Milne's hope for a new Mamoulian was, of course, never realized. Quite to the contrary, following *Finian's*, Coppola embarked on a series of five of the most serious-minded, tragic, and darkly violent films in American cinema. However, in 1981, Coppola hired Gene Kelly to produce a string of Arthur Freed-like musicals for Omni-Zoetrope and began work on a musical of his own, *One from the Heart*, a film that made *Finian's* financial disappointment seem mild. Coppola began a 1982 dialogue with Gay Talese in *Esquire* with this statement: "I see myself becoming more of a film composer. All my future films will be musical—with songs and dances and more fluid imagery."[41] Coppola collaborated on the musical score for *Rumble Fish*, and when the musical elements of *The Cotton Club* were allowed to dominate, they were the saving grace of the film. Perhaps Coppola will yet bear out Milne's prophecy of a new Mamoulian and

*Finian's Rainbow* will be regarded as an important apprenticeship. Until that time it remains even in its failure an interesting confluence of the Hollywood profit motive and the developing artistic sensibility of a young, soon to be important director.

## NOTES

1. Siegfried Kracauer, *Theory of Film* (New York: Oxford Press, 1971), 72.

2. Kracauer, p. 19.

3. Stephen Mamber, *Cinema Verité in America: Studies in Uncontrolled Documentary* (Cambridge: MIT Press, 1974), 4.

4. Fred Baker and Ross Firestone, eds., *Movie People* (New York: Douglas, 1972), 63.

5. Joseph Morgenstern, "A National Anthem," *Newsweek*, February 20, 1967, p. 96.

6. In Richard Koszarski's interview in *Films in Review*, 19, no. 9 (November 1968), p. 533, Coppola comments: "I began writing the script for *Big Boy*—I had bought the novel, from which it's loosely adapted, from this boy in England, with my own money—as sanity-therapy while I was working on *Is Paris Burning?* I was writing two scripts at once."

7. Koszarski, p. 533.

8. Baker, p. 59.

9. Rex Reed, "Offering the Moon to a Guy in Jeans," *New York Times*, August 7, 1966, p. 11D.

10. Reed, p. 11D.

11. Morgenstern, p. 97.

12. Baker, p. 63. Coppola made the parenthetical remark before publication.

13. I want to be careful about how much intentionality is implied here. The cinematographer, Andrew Laszlo, claims it was his original idea to shoot the scene in available light and unprepared with hidden cameras, after the production department announced that there were no funds left to shoot it conventionally. Upon checking the lighting in Macy's, however, his enthusiasm was dampened, but he felt "the point of no return had been passed, as I felt that, based on my suggestion, nothing short of a national disaster could now stop the director from going ahead with the sequence." Laszlo eventually solved the lighting problem with considerable help from the lab, but the overall tone of the article suggests Coppola was constantly pushing Laszlo to use unorthodox techniques. "The Far-Out Photography of *You're a Big Boy Now*," *American Cinematographer*, June 1967, p. 414.

14. David Benedictus, *You're a Big Boy Now* (New York:E. P. Dutton, 1964), p. 178. Hereafter all references to the novel will have page quotations in the text.

15. Robert K. Johnson, *Francis Ford Coppola* (Boston:Twayne, 1977), p. 176.

16. Robert Philip Kolker, *A Cinema of Loneliness* (New York: Oxford Press, 1980), p. 146.

17. The shooting of this scene is very reminiscent of Hitchcock. The attack by the rooster reminds one of Tippi Hedren being attacked in *The Birds*. Miss Thing's falling down the stairs echoes the detective who falls down the stairs in *Psycho*.

18. Richard Schickel, "A Disaster Area," originally in *Life* magazine. Reprinted in *Film 67/68*, Hollis Alpert and Andrew Sarris, eds. (New York: Simon and Schuster, 1969), 112, 113.

19. Morgenstern, p. 98.

20. Reed, p. 11D.

21. Michael Pye and Lynda Myles, *The Movie Brats* (New York: Holt, Rinehart, and Winston, 1979), p. 73–75.

22. In two interview/articles, Coppola has referred to *Finian's* as "basically a cheat." They are Stephen Farber's "Coppola and *The Godfather*" in *Sight and Sound*, 41 (Autumn 1972), and Susan Braudy's "Francis Ford Coppola: A Profile" in *Atlantic*, August 1976. In the Braudy piece he refers to *Finian's* as being a motivation for his daringness with *The Rain People*: "I hated *Finian's* and I was scared that I was incapable of writing an original script and directing it. So I forced my hand, invested my own money and got studio backing once we'd started" (p. 70).

23. Gerald Mast, *A Short History of the Movies* (Indianapolis: Bobbs-Merrill, 1981), 428.

24. Farber, p. 220.

25. The story is best told in the Farber interview, p. 220. There Coppola relates: "And somehow it happened, though I had resolved it wouldn't. Partly I decided to do *Finian's Rainbow* because I remembered the show. My father had been in the musical comedy business. It was a very romantic idea, like wouldn't my father be happy if I did a big musical." There has been speculation that the desire to please father was a powerful influence in Coppola's handling of the relationships of the family in *The Godfather*. Joseph McBride, in "Coppola Inc.," *American Film* (November 1975), p. 18, suggested: "Some think the real clue to the Michael Corleone analogy is in the August-Francis relationship, which has been compared to the rivalry in *The Godfather* between Michael and his flashier brother, Sonny, for their father's love and for custodianship of the family tradition."

26. *Variety*, "W7 Plans $2,000,000 Promotion Campaign for 'Finian's Rainbow' " (August 14, 1968), 4.

27. Coppola gave his own estimation of why the film had not been made before in an interview with Joseph Gelmis that is published in that writer's *The Film Director as Superstar* (Garden City, NY: Anchor Press, 1970), p. 182: "There were political reasons, partly. It came out right before the McCarthy era. I guess lots of people felt there were leftist radical things in it. And the people who wrote it wanted lots of money for it. And by the time that subsided, it was already an old show. People had tried to make it, on and off. John and Faith Hubley were planning to make a full-length cartoon out of it back in the '50s."

28. Brooks Atkinson, "*Finian's Rainbow*," *New York Times*, January 11, 1947.

29. Gelmis, p. 183.

30. Renata Adler, *A Year in The Dark* (New York: Random House, 1969), 266.

31. Koszarski, p. 534. In the same discussion comes the following exchange: "Q. Did you do the screenplay for it? A. I did, but I don't get credit." Credit on the film was listed as Harburg and Lane, the play's authors.

32. This is from the text of *Finian's Rainbow* that appeared in *Theatre Arts* (January 1949), pp. 56–76.

33. Gelmis, p. 184.

34. Taylor, p. 21.

35. Dan Georgakas, "The Man Behind Fred and Ginger," *Cineaste*, 2, no. 4 (1983), 27.

36. Adler, p. 266.

37. Pauline Kael, "The Current Cinema," *The New Yorker*, October 19, 1968, p. 213.

38. Arthur Knight, *"Finian's Rainbow,"* *Film 67/68*, Hollis Alpert and Andrew Sarris, eds. (New York: Simon and Schuster, 1969), p. 158.

39. Milne, p. 44.

40. Ibid. Mamoulian was a Hollywood director noted for big, colorful musicals with unabashed sentiment.

41. Francis Coppola and Gay Talese, "The Conversation," *Esquire*, July 1981, p. 78.

# 3
# *"Personal" Filmmaking*

## The Rain People

In his pre-*Godfather* period, *The Rain People* best demonstrates Coppola's aspirations toward seriousness and creative exploration, something other than commercial filmmaking. Throughout the wheelings and dealings of his earlier career, "Art"—with a capital "A"—was still a priority in Coppola's mind. *The Rain People* is a self-conscious attempt to depart radically from the way conventional feature films are made and in that departure to question the very methodology of Hollywood filmmaking. Despite its overly melodramatic ending, there is integrity in *The Rain People's* experimentation. Stephen Farber called it "one of the quietest, most uncompromising personal movies in American film history."[1] Had the film's critical or commercial reception been better, it seems safe to speculate that Coppola would have twice rejected the offer to direct *The Godfather* instead of once, and that his career would have gone in a very different direction.

As it happened, however, *The Rain People's* critical failure seems more the result of the film's singularity, and its commercial failure a result of its downbeat and poorly motivated plot outcome. Frontline reviewers had difficulty in reacting to or judging such an unusual film, which is often the case with reviewers working under deadline pressure. (This was apparent again with the critical response to *One from the Heart* and *Rumble Fish*.) Audiences may have been troubled by the narrative's lack of catharsis to the psychological problems exhibited by Natalie, the main character. The film defines her emotional crisis, but offers, perhaps realistically, no resolution. Coppola seemed to discard the commercial sense he exhibited in his earlier ventures: happy endings, romance, upbeat music and editing, gratuitous sex and violence (e. g., *Dementia 13*), and facile social psychology. Instead of the commercial elements, we find something, for want of a better term, "personal."

The "personal" aspects of the film production extend from the initial conceptualization of the film to the very eccentric production methods.[2] *The Rain People*'s plot germinated from an unfinished short story Coppola had written for a creative writing class in 1960, titled "Echoes." Initially the story concerned three women leaving their husbands and was developed from a time in the young Coppola's life when his own mother had become frustrated and suddenly left one weekend to spend time alone in a hotel. It seems the young child's inability to understand that action led to the later attempt to deal with the experience creatively. However, Coppola was unable to resolve the story satisfactorily, and he put it away for a number of years following the creative writing class. Then, at the San Locarno film festival where Shirley Knight's *Dutchman* was playing, Coppola noticed Knight outside crying over an unkind remark someone had made to her. Coppola was touched, approached the actress, and told her he would write a movie for her. Probably underlying the rather gallant gesture was an admiration for the European directors' practice of having female alteregos in their films: Antonioni/Monica Vitti; Fellini/Guilleta Masina; Bergman/ Liv Ullman, and so on. Knight had a reputation as a stage actress, someone of substance, opposed to the Hollywood approach to filmmaking. She seemed the ideal person to become Coppola's feminine alterego. As it turned out, however, Coppola and Knight had serious disagreements, Knight came to distrust Coppola, and Coppola felt this adversely affected the narrative, which characteristically was not finished when the film began.

Coppola initially conceptualized the production as a voyage of discovery. He would take a small crew, perhaps five or six technicians, with portable equipment and freely improvise the film from a loose screenplay as they duplicated Natalie's cross-country journey. His directing experience to this point had spanned the Roger Corman low-budget, shoot-quickly *Dementia 13* to the large New York and Hollywood union crews of *You're a Big Boy Now* and *Finian's Rainbow*, and he was looking for the best of both worlds. The first attempts at getting the film financed demonstrate the usual Coppola chutzpah. As with other projects, Coppola risked personal money, this time the money he had made from his previous film, *Finian's Rainbow*, to buy his own equipment, $80,000 worth. He began shooting *The Rain People* at an aunt's house with a small crew of friends before he had studio financing. This included George Lucas, Walter Murch, and others from the California film school community, which provided some buttressing from the lures of Hollywood. (Coppola reportedly turned down a $400,000 offer to direct *Mame* with Barbra Streisand during the same period.) George Lucas later released a 16mm documentary extolling the comraderie of the mission.

*The Rain People*'s production had preceded the premiere of *Finian's*, when the Warner's executives were still euphoric about that film's possibilities. With a gambler's bluff, Coppola had announced he would do the film with or without studio financing. Feeling $800,000 was not a big risk with someone of Coppola's talents, Kenny Hymans, of Warner Brothers, gave Coppola financing and a carte blanche to continue with *The Rain People*. Coppola welcomed the support, but with the Warner Brothers' trademark came problems with unions, which plagued him throughout the shooting and eventually forced him to use a larger, 17-member crew. This was still small by Hollywood standards, but a departure from his original vision. An interesting scene in Lucas's documentary shows Coppola pacing about, arguing on the telephone about the union requirements, making heated threats about what his new style of filmmaking would do to the old system. More was on Coppola's mind during the filmmaking than just how best to resolve the narrative.

Briefly, the narrative of the film went as follows: Natalie (Shirley Knight) awakens early one morning, while her husband sleeps, and sets the table, writes a good-by note, and leaves. On the way out of town, she visits her mother and explains that she is pregnant and upset about the potentially constricting responsibilities of being a wife and mother. Natalie's solution is to spend time by herself. Driving aimlessly, she encounters a hitchhiker named "Killer" Kilgannon (James Caan). Despite the name, Killer is a gentle innocent who played football until a brain-damaging injury cut short his career. His college gave him $1,000 and sent him away. (This was modeled on someone Coppola knew at Hofstra.) Natalie, initially unaware of his condition, begins to seduce him in a motel room. However, halfway into the seduction she discovers his scars, and from that point until the conclusion Killer is an unwanted responsibility for Natalie; metaphorically he is the child inside her. Natalie unsuccessfully attempts to unload Killer at his former girlfriend's house. In Nebraska, she gets Killer a job working for Mr. Alfred (Ron Aldridge), the unscrupulous owner of the "Reptile Ranch" who takes Killer's money as a fee for taking care of "the dummy." Natalie leaves distressed, and in her hurry to depart is pulled over for speeding by a motorcycle cop named Gordon (Robert Duvall). The two begin to flirt, but Gordon makes Natalie go reluctantly to the county clerk to pay her fine. The County Clerk turns out to be Mr. Alfred, and as Natalie returns to Alfred's she discovers Killer has run amuck and is freeing mistreated animals. After Natalie stops him, Mr. Alfred takes $800 of Killer's money for damages and Natalie takes Killer away. Killer is becoming increasingly dependent upon her, and as she calls her husband from a phone booth, Killer rips the phone cord out. Natalie leaves him in a rage, and we next see her with Gordon entering Gordon's trailer after a "date." Gordon's 9-year-old daughter is a bit wild and clearly jealous of Natalie; so Gordon kicks the daughter out of the trailer. The little girl wanders about the trailer park until she coincidentally meets Killer. Meanwhile, Natalie begins to feel Gordon is looking for someone to replace his dead wife. Her fantasies about an uncomplicated sexual encounter fade and she decides to leave. This angers Gordon, and he attempts to rape her. Killer breaks in, and in the ensuing melee, Gordon's daughter shoots Killer with her father's pistol. The film ends with Natalie hysterical, telling the dead Killer he can come home with her and that she and Vinny will treat him as family.

The central theoretical issue that dominates both the production of the film and the way we react to it is the effectiveness of the concept Siegfried Kracauer called the "found story." As Kracauer explained it: "The term 'found story' covers all stories found in the material of actual physical reality."[3] The best anecdote to illustrate the concept concerns Eisenstein, who had a completed script for *Potemkin*, but upon seeing a photograph of the Odessa steps conceived the famous third act of that film. The physical reality of the Odessa steps overwhelmed any imaginative work done with the content in the initial conceptual stages. The "found story" had much to do with quasi-cinema verité scenes in *You're a Big Boy Now* and also Coppola's initial frustration with both the studio sets in *Finian's Rainbow* and his inability to shoot on location. *The Rain People* is Coppola's most deliberate experimentation with the idea of the found story, and his most successful. (The Philippine jungle in *Apocalypse Now* came to have the same function, although less premeditated.) However, *The Rain People* does not pretend toward cinema verité, as *Big Boy* did. In discovering locations as he filmed along the way of a four month cross-country odyssey that moved from Long Island, New York, through West Virginia, Tennessee, and ended in Ogallah, Nebraska, Coppola sought to enhance and refine the loose narrative he had conceptualized with the inspiration of the locations they stumbled upon.

The most successful scene resulting from this method occurs toward the end of the film. Somewhere in Nebraska, Natalie gets Killer a job at "The Reptile Ranch," a disgusting place where Mr. Alfred raises chickens and Easter bunnies for children under very cruel and inhumane conditions. The squalor, yet authenticity of this location, make it difficult to believe it was anything other than a "discovery." However, the cinematic qualities of the location also underline and enhance narrative issues; the mise-en-scene heightens the moral dilemma Natalie faces in divorcing herself from Killer— will he be treated in a similarly inhumane fashion? Is her convenience more important than the ill-defined responsibility she feels toward Killer? The Reptile Ranch becomes a metaphor for the world that awaits Killer with no one to protect him. Natalie leaves emotionally upset. While she is away, Killer sees clearly enough the relationship he has to the animals and begins to set them free. (Not coincidentally, this conceit has parallels to the end of *Rumble Fish*; S. E. Hinton saw the film before she wrote her novel.) Finally, Natalie has to take Killer away from the Reptile Ranch, an indication that she is beginning to acknowledge a responsibility to Killer as well as to the fetus inside her. Clearly, the "found" location has much to do with the excellence of this section of the film.

On the other hand, the most disconcerting scenes seem to be the ones that feature what might be called a travelogue approach. At one point Killer and Natalie are in Tennessee. Momentarily separated, Killer searches for Natalie through a parade. The parade is just the sort of thing that would seem exotic to white university film school graduates: black high school bands strut down the street in free-form dance rhythms. The camera focuses on the faces of poor Southern blacks lining the streets as Killer walks among them. His movement is against the grain, which establishes his lack of direction of life. However, were this a film examining the living conditions of Southern blacks, the footage would be quite interesting, but in the context of this psychological melodrama concerning a New York woman who tries to find herself by a lonely escape, the footage is distracting and has no correlation. The forced quality of such a scene may have prompted some of the negative reviewers to question the sincerity of the production.

Still, *The Rain People* would have been far less compelling had it been shot in the sort of mundane, ordinary locations normally allowed by a Hollywood producer. There is a certain intensity in Knight's acting performance that seems engendered by strange locations, cheap hotels, and phone booths in the middle of nowhere. Likewise, a Nebraska trailer park or a desolate Midwest landscape subtly emphasize the existential aspects of the character's motivations: Natalie totally divorces herself from the environment that she felt was strangling her and replaces it with an ultimately more threatening, impersonal one. The edge to Natalie's desperation would have not been achieved in a convenient Hollywood location.

Experimentation has its risks. Mistakes such as the Chattanooga parade were made by a young director under pressure from labor unions to use a larger crew, under pressure because he was not getting along with his lead actress, and under pressure to manufacture a story as he went along. When one considers the production's background, the film might seem remarkable for the degree of integration it does maintain, except for the fact that Coppola has always thrived under pressure. Throughout the film there is a steady and unified exposition of Natalie's character, even in the segments where Coppola introduces new characters to push the narrative along. The film almost seems intentionally anti-commercial. Coppola experiments with long, real-time takes of Natalie in a phone booth talking to her husband, which demonstrate Knight's prowess as an actress. Coppola holds another shot while a traffic cop prepares to approach a car for an uncomfortably long length of time, seemingly challenging traditional film's reliance on ellipsis and time compression. This sort of experimentation is theoretical and interesting, but commercially risky. Stephen Farber, in an article about four low-budget films of the late 1960s by writer/directors, noted:

There is nothing about this film that is fashionable, nothing that makes it easy to sell to teens—no Arlo Guthrie record, no rock music backgrounds, no exaltation of youth against the Establishment, no documentary scenes of demonstrators in Chicago, no psychedelic parties. The film is an intimate exploration of Coppola's own interests and obsessions; it cannot possibly appeal to a mass audience.[4]

Thus, we are at the central enigma of *The Rain People* and perhaps, in a larger sense, Coppola's career. Financed by a multi-million dollar, profit-making corporation, Warner Brothers, *The Rain People* is nonetheless anti-commercial, individualistic, experimental, and finally personal. We have seen how Coppola through initiative, drive, talent, and a bit of historical timing was able to maneuver himself into a position to make such a film. Yet from a systematic view, the question remains whether Hollywood needs films like *The Rain People*, and whether there is some larger compulsion than profit and loss. The widely accepted equation is that Coppola makes commercial films to finance his artistic films, *Finian's Rainbow* for *The Rain People*, *The Godfather* for *The Conversation*, *The Outsiders* for *Rumble Fish*. It sounds like paying one's dues for artistic self-indulgence. Perhaps, however, the larger operative is that in their "failure," films such as *The Rain People* or *The Conversation* serve as cautionary warnings to any director that would drift too far from the mainstream. They become object lessons for what Hollywood should not attempt. Finally, we have to wonder how much Coppola himself has absorbed this lesson after twenty years of struggle with the constraints of such a system.

Despite the perception of the film's "failure," the film did win the Best Film Award at the San Sebastian film festival. In more recent years, *The Rain People* has attracted favorable critical interest as a film ahead of its time in its concern for issues central to the women's movement. In 1976, Diane Jacobs wrote a reappraisal observing that it was "a woman's film in the best sense of the word, which is to say a film about humanity filtered through a female experience."[5] Bert Cardullo, in "Re-viewing *The Rain People*" for *The New Orleans Review*, suggested it was "Coppola's most fully realized, if least spectacular film."[6] Marjorie Rosen, the author of *Popcorn Venus*, asked Coppola in an interview whether there was any chance for revival of the film, to which Coppola curiously remarked, "Movies are like old girlfriends: Once you've done them and you're finished with them, you don't go back."[7] Nonetheless, Natalie can be seen as a forerunner to Kay Corleone of *Godfather II* who says "No" to her husband's patriarchal domination and aborts their child. Both characters rebel at the role assigned women in their respective cultures; both end up leaving husbands who espouse respect for the concept of family and motherhood.

However, although Kay Corleone is not the center of *Godfather II*, as Natalie is in *The Rain People*, the questions her character raises are dramatically better resolved than those of *The Rain People*. Later feminist critics viewed Natalie as one of the first contemporary characters to address the constricting role of the housewife in modern society. These critics ignored the negative results of Natalie's rebellion—ultimately she is shown as irresponsible and dangerous for her rejection of the traditional "woman's role." As Richard Combs observed:

That Coppola's notion of fulfillment and love completed is finally bound up in the image of children and the family would not be so suspect if it were not so unargued—and if it did not lead straight to the banal contrivance of the ending, with the pairing of Natalie's crippled family with Gordon's. . . . By refusing to find any potential in his heroine's physical quest, Coppola sabotages the film dramatically, and the result has a forlorn, self-destructive air."[8]

"Unargued" perhaps because Coppola had a loose hold on the dramatic implications of Natalie's actions. He seemed to intuitively understand Natalie's frustration well enough to convey it convincingly, but intellectually lacked a strong sense of the larger women's issues that Natalie's dilemma addresses. By *Godfather II*, Coppola understood the dramatic implications of a woman's rebellion well enough to make Kay Corleone the primary counterpoint to the moral degeneracy of the male Corleones. Still, Kay's actions proceed directly from the 1970s' assumptions that a woman is not the property of her husband; they seem anachronistic in the 1950s time frame of the film. *Peggy Sue Got Married* (1986) is ultimately the only Coppola film that is thoroughly in synch with the modern woman in her own time frame, and with that film we have a female scriptwriter.

Nonetheless, although the dramatic conclusion to *The Rain People*'s experimentation is unsuccessful, in the rest of the film Natalie is a fully realized character. Her depth and complexity is always plausible and compelling. Perhaps some of the tension in the character portrayal stems from the troubled collaboration between Coppola and actress Knight. In an interview with Stephen Farber, Coppola claimed Shirley Knight was the only actor he never developed a rapport with and suggested she did not trust him. Coppola speculated Knight enjoyed the theatre more than Hollywood, and his promised revolutionary approach to filmmaking did not materialize for her. Farber observed that the Natalie character was lost as the film went along, to which Coppola responded:

That was an editorial decision. Maybe I was angry at her, I don't know. The character as I had written it had a lot of the schizophrenia that comes out in the film, but there was also a tremendously compassionate side. The whole basis of the character was that she was a mother, a mother figure. And I didn't feel that I was getting that from Shirley. I would get the high-strung, nervous intensity, I don't know how much I liked that character I saw, whereas I liked the character I had written. I think that affected the cut. I started to throw more weight to Jimmy Caan's character. That is definitely the flaw of the film.

Coppola went on to analyze that this "flaw" had to do with not fully exploring the existential premise of the film, that the continual introduction of new characters was an escape from his writerly responsibility. He concluded:

I'd like to rewrite *The Rain People*. I never resolved it. I never really said "What does all that mean? Does that mean that woman is destined, through her physiological make-up, to be at home with her husband?" I don't know if that's what it means, but I wish the film had answered that.[9]

Despite these problems, Coppola remarked in 1974 that *The Rain People* was his favorite of his film work. No doubt he recognized the moments of character revelation that went beyond the traditional limits of Hollywood feature films, regardless of the problems with Knight. As an interesting footnote, Lucas's documentary on the making of *The Rain People* showed a backstage argument between Coppola and Knight over whether Natalie should carry a purse in one scene. In the argument Coppola seems rather domineering and patriarchal; Knight seems sulky but stubborn. Whether or not the director's personal demeanor toward women had anything to do with his difficulties in resolving *The Rain People* is certainly a dangerous area in which to speculate, although some of Coppola's intimates have commented upon it in other contexts. Coppola's wife Eleanor later quoted the director in *Notes* as saying he would give a million dollars to have a wife who was just satisfied with being a housewife; this during their much publicized marital problems. On a publicity tour for *Rocky III*, Coppola's sister Talia Shire in an offhanded manner compared her relationship to her older brother in terms of the Adrian/Paulie relationship in *Rocky*:

Francis has always been loving and extremely protective toward me. But I think he came very much from the feeling that a woman, especially a woman related to him, should explore herself but not come too far out of the, well, kitchen.[10]

The fact remains that of the best characters Coppola has created as a writer, Natalie is the only female. Coppola has yet to create a fully developed woman character who is happily free of family responsibility. Perhaps in conclusion we should dwell more on what *The Rain People* is than what it is not. It is a film of high ambition and daring. Much more than Coppola's other early films, this is the film that in its production experimentation looks forward to the post-*Apocalypse Now* Coppola, when he would try to own his own studio and revolutionize studio film production with new video-playback shooting systems. Although Coppola throughout his career has been struggling with conventional Hollywood genre films, this is also the film that tips his hand as a filmmaker interested in serious, artistic themes that are usually the province of European film. If it also reveals a weakness or blind spot in the preeminently male Coppolian fictional universe, then it is also a weakness he intends to explore, not turn away from. The success of *Peggy Sue Got Married* suggests more felicitous results with women collaborators such as Arlene Sarner and Kathleen Turner, but we will also see in the discussion of that film a similar problem with the ending. Despite its flaws, *The Rain People* has an integrity in its uniqueness.

## NOTES

1. Stephen Farber, "Coppola and *The Godfather*," *Sight and Sound*, 41 (Summer 1972), 218. Farber wrote about the film at more length in "End of the Road?" *Film Quarterly*, 23 (Winter 1969), 3–16.

2. The production account is taken from a number of sources. Two sources that are very interesting and seldom cited are Philip K. Scheuer, "On the Road with *The Rain People*," *Action*, 41 (Jan./Feb. 1969), 4–6; and David People's "How to be a Film Director," reprinted in Thomas Fensch's *Films on the Campus* (New York: Barnes, 1970), 77–88.

3. Siegfried Kracauer, *Theory of Film* (New York: Oxford University Press, 1971), 245.

4. Farber, *Film Quarterly*, p. 15.

5. Diane Jacobs, "Lookback: Francis Ford Coppola's *The Rain People*," *Millimeter*, 4 (November 1976), 60.

6. Bert Cardullo, "Reviewing *The Rain People*," *New Orleans Review*, 11, nos. 3/4 (1984), 112.

7. Marjorie Rosen, "Francis Ford Coppola Interviewed," *Film Comment*, 10 (July/August 1974), 43.

8. Richard Combs, "*The Rain People*," *Monthly Film Bulletin*, 46 (January 1979), 11.

9. Farber, *Sight and Sound*, pp. 221–222.

10. Susan Stark, "Talia," *Detroit News*, May 28, 1982, p. 3D.

# 4
## Phenomenal Success

### The Godfather

It was *The Godfather* that gave force and immediacy to the inscription "a film by Francis Ford Coppola." There is no exaggeration in saying the film's success was phenomenal: record-breaking commercial performance, critical raves and industry accolades, and also a pervasive cultural impact. For a period of time it was difficult to get through a week without hearing an "offer you can't refuse" joke; this film touched America's collective unconscious. It appeared during a phase when 1960s' activism and rebellion was just beginning to turn to the cynicism and self-interest of the 1970s. The Corleone's contempt for establishment values and advocacy of taking care of one's own struck a nerve. In addition there was the film's emphasis on ethnicity and immigrant roots when perhaps a vague dissatisfaction with the traditional concept of being "American" led many to a nostalgic exploration of their own pre-American origins. Finally, there was the sheer entertainment value of the film—Mario Puzo's vivid, violent, sexy dynastic saga and Coppola's inspired control of the cinematic elements, a combination that will stand up in any era.

Still, it is curious that the film that put Coppola on the celebrity map, that gave him the magic adjective "bankable," is also extremely problematic in terms of his authorship, or "auteurship." Coppola coordinated diverse creative agents in this production, he was clearly the catalyst for the film's success, but in a career view, his creative control and his originality are far less than in other films that bear his directorial signature. This is particularly evident if we place this film up against its sequel, *Godfather II*. Coppola went from essentially a highly skilled hired hand on *The Godfather* to the dominant artistic personality on *Godfather II*. To use French auteurist terminology, the transition was from being a *met teur-en-scene* on the first to an *auteur* on the second, albeit within the Hollywood context.

That same context has made this study cautious of ascribing something like personal "worldview" to an entity prone to so many influences as a Hollywood big-budget film. Yet it seems that in the overall analysis two worldviews delineate the differences between *The Godfather* and *Godfather II*; Mario Puzo's view prevailed with the former, and Coppola's with the latter. This distinction goes beyond the fact that *The Godfather* is first and foremost Mario Puzo's exciting story, whereas *Godfather II* is more a conceptual film, and Coppola's concept. In fact, it is the more nebulous quality of outlook-on-life that informs the distinction: Puzo's in the first, Coppola's in the second.

Puzo's worldview is somewhat benevolent and nonjudgmental, with tolerance and understanding of human shortcomings, even a fascination for them as part of a larger, well-planned order. *The Godfather*, the film, shows clearly how Puzo applied this to the gangster milieu: killers are good family men with a certain code of honor. However, the more sprawling novel extended this view to: 1) policemen, who mostly take bribes to put their children through school (and draw the line at ignoring victimless crimes); 2) celebrities, who are seen as average people thrown into unusual circumstances; and even 3) individual doctors, who are oppressed by a rigid, self-serving medical community. Societal institutions are inept in the Puzo worldview, but the individual, nevertheless, has a way of working out his own justice in this world. Puzo's view is strong in the novel, less strong but evident in the first film, but consumed by Coppola's worldview in the second film.

Coppola's view is much angrier. Rather than seeing the Mafia as a metaphor for how individuals cope in an unjust world as Puzo does, Coppola sees it more as a metaphor for the predatory, selfish, and ruthless aspects of modern corporate America. Perhaps the key contrast would be the two respective artistic views of Michael Corleone. Puzo treats Michael sympathetically, tragically, as an individual forced reluctantly to become his father, yet not quite up to the task. Coppola is unsympathetic, seeing Michael as the epitome of the failure of vision of the leaders of modern America. Coppola's shaping of *Godfather II* suggests Michael as almost a personal demon that Coppola needed to exorcise, as a moral lesson in how individuals lose their humanity with the acquisition of power. This will be discussed at greater length in Chapter 6, which focuses exclusively on *Godfather II*. Nonetheless, with reference to the evolution in control and tone in the *Godfathers*, consider Puzo's reaction to the sequel:

> *Godfather II*, which I think is a very good movie, and I'm surprised that Francis could even pull it off, descended into a moral point of view, which I disapprove of in art. In *Godfather II* we have Michael defeated and desolate, and that's not my

concept of how it should have ended. That's a concept that conforms to the morals of our society and that I don't think happened to be true. The book ends with Michael's wife lighting candles to save his soul. That's my moral comment, that's all. But the concept of power desolating someone, the way they showed it in the picture, all alone by the ocean with just his sister, I think is just baloney.[1]

By extension, the "morals of our society" that Puzo referred to comprise the myth that the rich are unhappy, which traditionally made the common man's inevitable jealousy easier to endure. Puzo's is the classic writer's personality, the introverted observer, looking for explanations for the way people behave and the truth behind the myth. Coppola's personality as a filmmaker is much more extroverted, oriented toward affecting rather than observing people. He has seen himself as a revolutionary, as an artist out to overthrow a dead establishment, and it may be that Puzo is reacting to a strain of self-righteousness that Coppola threads through the sequel. To Coppola, Michael Corleone is the same unthinking, insensitive, powerful-but-failed corporate executive that blocks Coppola's own ambitions for a new kind of filmmaking. His dealings with Warner Brothers/Seven Arts and the dissolution of Coppola's American Zoetrope just prior to his work on *The Godfather* may have provided some handy models.

But before falling too deeply into the trap of artistic intention, let us return to an examination of the production background of this enormously successful film, the film many feel initiated the "blockbuster syndrome" of the 1970s. Unlike Coppola's preceding film, *The Rain People*, and perhaps more like *Finian's Rainbow*, Coppola walked onto an ongoing, studio-controlled production and with a talent for behind-the-scenes infighting gained a modicum of control over the creative decision making that led to the film's success. The coups Coppola accomplished are legendary—securing Brando and Pacino against the executives' wishes, coercing Paramount in to paying for Sicilian location shooting, and so forth—but it should not be forgotten that it was someone else's film upon which these artistic victories were performed. There are problems with terming this a Francis Coppola film.

Mario Puzo had long cherished the dream of being a writer/artist, if we are to believe his *The Godfather Papers*,[2] a paperback hastily issued during the height of *The Godfather*'s popularity as a film. Included in the collection are painful excerpts from his "Writer's Diary" in the 1950s, a time when he was toiling without financial encouragement, in debt, and having difficulty supporting his family through a minor bureaucratic post. Two novels, *The Dark Arena* (1955) and *The Fortunate Pilgrim* (1965), received excellent reviews but netted him only $6,500 combined. Gay Talese called the latter "perhaps the best novel ever written about Italian immigrants in America."[3] Nonetheless, Puzo supported himself during the period by cranking out quick adventure stories for popular magazines. He also nurtured a lively interest in the Mafia, sending to Washington for all transcripts related to the Senate hearings—he brags he never knew anyone in the Mafia, which is a tribute to his imaginative power.

After the critical, but not financial, success of *The Fortunate Pilgrim*, Puzo went to his publisher to get an advance on his next novel. The publisher refused, but told him he should have emphasized the Mafia element in the preceding book (a minor character is tempted to join the Mafia) and that they would give him an advance on the receipt of one hundred pages of a Mafia novel. Puzo was not pleased, but being $20,000 in debt he produced a 10-page outline, which they refused. Puzo passed the time "working on a string of adventure magazines, editing, writing freelance stories. . . . I was ready to forget novels except maybe as a puttering hobby for my old age."[4] A writer friend, however, was regaled by Puzo's Mafia stories and arranged a meeting with G. P. Putnam. They gave him a $5,000 advance and Puzo took three years to write the book, continuing his free-lancing during this time. With one hundred pages completed, he sold an option to Paramount for $12,500 versus $50,000 if the film was made. In retrospect, Puzo admits this was a mistake, a ridiculously low price in view of the eventual film earnings. On completion of the book, however, the paperback rights were sold for $410,000 a record at that time.

Puzo was surprised at how good the reviews of the book were. Besides Gay Talese's admiring review for *The Washington Post*, Roger Jellnick wrote in *The New York Times*: "*The Godfather* is bound to be highly successful, and not simply because the Mafia is in the news. Mr. Puzo's novel is a voyeur's dream, a skillful fantasy of violent personal power without consequences."[5] In *The New York Times Book Review*, Dick Schapp wrote: "Allow for a touch of corniness here. Allow for a bit of overdramatization there. Allow for an almost total absence of humor. Still Puzo has written a solid story that you can read without discomfort at one long sitting."[6] In the favorable reviews there was a grudging admiration for the skill of its commercialism. Of the negative reviews, perhaps the *Times* (London) *Literary Supplement* blast best demonstrates the sort of highbrow disdain that Pauline Kael would echo in her review of *Godfather II* when she called Puzo's work "trash." *The Times* called it: "At best pretentiously literary, at worst as in the recurrent scenes of murder and assault, mechanically sensational."[7]

Initially the Paramount executives were reluctant to make *The Godfather*. An earlier Mafia film, *The Brotherhood* (1968) had lost money for Paramount, and Puzo claimed the plot of that film had been pirated from the early galleys of *The Godfather*.[8] However, the phenomenal sales success of *The Godfather* made the film obligatory, and they resolved to up-date the story to the present, set it in St. Louis, and shoot it on a quick, low budget to capitalize on the paperback's popularity. Somewhat against usual practice, they hired Puzo to distill the novel down to script form.

Puzo worked on the initial script from April to August 1970, and then it was time to hire a director. In lists of potential directors, Coppola's name kept turning up because of his Italian ancestry. Coppola was fresh off the commercial failures of *The Rain People* and *Finian's Rainbow*, and his first attempt at forming his own company, American Zoetrope, was falling apart with Warners' lack of support. He was again attempting to get *The Conversation* off the ground. His stock had gone up somewhat in the spring of 1970 with the release of *Patton*, which had a screen credit for work he had done in 1966. There was the feeling that because he was young and had just suffered some failures, he could be controlled, and he became the third or fourth choice behind Richard Brooks, Peter Yates, and Constantin Costa-Gavras; Costa-Gavras declined the film, professing his admiration for the novel's treatment of capitalism, but bowing out because of his ignorance of the nuances of American culture.

Coppola's reaction to his first offer to direct *The Godfather*:

I started to read the book I got only about 50 pages into it. I thought it was a popular, sensational novel, pretty cheap stuff. I got to the part about the singer supposedly modeled on Frank Sinatra and the girl Sonny Corleone liked so much because her vagina was enormous—remember that stuff in the book? It never showed up in the movie. Anyway, I said "My God, what is this—*The Carpetbaggers*?" So I stopped reading and said "Forget it."

Four or five months later, I was again offered the opportunity to work on it and by that time, I was in dire financial straits with my own company in San Francisco, so I read further. Then I got into what the book is really about—the story of the family, this father and his sons, and questions of power and succession—and I thought it was a terrific story, if you could cut out all the other stuff. I decided it could be not only a successful movie but also a *good* movie. I wanted to concentrate on the central theme, and that's what I tried to do.

So the fact is, it wasn't a piece of trash.[9]

Initially Coppola was just to direct. But with the characteristic energy and drive he invests in all his projects, he decided to write as well. Puzo recalls their writing habits:

He rewrote one half and I rewrote the second half. Then we traded, and rewrote each other. I suggested we work together. Francis looked me right in the eye and said no. That's when I knew he was really a director.

I liked him. And he earned his half of the screen credit. And I was glad to see him get it. I could blame all the lousy dialogue lines on him and some of the lousy scenes. He was never abrasive, we got along fine; and finally there was a shooting script.[10]

After the screenplay was finished, some of the most important creative battles of the film were fought over the casting and location shooting. Puzo wrote that he felt that it was "their movie," meaning the producers had the final say over these key elements. However, Puzo did not wash his hands of the affair, remained to give his input, was an ally of Coppola's, and was the first to suggest the casting of Marlon Brando. The Paramount brass were much opposed to Brando because of his reputation as a difficult actor who made films go over budget. However, at this point in the pre-production process, Coppola seems to have begun dominating the decisions made on the film. In the most widely recounted anecdote of the production, Coppola talked the executives into at least grudgingly looking at a screen test of Brando. Brando, unaware of the executives' antipathy, agreed to do a video improvisation with Coppola as an experiment, and impressively *became* the godfather on the tape. Coppola showed the evidence to a board-room full of hostile studio executives and won them over. James Caan and Robert Duvall, both Coppola protegé from *The Rain People*, were given the key roles of Sonny Corleone and Tom Hagen.[11] Caan, at one point, was the leading candidate for the role of Michael, but Coppola, having seen Al Pacino in a highly successful run on Broadway, could not get the actor's face out of his mind for the role of Michael.

Although Pacino eventually was nominated for the Best Supporting Actor Oscar, his character had the most screen time in the film. The executives wanted a bankable name in the role. Robert Redford was frequently mentioned, but Coppola, in another test of his influence over the film, finally won out. Puzo observed: "Francis Coppola is heavy-set, jolly, and is usually happy-go-lucky. What I didn't know was that he could be tough about his work."[12] Coppola and Puzo teamed up to argue for the casting of Brando and the location shooting in Sicily, but the evidence suggests Coppola was the more tenacious persuader of the duo.

In looking at the importance of pre-production decision making, it is difficult to imagine *The Godfather* without Duvall, Pacino, Caan, or Brando, but it is conceivable that other actors would have also been impressive. However, clearly the decision to shoot the Sicilian location scenes was absolutely essential to the success of *The Godfather*. Besides the authenticity these scenes add, there is the simple pleasure of watching the scenes: the light in contrast to the darkness of the New York scenes touches off mythic resonances of innocence versus experience, good versus evil, nature versus the city, and so forth. Ironically, of course, this is all turned around: it is Sicily that gives birth to the violent methods of the Mafia; it is New York that the immigrants go to with the dream of something better. The killing of Apollonia in this "garden" is a metaphor for the death of any hope for another sort of life in the consciousness of Michael. Without the physical setting of Sicily in the film, all the tensions and dichotomies would become polarized and rigid, like those of standard urban gangster films. The executives initially wanted to shoot these scenes in up-state New York before Coppola's browbeating freed up additional funding.

Furthermore, the issue of the Sicilian scenes illuminates a certain courage about the film that explains why it was so well received. Despite considerable pressure from the Italian-American League, the film never backed off from the fact that the gangsters under consideration were Italian. Some of the earliest Hollywood gangster films were about recognizably ethnic gangsters—Paul Muni as the Italian Tony Camonte, modelled on Al Capone in *Scarface* (1932); James Cagney as a noticeably Irish gangster in *The Public Enemy* (1931); Edward G. Robinson as Rico in *Little Caesar* (1930), and so on—and their attraction to gangsterism was depicted as one of the more lucrative avenues open to an immigrant's son. With the Hays code of 1934 the gangster became outwardly more sanitized, less distinguishable as an ethnic type. Crime as a solution for the unjust lack of opportunity for immigrants in America ceased to be an issue in the important gangster films of the 1950s and 1960s that preceded *The Godfather*; the psychologically disturbed personality of the gangster became the more important issue.[13] That the film did not try to whitewash cultural sore points (and, in fact, by *Godfather II* was directly commenting on this reality of the American experience) enhanced the film's status as serious art. At one point in the film, one of the dons at the gangster convention remarks that the narcotics trade should be kept to "the coloreds"; "They're animals anyway, let them lose their souls." No obvious, didactic attempt is made to discredit this character's racism; the viewers must supply their own moral judgment. Most Hollywood films would have deleted the line for fear of offending someone—and lost a dimension of the subject being considered. *NBC* showed far greater timidity by running extensive disclaimers before each airing of the film denying that the film was meant to represent any ethnic group.

The Sicilian scenes suggested that there was a link in the violence of the native Sicilians and the immigrant Sicilians. But it suggested more than that; it suggested that the family relations, the physical look of the people, the social customs, the food, and so forth had links to a homeland. That there is a relation between our ancestors and our contemporary selves was dramatized for more than just the Italian-Americans, and some of the upsurge in interest in geneaology among all ethnic groups in America in the 1970s can be attributed to the chords *The Godfather* struck in our national consciousness.

Although Coppola seems to have had major input in pre-production decisions such as whether to film in Sicily, in the early phase of the production process his relationship with some of the other creative personnel was less than harmonious. Cinematographer Gordon Willis and the crew of technicians were very skeptical about the kid director; rumors coming off the set to the effect that the film would be a disaster almost got Coppola fired. Most probably, any improvisational style left over from the experiments of *The Rain People* grated against a seasoned professional crew. For instance, Coppola decided to shoot some of the wedding sequence in cinema verité style. Coppola also has a penchant for indulging actors, giving them extensive rehearsal time, allowing them to pull pranks on the set, and Gordon Willis reportedly has something less than admiration for actors.[14]

For visual style, Coppola and Willis, without going to black and white, wanted to evoke the films of the 1940s by using a grainy film stock, and avoiding the zoom lens, fast cutting, and abundant close-ups. Muted colors dominated by yellow and brown were to give the film a nostalgic feel. Coppola's initial encounters with Willis were antagonistic: "I'd tell the guy how I wanted to shoot the scene, and he'd say, 'Oh that's dumb.' "[15] The pair gradually became accustomed to each other, Coppola grew to admire Willis' talent, and they worked together on the sequel at Coppola's request.

The unusually large number of accounts of the production universally point to Coppola as the prime mover in the creative production decisions, the artist with the most impact on the final result. Often, however, the most creative production practices will not save a film with a poor screenplay. Coppola has never been one to affect humility, but he has often been quoted as saying he felt the essence of *The Godfather* was Puzo's, indicating a bias on his part toward narrative and characterization over the non-narrative elements of cinematography, acting style, editing, and other traditional production concerns. Coppola remarked to Charles Higham: "There's no doubt there's more of Mario Puzo in the picture than anybody else. The film, after all, is extremely faithful to the book."[16] However, it is interesting that the film's faithfulness to the novel is more a result of Coppola the screenwriter than Puzo the screenwriter as revealed in this *Time* magazine production account:

[Coppola said] "Puzo's screenplay had turned into a slick contemporary gangster picture of no importance. It wasn't Puzo's fault. He just did what they told him to do." With Puzo's collaboration, Coppola rewrote the script along the broader lines he envisioned. "It was my intention," he says, "to make this an authentic piece of film about gangsters who were Italian, how they lived, how they behaved, the way they treated their families, celebrated their rituals."[17]

Coppola returned the story to 1945 and returned it to New York, maintaining the historical perspective toward the development of modern organized crime. However, while Coppola was faithful to Puzo's original narrative, he was clearly interested in adding non-narrative dimensions: rituals, glimpses of typical immigrant behavior, and so forth. These embellishments certainly were a factor in the film's success. Still, the issue of narrative "faithfulness" deserves further examination here, particularly because a host of reviewers, led by Pauline Kael, insisted that Coppola removed narrative elements that made the book "trash" and injected a more artistic perspective. Kael wrote: "Puzo didn't write the novel he probably could have written, but there was a Promethean spark in his trash, and Coppola has written the novel it might have been."[18] The concept of "writing" is more problematic than Kael makes it, because Puzo was involved with the "writing" on the film, as was Robert Towne in the capacity of "script doctor."

## Novel versus Film

What I will do in the remainder of this chapter is examine the notion of "writing." We have two texts at issue: that of a bestselling novel and that of a phenomenally popular movie. It almost seems a basic human instinct to ask the question: "Did you like the novel better than the film?" but that is not my concern here. Rather, the concern is with the title "a film by Francis Coppola" and what it signifies. Is that title merely a construct of the publicity apparatus that works to sell the product—and Coppola generated some colorful copy of this film. Or is it an authorial signature, an indication of a creative sensibility that shaped diverse elements into a work of art with its own coherence?

A film adaptation is in a way parasitic, it takes its basic narrative structure from the preceding novel. But then the non-narrative elements that shape the experience of reading a novel versus seeing a film make the respective entities extremely different. I have no interest in prescriptions for what makes a good adaptation of a novel. Coppola felt that because so many people had read *The Godfather* there were certain narrative elements he could not leave out—the horse head scene, for instance. But, there is really no good, non-financial reason a film should be true to anything but itself. Still, by examining closely some of the differences between the novel and the film we should get some idea of how the respective authorial agents—Mario Puzo and Francis Coppola—functioned in the filmic text of *The Godfather*. This will give us an idea of how problematic film authorship is—particularly in Hollywood, big-budget commercial epics. First a plot outline of the film.

The film opens with Don Corleone's daughter Connie's wedding to Carlo. During the festivities, the Don grants favors to visitors, among them: Bonasera the undertaker, Nazorine the baker, and Johnny Fontane, who needs a part in a new Hollywood movie. Following the wedding, Tom Hagen, an adopted son and the Don's lawyer, goes to Hollywood and "persuades" the intransigent Jack Woltz to give Fontane the part in the film. (The head of Woltz's prized racehorse is placed in Woltz's bed.) The Don's "Family" then meets with Sollozzo, a drug dealer seeking to capitalize on the Corleone's political connections, and the Don refuses him. Sollozzo notices Sonny Corleone's interest in the deal and orders an unsuccessful assassination attempt on the Don. A crime war begins. Previously independent of the family business, Michael Corleone is drawn into the fight when he discovers a second assassination attempt on his father at the hospital. Angered, he arranges a meeting with Sollozzo where he kills the drug dealer and his corrupt police captain accomplice. Michael escapes to Sicily and gang war rages. While in Sicily, Michael marries a Sicilian peasant girl, Apollonia, who is inadvertantly killed during an attempt on Michael's life by the Corleones' enemies. Sonny is killed when he goes into a rage over his brother-in-law's beating of Connie and leaves the protection of the family compound to go avenge his sister. The Don leaves his sick bed and makes peace with the five Families. Michael returns to take leadership of the family and marries Kay, his former (WASP) girl friend. After the father's fatal heart attack and Michael's move of the Family to Las Vegas, Michael orders the murder of all their enemies in one fell swoop. The film ends as Michael lies to his wife about his culpability in the murder of his brother-in-law.

Strictly on a narrative level, what follows is a listing and brief discussion of the key subplots that were removed from Puzo's novel for the film:

1) *The Johnny Fontane story*. It was common knowledge that the novel's Johnny Fontane character was modeled on Frank Sinatra, especially his alleged links to the Mafia. Coppola in several interviews professed a disdain for using celebrities' lives to give any story sensationalism and claimed he avoided this aspect in the film. There are several anecdotes about Sinatra's reaction to the novel: in one he is said to have approached Coppola about the two of them buying the book with Sinatra playing the Godfather; in another there was a public confrontation between Puzo and Sinatra, during which Sinatra burst into a rage and screamed at Puzo. The reaction was overblown. Puzo basically took a brief narrative sketch of the relationship between Sinatra and Harry Cohn in Bob Thomas's *King Cohn*[19] and gave his imagination free rein.

*The Godfather* was hardly a *roman à clef*, but rather a fanciful expansion on some loose facts by Puzo. The meat of Puzo's characterization is the psychological analysis of how a normal guy deals with becoming a sexual idol. The film reduced the Fontane narrative to the elements that demonstrate Don Corleone's power: Johnny cannot sing, he needs the non-singing movie part, his Godfather obtains it for him; later he helps the Godfather's casinos. Puzo uses Johnny's adventures in Hollywood to contrast the New World sexual decadence with Don Corleone's Old World sexual prudishness. The omniscient narrator suggests that the Hollywood *pezznovantes* (leaders) are not equal to the Mafia pezznovantes because of their sexual dalliances and are ripe for a takeover. Such analysis is not terribly insightful, and the simple scene in the film, wherein the Don chastises Johnny for not seeing his children, economically tells us all we need to know about the Don's conservative, old world ways.

2) *The Jules/Lucy Mancini story*. The film's omission of Jules, Puzo's rogue doctor who always has the right diagnosis for people who distrust doctors, is perhaps the most sensible omission of the adaptation. Puzo's unconvincing

details about Jules offer a somewhat unintentional comic relief to the pre-dominating darker themes of the novel. Lucy, in the film, is simply a buxom looking bridesmaid with whom Sonny has an affair. A brief cut establishes Sonny's wife gesturing about the size of her husband's penis and then giving a pathetic look as she notices his departure with Lucy. (Full comprehension of this scene probably demands familiarity with the novel.) The film leaves the affair essentially in place: Sonny's inability to restrain his sexual impulses matches his volatile temper in the violent world of crime. Puzo's novel, however, goes on quite ludicrously to portray Lucy as a woman unable to attain sexual pleasure because her vagina is too big. Sonny's giant penis, which makes his wife fear the marriage bed, proves the "perfect" match for Lucy: "It was love of the coarsest nature, a fleshy love, a love of tissue for opposing tissue." She pines away after Sonny's death, until she meets Jules, a former brilliant surgeon/abortionist, who was saved from prison by the Corleones and installed as house physician at one of the Las Vegas hotels. He falls in love with Lucy, discovers her problem, performs cor-rective surgery, and remarks, "Tonight's the big night. Do you realize I'll be the first surgeon in medical history who tried out the results of his 'medical first' operation . . . "[20] Later he discovers Johnny Fontane's throat tumor and saves him. For all these good deeds Michael Corleone makes him the director of a hospital the Family builds in Las Vegas. Although time length of reading a book versus seeing a film probably had most to do with the elimination of these racy, "soap opera" elements, their omission no doubt contributed to the notion that the film was more "serious" than the novel.

3) *The Al Neri, Captain McCluskey, and Luca Brasi expositions.* These deletions are more indicative of the differences between the worldview of Puzo's novel versus that of the film than are the Johnny Fontane, Jules, or Lucy Mancini deletions. These New York City characters—a cop turned gangster, a crooked police captain, and a murderous thug—are sketched boldly and vividly by Puzo in brief outlines of their background and the circumstances leading to their inclusion in the novel's narrative. The func-tion of these characters in the novel was to add texture, realism, and a feeling of deeper penetration into the gangster's world. The police captain, McCluskey, is a cop on the take, and Puzo provides ample description of his middle-class family background and his quite seductive rationalizations for taking mob money. The film reduces McCluskey to Sterling Hayden's swaggering hot-head with no background. When in the novel we know McCluskey's own rationalization for his vice, we can understand his sudden outburst and his slugging of Michael as an eruption from a repressed con-science. In the film, however, there is more of an us-versus-them mentality. There is incredible audience gratification when McCluskey gets shot. We never for a moment feel that there might be similarities between his view of the world and the Don's.

The Luca Brasi exposition in Puzo's novel is not as complex or unsettling as the Al Neri exposition, but its deletion, like the Neri deletion, suggests that Coppola softened and romanticized the Mafia in the translation of novel to screen. The book details how Brasi systematically axed to death several of Al Capone's gunmen as well as ordered a midwife to throw a newborn of his in a furnace. In the novel, our allegiances to the "good guys," the Corleones, must be tempered by the knowledge of their use of such psychotically violent accomplices. Coppola chose Lenny Montana to play Brasi because of his fearsome looks, but then undercut this impression by having Brasi act like a buffoon at the wedding, a product of Coppola's eye for spontaneous images and not a product of a comprehensive view of how the characters function in the original narrative.

The pattern that emerges from these narrative details, which were omitted from the film, is that Puzo in a nonjudgmental, nondidactic way presents a vision of reality that vacillates between a seemingly closed, insulated world and a world that is psychologically familiar to our experience. Our emotions are played upon by the titillation, fantasy, and exposé, while at the same time, judgment of the crimes, the greed, the vice, and the human frailties is left to the reader. While clearly we identify with the Corleones in both the novel and film, the film has much less facility with the question of judgment as we are taken on a rollercoaster ride of suspense about whether the Corleones, the good guys, will conquer their enemies, the bad guys. Although the film eliminates the trashy, soap opera elements of Puzo's narrative, which helped to gain the film a more serious veneer, it also removed some of the more interesting moral ethos of Puzo's world. What begins to emerge in a consideration of the film, and even more so in its sequel, is that Coppola is an angrier, more easily outraged, more opinionated narrator than the more benign Puzo. What also emerges is that Coppola casts a softened, romantic eye toward the Corleones, particularly toward the elder Don.

This is revealed in a host of details smaller than the above elisions. For instance, there is the Don's sardonic remark: "A lawyer with his briefcase can steal more than a hundred men with guns," which was dropped at Brando's insistence. Robert Duvall later claimed Brando would not use the line because: "He wanted the guy to be a saint."[21] In the novel, on the other hand, we learn how the Don ordered executions of honest competitors. We find out that the Don often created the problems for people like Johnny Fontane that he so charismatically solves in the film. The Don is also more openly male chauvinistic in the novel. Sonny is more a psychotic killer than the jovial charmer James Caan makes him. In the novel, while Michael is in Sicily, there is a long discussion of the "cancer" that the Mafia had become. From this comes a revelation: "Michael thought about his father's organization. If it continued to prosper it would grow into what had happened here on this island, so cancerous that it would destroy the whole country." That threat is not presented dramatically in either the first film or the novel; it does become the subject of *Godfather II*. However, the development of self-realization, which could contribute to a tragic vision of Michael as seeing his fate but unable to avoid it, is omitted from Part I.

There are other subtle differences between Michael Corleone of the film and of the novel. For example, in *The Godfather* film, before the final massacre of Michael's enemies, Michael very curtly tells Tom, "You're out" of the highest strategy decisions of the family. The coldness Michael displays looks forward to the Michael of *Godfather II* who eventually isolates himself from everyone. The purpose of the same scene in the novel was to show Michael's difficulty in learning to say "No" in a polite way to those denied. The intent was to show Michael's difficulties in filling his father's shoes rather than to show Michael as an arrogant, cold-hearted autocrat. Puzo shows more compassion and tolerance for Michael than does Coppola, who seems to shift more sympathy to Brando's Vito.

Puzo was never reconciled to the ending of the film.[22] The final image of the novel is Kay praying for Michael. This finale was built on Kay's conversion to Catholicism, and her realization that Michael had Carlo put to death and had lied to her about it. Puzo said simply that this was the only moral comment he was going to make and that the film should have used a 30-second cut to honor that. It's an ambiguous comment, but it has the effect of emphasizing the tragic in Michael's fall from innocence, rather than the coldness of Michael's lying to Kay, which the film's ending emphasizes. Not surprisingly, in Hollywood tradition the original author's wish was violated, but not in this case by Coppola, who shot the scene as Puzo wrote it. Robert Evans overrode Coppola and ordered that the film end on Michael's closing the door to Kay, one of the rare instances in Coppola's career where he lost the right to final cut. Later, when the film was combined with *Godfather II* for the nine-hour television showing, Coppola restored the scene of Kay lighting the candles.

Although Coppola dominated the successful pre-production decisions, it may be that in the one key area where he lost that domination to Evans, Evans was right. The film as shot does not prepare us for the ambiguity of Puzo's ending. The film does not explore Mama Corleone and Kay's interaction with her. As the film stands, after the montage of executions, Kay asks Michael, in his office, whether Connie's accusations were true about his ordering Carlo's execution. Michael rages that she is never to ask him about business, and then relents, telling her she can ask him just this one time. She repeats the question; he pauses and responds "No." A very effective visual cue follows: the door shuts on Kay and we see Michael with his cronies in the inner sanctum being called "Don Corleone."

In Puzo's ending, that Kay has embraced the old world Catholicism of Mama Corleone suggests the impossibility of moral defiance of the code of violence expressed in the novel. A possibility of Michael's change is not suggested. Kay is no longer the single outside observer; she has taken her place in the scheme of things. In a sense her submission matches most readers' undeniable feelings of endorsement for the murders Michael orders. In terms of our usual experience of fiction, the violent deeds of Barzini, Tataglia, Tessio, or Carlo demand vengeance of a similar nature, and vengeance Michael exacts. The film version, in which Kay seems naively to believe Michael before being symbolically shut out of his life, does not suggest Kay's submission to the Mafia world. The sequel would have been much more difficult had the first film ended with Puzo's scene: Kay's rebellion would have been much more abrupt. In some ways, the sequel is Kay reopening the door and shouting "You're a liar." But in terms of our empathy with Michael's vengeance, it is not surprising that boisterous movie audiences have cheered when Michael slams the door on Kay. She is a nagging conscience whose presence suggests there is a world where problems are not resolved with machine guns.

Coppola felt that the ending of the film established how cold blooded and cynical Michael had become, and certainly the scene can only be interpreted as establishing this. However, the effectiveness of the preceding three hours of empathy with the Corleones and their struggles completely annihilates any antipathy we should feel for Michael in the end.[23] This is caused in no small part by the shadings Coppola added to the narrative, as described above. In 1972, in an America that had become cynical about establishment values due to the Vietnam War, many embraced the Corleones and their efficient and effective protection of their own. The Corleones, in terms of what we saw on screen, did not hurt anyone who did not deserve to be hurt. The novel's ambiguous ending fit the tone of the rest of the book, but the film's pointed ending was submerged by the weight of the preceding images.

Up to this point, the discussion has focused on what the film eliminated or changed from the novel, a fairly inevitable step when translating 446 pages of prose to three hours of screentime. Despite the inevitability, it is being suggested that the deletions were not innocent and that a certain outlook guided them, mostly the outlook of Coppola, but often the outlook of others such as Evans. The changes from novel to film are not as wholesale as, for instance, *You're a Big Boy Now*. They are, on the contrary, rather subtle. The producers of the film, Coppola included, were bound by the fact that a large portion of the viewing audience would have read the novel and would be offended by any major discrepancies. Coppola later spoke of this fact in terms of obligations:

There were so many obligations that I had. I had to do the Hollywood producer. I hated that whole Hollywood section, but I had to do it because I had to cut off that stupid horse's head. I had to do this, I had to do that. And by the time I did what I had to do, I had already used up the movie. So I never had time to make some of the points I wanted to make. Brando's death scene was very self-indulgent, in that it didn't just say what it had to say and get out. It was like four minutes with this little kid. That's the best scene in the film, I think.[24]

The above comments are an understatement of the fecundity of Coppola's imagination and creative energies with a film that abounds with additions, rephrasings, and cinematic stylizations that go beyond the simple function of transferring a novel to film, or doing what one "had to do." *The Godfather* in and of itself is a powerful film, far beyond a good adaptation.

Cinematic Stylization

In the remainder of this chapter the discussion will dwell on the cinematic vision Coppola brought to the project. The discussion of the cinematic aspects of the film will be divided into four areas: 1) cinematic stylization: instances where cinematic technique (lighting, editing, sound, etc.) went beyond the description offered in the novel; 2) *mise-en-scene*: elements of the mise-en-scene not suggested by the novel, which work to heighten the film experience; 3) performance: work with the actors to elicit a greater authenticity than supplied by the dialogue and description offered by the novel; and 4) narrative additions: written or improvised scenes that depart from the novel's narrative and enlarge the scope of the work.

The greatest demonstration of the cinematic sensibilities Coppola brought to bear on the adaptation is undoubtedly the baptism/execution montage. In juxtaposing the execution of Michael's enemies with the baptism of his godson, a crescendo of music, parallel montage, and editing contribute to a bravura exposition of the essential transformation Michael Corleone has undergone, from innocence and ignorance of his father's world to total participation and mastery of it: a baptism of his own. Puzo, the literary mind, pays tribute to Coppola, the cinematic mind, in the following description of the "birth" of the scene:

There was only one thing wrong, and that was that there was something missing at the end of the screenplay. I said to Francis, "Look, there's something missing; I don't know what it is. I know there's something we have to do, but I really don't know what it is." He took one look at it, and he said he knew what it was. He said, "We'll have them all killed while the baby is being christened." Oddly enough, that technique wouldn't have worked in a novel. It would have been absolutely awful in a novel. On film it was terrific. Francis saw that in just two seconds.[25]

It could have worked in the novel: Flaubert's agricultural fair scene in *Madame Bovary* used a similar sense of juxtaposition. Nonetheless, the scene is probably one of the best examples of Eisensteinian montage of collision in the American cinema, certainly the most flamboyant. The notion of presenting two opposing concepts—the gangland violence and the rituals of the Catholic church—and by their linkage creating a third idea, that there is a connection or similarity, brilliantly summarizes the major thrust of the entire film. It begins as we see a priest ritualistically preparing for the baptism intercut with the various gangsters' own rituals of preparation for murder. Spiraling Bach organ music abruptly halts, the priest asks, "Michael, do you renounce Satan?" Michael assents, and the graphic violence explodes as we see cuts of Michael's enemies assassinated. Michael, once innocent like the godson before him, has now been fully baptized into the violent consequences of his power. Religious metaphors were in the story from the beginning, especially in the very term "Godfather," in Catholicism a figure who ensures the safety and religious education of a child should something happen to the parents. In the metaphoric use in connection with the Mafia, it denotes the benevolent aspects of the Mafia chieftain: he supposedly looks out for those under his protection. However, the darker implications of the guardianship and the violent underpinnings of its power are cemented at once in the baptism/execution montage. In a sense, the "family" has conducted itself not unlike a religious order with their hierarchal relationship, their codes of behavior, and their rituals. For those not accepting the religious metaphor, the montage simply conveys Michael's hypocrisy: he sits stoically in a sacred place, renouncing Satan, while satanic acts he ordered go on elsewhere. It is a brilliant example of cinema's potential in a complex, multi-faceted metaphoric mode most effective to this art form.

Coppola uses the idea of collision in editing elsewhere as well. The eroticism of Michael's nuptial night with Apollonia is jarred when Coppola cuts back to New York with Kay arriving in a garish red dress at the Corleone compound to ask about Michael. The montage emphasizes Michael's unfaithfulness to Kay. Another collision comes as we cut from a shot outside the Woltz mansion, with the voice-over of Woltz screaming in horror, to a tranquil close-up of Don Corleone talking softly to his emissary Tom Hagen. The editing reminds us that beneath the surface of this affable man is a conscience capable of ordering gruesome deeds, a concept the charismatic presence of Brando all too often undermines.

A classic Hollywood linkage montage is utilized as the gang war commences. A man (Coppola's father, Carmine) playing a nostalgic song on the piano for the men who have "gone to the mattresses" links together a series of dissolves of newspapers detailing the war, photographs of brutal murders, and the men eating spaghetti and relaxing. The oddly warm, melancholy feel of the men forced to share adversity together is chilled by the repulsive murders.

Sound is used in a distinctly cinematic way throughout the film. The most obvious scene is Michael's murder of Sollozzo and McCluskey. Puzo, in the novel, described Michael as hearing a pounding of blood in his head just prior to the act of murder. Coppola found a cinematic equivalent by establishing the restaurant as being near a subway: As Michael readies himself for the murder, the grating, loud sound of the subway becomes an objective correlative to his and our emotions at the act. More subtly, in a scene in which Sonny is pacing about the kitchen waiting for news about the wounded father, a baby's screeching is used to set us on edge, and a loud rattle of a door as Clemenza arrives makes us think a gun has been shot. In a more traditional Hollywood technique, thunder crashes as McCluskey enters the frame to come and strike Michael.

Camera placement is consistently expressive; for example, in the ending of the scene in which Michael lies to Kay: Kay goes down the hall to fix a drink. A two-shot shows Kay in the foreground with Michael at the end of the hall, emphasizing a physical and metaphorical space between them, compounded by the physical fact that he is in the office where several gangsters join him, calling him "Don Corleone." The subtlety of this placement is then exploded by the medium shot of Kay peering toward the inner sanctum and having the door closed in front of her. Another example, more light and witty, would be the fixed tilt down, rear angle on Michael and Apollonia's first walk together. We see them walking deep into the frame. She intentionally stumbles (according to the novel) and Michael grabs her arm. Suddenly the old women chaperones enter the frame giggling. Our mirth about the women is then chastened as the two bodyguards walk into the frame with shotguns (*luparas*) on their shoulders. Several camera placements seem homages to the past masters. A sudden high angle view as the Don is shot by two hoods in the street is reminiscent of Hitchcock's penchant for distancing at crucial moments. The increasingly closer shots of Woltz's mansion before the horse head scene, and then the same receding shots following it are suggestive of Welles' shots around Xanadu at the opening and close of *Citizen Kane*. The cine-literacy of the "movie brats," noted by Pye/Myles and Jacobs, is much in evidence in this film.[26]

### Mise-en-Scene

*Mise-en-scene* was defined by Bordwell and Thompson as "the elements placed in front of the camera to be photographed: the settings and props, lighting, costumes and make-up, and figure behavior." The visual density and richness of *The Godfather* make its mise-en-scene one of its greatest appeals. Robert Kolker insightfully noted that *The Godfather* was visually striking "at a time when the visual component of American film was becoming weaker and weaker, due partly to the influence of filming for television."[27] Kolker went on to argue that Art Director Dean Tavoularis had a significant impact on the look of the film. Coppola has used Tavoularis as a production designer for every subsequent film. Some examples of their collaboration in this film:

Most of the seasonal chronology is suggested by Puzo's novel. The August wedding in the novel and film suggests the Corleone family at the summer of their power. The assassination attempt against the Don and the subsequent erosion of the Family power take place in the winter. However, the film's production design people emphasized the Christmas season more than did Puzo: Tom is picked up by Sollozzo buying presents for his family, Michael is coming out of the Christmas showing of *The Bells of St. Mary's* when he sees a paper announcing the attack on his father. With the use of Christmas, Puzo suggested that even gangsters have ordinary family lives. The film enhances this element and makes the character even more sympathetic than did Puzo. However, the film's most evocative use of seasonal setting is the fall setting for Michael's reunion with Kay. The scene was changed substantially from the novel in which Mama Corleone engineered Kay's visit to the family compound after Michael had returned from Sicily. In the film Michael unexpectedly approaches Kay while she is shepherding some school children outside the school where she teaches. Michael, dressed in black with a black hat, looks deathly. He walks with her and his bodyguards follow, visually reminding us of the chaperones on his first walk with Apollonia, and establishing his embrace of the cultural habits he once spurned. Contrasting with this are the swirling fall leaves on the ground and the muted colors. The mise-en-scene, the ambience, suggests that the bloom and passion have gone out of Michael and Kay's relationship. The tone of this scene's mise-en-scene prepares us fully for the Michael who will deceive Kay and eventually shut her off from their children in *Godfather II*.

The look of the Don's office is also a function of the cinematography. The quite obvious visual contrasts between the dark offices of Don Corleone and the bright daylight of the wedding established an appropriately sinister quality to the actions discussed and ordered in this area. Later, this locale becomes the obvious choice for the area where Michael lies to his wife. He has assimilated the priorities that go with this space.

The film begins with Bonasera intoning: "I believe in America" in the same dark recesses of Don Corleone's office. The novel begins with Bonasera waiting for vengeance in a New York courtroom. In general, both openings support the idea of the injustice of the American system versus the justice of the Don's system, but the "I believe in America" has an ostentatiousness that matches the giant American flag at the opening of *Patton* or the American landmarks at the opening of *Finian's Rainbow*. Coppola in no uncertain terms establishes immediately one of the overriding themes, the perversion of the American dream; Puzo lets this evolve more slowly.

Aside from the striking "I believe in America" scene shot in the Don's office, perhaps the first shots that really tip a sensitive viewer off to the fact that this film is meticulously crafted visually are the establishing shots of the wedding. Close inspection shows that they were framed to emphasize both a cluster of telephone wires around the compound and the compound's stone walls. This creates a sense of a highly enclosed, difficult-to-penetrate world. While the appeal of the film, and perhaps the film experience in general, is that we, the viewers, penetrate this world, these walls sometimes remind us of our privileged status, as later when Kay tries to get by them to find out about Michael. A smashed car by the gate is a visual reminder of the danger of such a world.

In the novel Sollozzo takes Tom Hagen, blindfolded, to a basement apartment. In the film, much more effectively, they take Tom to an abandoned warehouse. It is cold inside and the bodyguards warm their hands by a fire as if they were hunters in the forest. The contrast between this, Sollozzo's world, and that of the warm, congenial Corleone world is indicative of why we are so thoroughly seduced into empathizing with these criminals. We want the home protected from the wolves.

Based on Coppola's Hitchcockian affinity for characters set against monuments, exhibited at the beginning of *Finian's Rainbow*, it would seem a safe guess that it was his decision to film the execution of Paulie Gatto with the Statue of Liberty far in the background. Robert Kolker called attention to the appropriateness of Clemenza's comment in this particular scene, "Leave the gun, take the cannoli," which is at once amusing and horrifying because of the nonchalance of the murder. (The line was not in the novel.) The Statue of Liberty takes the crime further, asking the reflective viewer to consider whether the immigrant's American dream has become completely perverted by these killers with whom we find ourselves empathizing. Coppola uses the motif again several times in *Godfather II*.

A final point that should be made about the mise-en-scene is that often brilliantly cinematic details emerge from the novel. Some critics accused Puzo of writing with a screenplay in mind, a suggestion Puzo has dismissed. The placing of the Don's death scene in a tomato garden was an inspired use of setting. Gangsters typically die in gutters, shattered automobiles, or sleazy nightclubs—there is a good deal of that in both the film and book— but this gangster dying in a tomato patch had a way of forcing an entire rethinking of the gangster myth. Was this more authentic? Was it really only a few cheap thugs who found that "crime does not pay"? Were our sympathies once again being manipulated by the pathos of a man dying in a garden while his grandson looked on? Finally, in the film version, the mise-en-scene was extended: the smashed tomato vines and glaring sun gave us a vicarious feel for the physical sensation of Vito's death.

Another cinematic detail was suggested in the novel, following the thwarting of the assassination at the hospital. Michael lights a cigarette for the shaking Enzo and notices his own hands are steady. We share his realization that he is a man like his father, capable of coolly dealing with danger. A detail that is less effective in the film than in the novel was Michael's scarred face after the McCluskey beating. Michael perversely refused to get his face fixed out of an unstated need to project the change in his personality. Some hope is offered for Michael when Kay compels him to have it repaired; it seems that the wounds will heal. However, his later lying to her about Carlo's murder suggests that the inner damage is irreparable. To notice this in the film, one has to be familiar with the novel.

Throughout this study the cine-literacy of Coppola has been noted, but it is interesting that Puzo seems to have been influenced more by the classic 1930s gangster films than was Coppola. The idea of Michael's scarred face as an objective correlative to his embrace of criminality was probably suggested by Howard Hawks' *Scarface* (1932), wherein the otherwise handsome Paul Muni wears a scar on his face much like Al Capone. Another parallel to that film is the demise of Sonny, which comes about because he leaves the protection of his bodyguards in a fit of rage over Carlo beating his sister. A similar predicament spells the downfall of Tony Camonte. Puzo acknowledged his imaginative debt to the old gangster films in his depiction of the gangsters taking Tessio "for a ride."[28]

### Performance

Although in *You're a Big Boy Now* and *Finian's Rainbow* Coppola had developed techniques for rehearsing actors in their roles well in advance of shooting, it was *The Godfather* that made his reputation as an actor's director. Much of the appeal of the film came from contributions made by actors, but they were contributions shaped and elicited by Coppola's expertise. One incident often recounted in the writing about *The Godfather's* production process is the dinner Coppola arranged at an Italian restaurant in which all the actors came in character and improvised. All the younger actors were doubly anxious to impress Brando, both as characters and as real actors in awe of a legend. Brando's support and attention to the younger actors apparently encouraged a chemistry that is evident on the screen. In addition, Brando brought his usual variety of method-acting tricks to the film. In the opening scene he decided to play with a cat while listening to Bonasera. This worked both to establish a certain haughtiness about this man who would play with an animal while deciding an important life and death matter for another man, as well as the somewhat opposite sympathy we usually attach to someone who likes animals. Likewise, there is the improvised scene in which Brando places orange peel fangs in his mouth to scare his film grandson—endearing him to us as a man who plays with children but also appropriate, as Coppola realized immediately, in that the film gangster dies as a "pretend" monster. Throughout the film Brando adds little mannerisms that suggest a character who has lived outside the confines of the film we watch: the way he sniffs a rose in his lapel, the wave of the hand dismissal after hearing Michael is a murderer, the way he holds a fixed position dancing with his daughter when she emotionally embraces him. Brando conveys a worldliness, a grace, a threat, a power in this character.

Coppola complained about not being able to do as much experimentally as he would have liked with the film, but did offer the following anecdote as an example of some of the creative work done in the performance process:

> Lenny Montana, who plays Luca Brasi, a *mafioso* in the picture who calls on the Godfather to thank him for being invited to the wedding—that's before he gets his hand pinned to the bar with a knife, of course, is not a professional actor, and he was terrified of playing the scene with Brando. We shot the scene a dozen times, but he froze on every take and forgot his lines. We finally gave up. Later, I wrote a new little scene where he was at the party, before his visit to the Godfather, practicing his speech perfectly over and over. We shot that and kept one of the scenes with Brando where Brasi froze, and it made the whole thing work well with the context of the story.[29]

Knowing this story and watching the film closely, one can see that Brando is barely containing his laughter in one of the cuts in which he is supposedly solemnly listening to Luca Brasi. While Coppola is right that the scene works well, it also undercuts the psychotic killer Brasi as portrayed in the novel, and once again has a way of making the Corleone family seem less sinister. Coppola conceived that the wedding sequence be shot partially in cinema verité. Although that sequence takes the first 27 minutes of the film, it was shot later in the production process, when Coppola was on firmer footing with the crew.

A number of the supporting performances go beyond the characters sketched in the novel and were a product of Coppola's extended rehearsal time. Mama Corleone's (Morganna King) best scene in the film is when she sings "Che La Luna" with an old immigrant at the wedding celebration—there is no suggestion in the novel for this vignette. Fredo's (John Cazale) introduction to Kay, not present in the novel, seems improvised: In a slightly inebriated but deliberate movement to kiss Kay, Cazale evokes the pathetic, affectionate, and lost qualities of Fredo, the passed-over son.

Throughout the film Richard Castellano as Clemenza has some of the best lines not present in the novel, perhaps ad-libbed. It is Clemenza who explains to Michael how to cook spaghetti for a group of men—one of the "Italian touches" Coppola wanted to encourage. "Leave the gun, take the cannoli," mentioned earlier, was also his line. When Michael refuses to talk to Kay because men are in the room, Clemenza cracks: "Hey Mikey. Why don't you tell that girl you love her? [sings] 'I ah love you with all my heart. If I don't see you I'm a gonna die.' " Paulie tells Clemenza that the mattresses will be exterminated: "Exterminate them? Ooh, that's a bad word to use." Castellano's "pain-in-the-ass innocent bystanders" comment is new to the film and nicely sums up the film's attitude about anyone besides the immediate characters. The producers could not come to terms with him for the sequel, replacing him with Michael Gazzo as Pentangeli. One of the problems reportedly was that Castellano wanted a personal writer on the set.

One of the best performance decisions Coppola made was to have the actors frequently speak in Italian. At one point while speaking Italian to Sollozzo so that McCluskey cannot understand, Michael breaks into English to convince Sollozzo of his seriousness about his father not being harmed and perhaps to feign uneasiness with the language. Later in the film, Michael has been speaking Italian in Sicily, but to impress Apollonia's father, has Fabrizzio translate from English a marriage proposal. Such touches give the film an authentic texture and add to our interest in the ethnic qualities.

### Narrative Additions

Coppola's attitude about the script additions is best summed up in the following remark to Marjorie Rosen:

I wrote the *Godfather* script. I did the adaptation. I credit Mario completely with creating the characters and the story. On the other hand, his book took in a lot more than what the film took in. I feel that I took the right parts. I also did a lot of things in that movie that people *thought* were in the book that weren't. The art of adaptation is when you can lie or when you can do something that wasn't in the original but is so much like the original that it should have been.[30]

However, one of the more interesting developments in the script writing stage was the solicitation of Robert Towne to do some "script doctoring." Five or six weeks into the shooting of the film, Coppola was still having doubts about the screenplay and felt unable to do much revision because of his directorial chores. In line with his desire to focus the film more on the family relationships, Coppola wanted Towne to do a scene that would accomplish the following:

*Towne*: Mainly, Francis was perplexed. In the book there wasn't any resolution between Vito Corleone and his son Michael—their relationship. He needed a scene between the two of them. Francis kept saying, "Well, I want the audience to know that they love each other." He put it that way.[31]

Reading the novel we understand the love of father and son because of the novelist's ability to place us inside the characters' heads. Film requires more dramatic exposition and Coppola was correct in that there was no dramatic demonstration of their love. In the novel, Michael tells Tom that his father had told him that the traitor would come to propose a meeting with Barzini. In the adaptation, this scene was fleshed out to establish the relationship between the Don and his heir. Brando rejected one draft of the scene and made the important suggestion: "Just once in this part I'd like to not be inarticulate." Consequently, Towne drew on what the omniscient narrator had told us and fashioned a speech in which Vito explained that he wanted a different destiny for his son, although like himself, Michael would not be a puppet dancing on someone else's strings. One of the collaborators, probably Towne or Brando, added the touch of the Don repeating himself, seeming forgetful, to which Michael responds with compassion and understanding. What occurs is a very human moment. No one would ever suspect that these loving family members are setting in motion the mechanics for an orgy of revenge and violence, a contradiction typical of the film.

In line with the discussion of the authorship of the film, from what Towne saw of the production he felt Coppola was the dominating force. When asked what he thought of the *auteur* theory, he responded:

That's like waving a red flag at a bull. You don't say that to *any* writer! But in some cases it's truer than in others. In the case of Bergman, who else is it going to be? To some extent Stanley Kubrick—or Coppola in his collaborations with Mario Puzo—is the overpowering force. But even then, a movie is always collaborative. I believe the *auteur* theory is merely one way it is easier for historians to assign credit or blame to individuals.[32]

Two other new scenes in the film should be mentioned: the family portrait scene and a Corleone family dinner before Sonny's death. Both dramatically develop undercurents of Puzo's exposition. In the first scene the Don will not have the family portrait taken until Michael is present, emphasizing both Michael's black sheep status, his aloofness and ambivalence toward the family rituals, and also the Don's special concern for the favored son. Later, the portrait is about to be taken and Michael drags a protesting Kay into the family grouping. This is a shrewd use of a situation many of us have experienced: the tension of the family's cautious skepticism about an outsider with the potential to become one of them, as well as the anxiety the outsider feels about the fixed commitment represented by being photographed as a family member before actually entering the family.

The other scene involves Sonny at the head of the table talking family business with Tom. Connie protests that their father never did such a thing. Carlo tells her to shut up; Sonny flares at him. Then Carlo asks something about business and Sonny reproaches him that business is never discussed at the table. In both the novel and the film, Carlo's treachery, like Paulie Gatto's, occurs off-stage. Puzo in the novel was very descriptive of Carlo's dissatisfactions with his position in the family business. The added scene capsulizes his unhappiness and Sonny's negative reaction to him in quick, bold strokes. Stylistically, we should note that while this scene will in a sense lead to Sonny's murder, Coppola never cuts to a dramatic close-up of Carlo's face to indicate the importance of this exchange or tip us off that something will come of it. The film does not lead us by the nose. Coppola emphasizes situations and lets us take out of the dense images what we will.

A number of other scenes are rephrased, slightly rewritten, or changed in context. Particularly striking is the scene at the studio when Woltz starts insulting Hagen with Italian slurs. Hagen responds that he is German-Irish, to which Woltz angrily retorts: "Well let me tell you something my Kraut-Mick friend..." Not in the novel, the line cogently summarizes how sometimes racism is more a tool than a real attitude.

The paradox of Coppola's participation on *The Godfather* is that he had so much control, made so many editorial deletions, additions, rephrasings, equivalences, but yet finally stayed relatively consistent with the vision of the novel. We can see that Coppola brought a desire to emphasize the family traditions, the ethnic context, and in the process romanticized Vito and the Mafia a bit more than the novel. There was also the decision to downplay the sensational sex, the Frank Sinatra/Hollywood section, and a few of the minor characters; but there was never the obvious attempt to use the novel simply as a jumping-off point for his own vision in the fashion of Coppola's work on *You're a Big Boy Now*. Perhaps the best analogy is that Coppola was like a brilliant orchestra conductor who brings new emphasis and insight into someone else's composition.

Some reviewers commented that based on his earlier "failures," Coppola had always had cinematic talent—he could direct actors, reveal character, and use an array of technical devices—but now with Puzo's strong narrative drive, which he could not develop on his own, he was the complete filmmaker. *The Conversation*, Coppola's next film and one from his own original screenplay, became an immediate test case for this assertion, as we will see. Coppola said in connection with *Apocalypse Now* that because of *The Godfather's* phenomenal success he worried that he would forever after be the guy with *The Godfather* in parentheses after his name. The worry now seems unfounded.

## NOTES

1. Mario Puzo, "Dialogue on Film," *American Film*, 4, no. 7 (May 1979), 43.

2. Mario Puzo, *The Godfather Papers* (Greenwich: Fawcett, 1972).

3. Gay Talese, "The Hazards of Great Gangster Fortunes," *Book World*, in *Washington Post*, March 9, 1969, p. 3.

4. Puzo, *The Godfather Papers*, p. 34.

5. Roger Jellnick, "Just Business, Not Personal," *New York Times*, March 4, 1969, p. 41.

6. Dick Schaap, "*The Godfather*," *New York Times Book Review*, April 27, 1969, p. 34.

7. "Packaged for Gluesville," *Times* (London) *Literary Supplement*, July 24, 1969, p. 808. No author given.

8. Puzo, *The Godfather Papers*, p. 40.

9. William Murray, "*Playboy* Interview: Francis Coppola," *Playboy*, July 1975, p. 56.

10. Puzo, *The Godfather Papers*, p. 17.

11. The casting of Talia Shire, Coppola's sister, would seem to be another move by Coppola to surround himself with known quantities. It turns out, however, that Coppola was not happy about her casting, as she recounted recently during a *Rocky III* publicity tour. Puzo got her an audition and Robert Evans hired her without consulting Francis. From Susan Stark, "Talia," *Detroit News*, May 28, 1982, pp. 1–3D.

12. Puzo, *The Godfather Papers*, p. 59.

13. As an example of the evolution of the gangster persona in this regard, we might think of James Cagney, first in *The Public Enemy* (1931) and later in *White Heat* (1949). The first film contained scenes depicting the sociological conditions of the 1920s; unemployment for returning veterans, crime gangs fostered by Prohibition, the loose morality of the speakeasy. The conditions seemed to foster Cagney's gangster persona. By *White Heat*, his drive toward crime seems much more pathological with an incestuous relationship with his mother.

14. Susan Braudy probed this relationship: "Coppola remembers the crew's snide asides as he worked through scenes with Brando and Al Pacino, sometimes requiring as many as fifty camera setups. Gordon Willis, the film's brilliant cinematographer, led the jeerers. Coppola says, 'I agreed with Gordy on how both *Godfathers* should look—no zoom shots, and grainy like old period photographers. But he hates and misuses actors. He wants them to hit marks. I said no. They're not mechanics, they're artists. I was their protector. Gordy acted like a football player stuck with a bunch of fag actors. I was in the middle.' " Susan Braudy, "Francis Ford Coppola: A Profile," *Atlantic*, August 1976, p. 71.

15. "The Making of *The Godfather*," *Time*, March 13, 1973, p. 58. No author given.

16. Charles Higham, "Director's Guild Winner: Francis Ford Coppola," *Action* (May/June 1973), 11.

17. *Time*, p. 57.

18. Pauline Kael, *Reeling* (Boston: Little, Brown and Co., 1976), p. 398.

19. Bob Thomas, *King Cohn* (New York: G. P. Putnam, 1969).

20. Mario Puzo, *The Godfather* (New York: G. P. Putnam, 1969), p. 319. All subsequent references to the novel will be followed by page number in parentheses.

21. Chris Chase, "Quick—What's This Man's Name?" *New York Times*, April 23, 1972, A&E, p. 16.

22. Puzo recounts that the executives did not want him to bring some friends to look at the rough cut and explains: "Or maybe because I was opposed to the ending they used. I wanted an additional thirty seconds of Kay lighting the candles in church to save Michael's soul but I was alone on this. So I said the hell with it, if my friends couldn't see it with me, I didn't want to see it. Again kid stuff. Just because I still found it hard to accept one basic fact. It was not MY movie." *The Godfather Papers*, p. 65.

23. My wife, who is of Sicilian ancestry, recalls how as young teenagers she and her siblings came home from seeing the film and were crushed to learn that their father had never been connected with the Mafia.

24. Stephen Farber, "Coppola and *The Godfather*," *Sight and Sound*, 41 (Autumn 1972), 223.

25. Puzo, *American Film*, p. 42.

26. Assistant Director Ira Zuckerman wrote of Coppola's script: "The margins are covered with notes and reminders in which he refers to other films (Bergman's, Hitchcock's, and some of his own) concerning the treatment of certain moments or scenes. Coppola anticipates specific reactions of the audience to parts of the story and the way they are handled." Ira Zuckerman, *The Godfather Journal* (New York: Manor, 1972), 24.

27. Robert Kolker, *A Cinema of Loneliness* (New York: Oxford University Press, 1980), 159.

28. Puzo, *American Film*, p. 39.

29. Murray, p. 58.

30. Marjorie Rosen, "Francis Ford Coppola," *Film Comment* (July 1974), 47.

31. John Brady, *The Craft of Screenwriting* (New York: Simon and Schuster, 1981), 398.

32. Ibid., pp. 426–427.

# 5
# The Challenge of Originality

## The Conversation

In interviews attendant to the premieres of *Godfather II* and *The Conversation*, Coppola spoke of the films, and the preceding *The Rain People*, as personal challenges to his conception of himself as a *writer*. At this point in this career he still viewed himself as a writer who directed, rather than a director who wrote (a conception that seems to have fallen by the wayside with the post-*Apocalypse Now* struggles with Omni-Zoetrope and his new role as a producer/mogul). The challenge was to generate a film straight from his imagination, an original work, with no pre-existing play, novel, or other writer's script to use as a springboard. His career until *The Godfather* had been established on clever self-promotion, shrewd business sense, a not-to-be-slighted cinematic sense in translating others' work to the screen, and energetic entrepreneurship. With *The Godfather* any questions about his cinematic talent were removed, as were any financial problems after his profit participation on that film. Now was the time to prove he was an artist with vision and an author.

The result was a film that was Coppola's closest approximation of the style of filmmaking more often associated with Ingmar Bergman and the European directors in the degree of personal experience invested in the narrative, the relatively small scale intimacy of the production, the independence of the production from studio involvement, the literary pedigree of the film's intellectual fibre, and the marked departure from the standard subject matter of other feature films being made. Perhaps the final resemblance to a Bergman film was its depressing subject matter and plot outcome, which contributed to its disfavor with general audiences. This

disfavor came despite the timeliness of the film's appearance in the midst
of the revelations of Watergate. (Coppola felt post-Watergate cynicism adversely affected the film's box office, as audiences sought out more escapist
fare such as *American Graffiti*, which he produced for George Lucas the year
before.) Those that did find pleasure in *The Conversation* had to work toward
that end, given the convoluted plot and the minuteness of some of the key
details that advance the narrative.

The artistic aspirations of *The Conversation*, at the expense of entertainment, come in stark contrast to Coppola's preceding film, *The Godfather*,
which has been described as an entertainment machine, in spite of the general
respect for its artistic merits. Perhaps, because *The Conversation* is so sin-
gularly Coppola's project—he conceptualized, produced, wrote, and directed it—it seems more of a piece than does *The Godfather*, which on close
inspection seems to have so many competing elements (e.g., the sensation-
alized violence versus the more serious metaphor of the Mafia as America).
Because this is a more writerly film, in this chapter I would like to dwell
more on it as a literary creation—examining its sources and influences, its
creative germination, and its internal structure. *The Conversation* is the film
most revealing of Coppola's intellectual pedigree, which is a key distin-
guishing feature of his orientation to film versus other film school generation
directors, who often see film as more of a rollercoaster ride.

The first germ of an idea for *The Conversation* came in 1966 when Coppola
and director Irvin Kershner (*The Empire Strikes Back*) were discussing advanced uni-directional microphones, which Kershner told Coppola were so
powerful that they could separate someone's voice out of a crowd, previously thought to be the best place to avoid bugging. Coppola instantly
riveted on this detail as a possibility for a film. He had a fascination with
electronics and gadgetry dating back to a year-long confinement in bed with
polio at age nine when he whiled away the time with tape recorders, 8mm
projectors, and puppet shows. Later as a young teenager he prankishly
tapped his tenement's telephones, which would seem to relate to the theme
of technology as voyeurism in *The Conversation*.[1]

Around the time of the discussion with Kershner, Coppola was also
reading Herman Hesse's *Steppenwolf*, the story of a misanthropic man living
alone. Coppola began to conceive of the eventual film as a character study
of the bugger-Harry Caul, modeled on Hesse's Harry Horner—rather than
the victims of the bugging. Hesse's Harry Horner also meshed nicely with
an interesting account of real-life bugger Bernard Spindel, who was featured
in a *Life* magazine article in May of 1966.[2]

The final major influence was Antonioni's *Blow-up* (1966)[3] with its central
scene and metaphor of a photograph being enlarged to reveal a murder as
well as the ephemeral qualities of human perception. In the same sense, a
recording in *The Conversation* is "blown up" to reveal an apparent murder
plot. Other references appear: A mime wanders about the opening Union

Park scene, echoing the troupe of mimes who appear at the beginning and end of *Blow-up*. Harry Caul meets a woman, has casual sex with her in his work area, and later finds she has stolen evidence, much like the David Hemmings/Vanessa Redgrave encounter in *Blow-up*. Early in *The Conversation* two girls adjust their make-up in the one-way reflection of the bugging van's windows. Unknown to them, Stanley, Harry's assistant, is passionately photographing them from behind the glass, muttering "Come on, give me a nice wet French kiss." The conception is modeled on David Hemming's sexy photo session with the model Veruschka in *Blow-up*. However, how the photographing is handled in the two films—one unseen, voyeuristic; the other a powerful interaction—reveals just how far apart the characters of the respective films are. *The Conversation* is by no means a straight adaptation of *Blow-up*. Harry uses the technology of surveillance as a way of hiding himself, of protecting himself from the outside world. The photographer in *Blow-up* uses the technology of photography to extend himself, to force himself upon the outside world. Ultimately, both films are about the subjectivity of perception, but the mindsets of the respective protagonists are radically different.

So we have a mixed bag of influences: technological discovery, European philosophical novel, European art film, and American journalism. In the early writing the film was to be a character study. As the scripting evolved, however, Coppola realized that he could not simply explore a character and have a marketable film, especially with an unattractive character who lacked the sex appeal of *Blow-up*'s photographer. Hence, Coppola began to review Hitchcock films in order to add a "thriller" aspect to the narrative. Antonioni never provided a solution to the murder mystery of *Blow-up*, but sensational sex scenes and a "hip" timeliness made the ticket-buying public unconcerned with the lack of narrative closure. Close inspection of Coppola's finished film will reveal the "thriller" aspects being somewhat at odds with the character study aspects. Scenes wherein Harry visits his "kept" woman, attends confession at a Catholic church, or spars with his landlady over her entrance into his apartment are psychologically revealing and make Harry's behavior understandable, but do little to advance the murder-mystery element, which seems rushed, vague, and a bit obtuse. Some have argued that we are viewing the murder-mystery through Harry's eyes, and therefore our confusion mirrors Harry's, but this may be an excuse for some sloppiness in the film's editing, which will be discussed later.

Coppola's initial work on the film's screenplay began just prior to his acceptance of the directing assignment for *Finian's Rainbow* (1968). Following *The Rain People* in 1969, he completed his first draft, and *The Conversation* was to be Coppola's first effort for his new company, American Zoetrope. Warner's withdrew funding of American Zoetrope following the disastrous reception of Lucas's *TXH-1138*, and *The Conversation* was on hold again. *The Godfather* assignment was taken to stay afloat, and that film's success led to Paramount's backing the relatively small budget *The Conversation* ($1.6 million; came in at $1.9 million). The extended germination time was profitable, as Coppola kept abreast of developments in the wire-tapping field, met and consulted with experts in the field, read catalogues of their devices, and shaped and re-shaped the narrative.

Because of the extended research time and the relatively unexplored subject matter for a Hollywood feature film, *The Conversation* had a bit of the journalistic exposé about it. Critics described the film as warning of a dangerous direction our society was taking, particularly with its Watergate timing. Stephen Farber in the *New York Times* wrote: "After months of irrelevant movies, *The Conversation* hits with the explosiveness of the morning headlines. Fortunately it has a good deal more substance."[4] Because Coppola was known to have conceptualized the screenplay in 1966, he was portrayed by some critics as a savant. David Denby reflected: "Timeliness isn't necessarily a sign of triviality in an artist; it may be a sign of good instinct, an ability to connect personal concern with national obsession. I think Coppola may become this sort of nonexploitive 'public' artist, a kind of cinematic Dickens (all proportions kept)."[5]

It would seem that with this background of originality of subject matter, a personal slant on the material, primary research, and an original screenplay directed by the author, we would have the perfect example of a Hollywood *auteur*: a single personality with an undeniable imprint on the film in question. Michael Pye and Lynda Myles, however, have seen fit to argue with the assumption in their book *The Movie Brats*, claiming Walter Murch as a collaborator/author on the film and stating: "The film is a perfect test of the *auteurist* theory that tries to establish the director as a film's prime creator."[6] Coppola in several interviews has lauded Murch's soundwork and editing on the film and claimed to have written the script with Murch's capabilities in mind. Murch, whom Coppola met through the George Lucas/ USC connection, was an important contributor on *The Rain People*, and later won an Academy Award for his soundwork on *Apocalypse Now*. Pye and Myles base their claim for Murch's authorship on basically four points: 1) Murch conceived and executed a series of optical blow-ups of the visuals of the central conversation, which gives the film its title, that were designed to make us progressively more intimate with what we were both hearing and seeing. 2) Murch was left on his own in the editing room to structure the last one-third of the film while Coppola went off to New York to begin *Godfather II* (Pye and Myles claim Murch decided the end of the film.) 3) Murch gave the bathroom scene wherein Harry checks the shower for evidence of the murder a Hitchcockian feel by editorial decisions in the cutting room; and 4) Murch's soundwork was brilliant.

These claims seem exaggerated. The optical blow-ups fall into the category of embellishment of a pre-existing concept. That Murch edited the last one-third of the film with Coppola away is important, but one wonders if some of the confusing narrative turns would have been smoother had Coppola stayed to oversee the editing. Point three seems mistaken; a draft of the screenplay dated November 22, 1972, makes abundantly clear the reference to *Psycho* in the bathroom scene; Murch only shaped it. In addition, the same draft ends with Harry maniacally tearing his apartment apart searching for a "bug." Coppola may have shot alternative endings, but the one he ultimately used was present in the 1972 draft and was probably modeled on the story of Jimmy Hoffa's similar breakdown at the height of his struggles with Robert Kennedy. (Bernard Spindel, whom Harry was based on, was intimately involved with Hoffa's counter-surveillance efforts.) Finally, Murch's soundwork certainly can be argued as brilliant; he was daring in using a range of sound not thought of as acceptable in conventional practice. However, it could also be argued Murch was over-elaborate. In an above-average 35mm theatre or with a laser disc system with good stereo speakers, *The Conversation* is an exciting auditory experience. Whispers and peripheral noises become a dramatic presence. However, in 16mm, videotape, or in average 35mm theatres, this high quality is lost and the sound becomes murky and frustrating at points. A Boston theater showing the film placed a sign outside acknowledging previous patrons' complaints about the sound and absolving themselves of blame. Penelope Gilliat in her *New Yorker* review said at her showing ushers apologized to the patrons for the poor sound quality before the film began. Certainly Murch made contributions to the film's impact, as did Gene Hackman, but to claim either as an author of the film is to do a disservice to the imaginative faculty at work when one sits at a typewriter and generates a narrative.

But we should not take the ability to generate narrative as sacrosanct. Perhaps there is something to the claim that Coppola is at his best when he brings his cinematic talents to someone else's narrative. Answering this question requires close examination of what will prove to be a highly intricate and complex plot structure. For that reason, I will first supply a more detailed plot summary than I have in other chapters.

The film opens with a three minute zoom-in from a long shot of San Francisco's Union Square at lunchtime to a close-up of various people walking around the square. Another shot that seems through a gun sight shows a couple, Mark (Frederick Forrest) and Ann (Cindy Williams), walking through the square. However, an assassination is not in progress; we begin to understand that the couple is being bugged by surveillance people. Harry Caul (Gene Hackman) and Stanley (John Cazale) are operating out of a camouflaged sound truck, while several freelancers work outside. The conversation seems innocuous. To Stanley's complaints of boredom, Harry responds "All I want is a nice, fat recording." The initial tape completed, Harry heads home. Some character-establishing scenes follow: Harry has several locks and alarms on his door, but his landlady seems capable of entering his apartment and reading his mail, much to Harry's consternation. This becomes a recurring motif: though Harry is an expert in invading others' privacy, he is inexplicably incompetent in protecting his own. After the argument, Harry plays a saxophone accompaniment to a jazz record. From his mannerisms it is apparent that he is in a private fantasy world and would never think of seeking out live musicians to accompany. Further characterization continues as he visits his girl friend (Teri Garr), who though attractive, seems a shut-in simply waiting for Harry. Harry never removes a plastic rain coat as he attempts to make love to her. An argument ensues when she learns it is Harry's birthday and begins to ask innocent questions about his background. Harry considers this too personal. He puts rent money on the table and leaves as she threatens to discontinue the relationship. Back at the lab, Harry cleans up some of the ambient noise on the tape and then takes it to his employer, "the Director," in an ominous corporate skyscraper. An aide, Martin Stett (Harrison Ford) tries to accept the tapes for the allegedly absent Director; Harry refuses. By this point Harry is becoming troubled about the tapes' ultimate purpose.

The next day Harry has a fight with Stanley, as the assistant expresses curiosity about the nature of the tapes they are mixing. Harry accuses Stanley of not being professional. Stanley becomes upset and leaves. Harry works on the tapes further and clears up an obscured passage where the young man mutters "He'd *kill* us if he got the chance." This disturbs Harry and he goes to confession at a Catholic church.

That night, Harry visits a wiretappers' convention, where the latest technology is being marketed. There we meet Bernard Moran (Allen Garfield), the man "who told Chrysler Cadillac was dropping its fins," and it becomes apparent that the seedy Moran views Harry as his greatest rival, to the extent that Moran has hired Stanley. In a scene many reviewers found unlikely, Harry has a group of wiretappers back to his work area for an informal party.[7] Amid the festivities, Moran's female assistant, Meredith (Elizabeth MacRae), begins flirting with Harry. Moran bugs an intimate conversation between the two, and in a fit of rage Harry throws everyone out except Meredith. She seduces Harry while he distractedly listens to the tapes. Afterwards he has a nightmare about trying to approach Ann, the young woman of the tapes, and spouting off a flood of revealing details about his childhood. While Harry sleeps, Meredith apparently steals the tapes for Martin Stett.

The next day Stett invites Caul to the Director's office to receive payment, explaining the tapes were too valuable to let him keep them. As Harry arrives, it is apparent that the Director (Robert Duvall) is very upset about the tapes, accusing Stett: "You want it to be true." Harry asks what will happen to the couple and receives no answer. In the bugged conversation, the couple spoke of the meeting Sunday at the Jagtar hotel at 3:00, room 773. By this point Harry is convinced the Director will try to murder the couple at that time. Harry goes to the hotel, rents an adjoining room, drills a microphone through the bathroom wall, and begins listening. He hears his tape being played, which starts some heated shouting, and then a struggle. Harry creeps around the balcony and to his horror sees a foggy window splattered with blood. A listener, not a man of action, Harry retreats frantically to hide under the bedcovers. Later, more composed, he picks the lock of the next room and enters, hoping to find clues as to what happened. The room seems as spotless as Norman Bates' hotel. However, in the bathroom, Harry flushes a toilet, and in a gruesome moment, it overflows with blood soaked rags.

Harry rushes to the Director's building, but once there is restrained by guards who will not allow him up to the Director's office. Walking out he views Ann, the Director's wife. Later he sees a headline announcing the Director's death in a fiery auto crash, and then a horde of press people hounding Ann, flanked by Mark and Martin Stett. Harry's mistaken perception now is apparent: rather than the Director killing the young couple if he had a chance, the reverse is true. At home, playing his saxophone, Harry receives a call from a voice that sounds like Martin Stett. Harry is told that he is being watched, and a portion of a tape of him playing the saxophone is played back. Unnerved, Harry frantically tears apart his apartment searching for the "bug" he cannot find. The film ends with Harry sitting amid the rubble playing a solo on the saxophone.

The key line of the film is "He'd kill us if he got the chance," which Mark mutters to Ann while standing next to a loud jazz band during the bugged conversation. The first few times we hear the line from Harry's perspective and the words sound like those of a hunted person. Following Duvall's murder, however, we hear the line again with a new inflection: "*He'd* kill *us* if he got the chance," which becomes a rationalization for an intended murder. Coppola's use of the differing inflections on the line seems to suggest, somewhat like *Blow-up*, that however much technology increases our capacity to perceive the world around us, we will never escape the fundamental subjectivity of human perception. Because of guilt about a past role in a bugging operation that led to a grisly murder, Harry has projected a concern about this couple's safety that is not warranted. The film on one level is a liberal humanist warning against putting such technologies in the hands of people with stunted emotional development (Harry) or lack of ethical concern (Bernard Moran and his employers).

However, on another level this film is a "thriller," and some of the requirements of that aspect muddy the humanist "message" and do not seem as well conceived as the character study of Harry. For instance, innocent people are not being hurt by electronic surveillance in the film, although it initially appears that way. It seems the murderous couple, knowing the Director's propensity for bugging, is using their pre-planned bugged conversation as a means of luring the Director to a pre-established murder location. It appears that Martin Stett is an accomplice in this labyrinthine plot (surely there are easier ways to murder someone) by bringing the couple's affair to the Director's attention and ensuring that the Director gets the tapes before the couple's alleged tryst. (However, in the 1972 script, Stett—there Matthew Harrison—is removed in a purge after the wife takes power following the husband's death.) In *The Godfather*, average, innocent people were never portrayed as adversely affected by the goings-on of the Corleones. *The Conversation* teases us with the illusion that we are seeing innocent people abused by the more powerful, but then reveals the supposed innocents to be part of the same club—who else can afford $15,000 to stage a bugging in the park? This reversal is a product of the "thriller" narrative's need for surprising narrative turns.

In the critical reaction, the film elicited an unusual amount of complaint among reviewers over the plausibility of varying plot points. For instance: why did Harry not recognize Moran's pen was a bug when it was placed in his pocket? Why would Harry, such a private man, have his colleagues back to his work area for a party? (Perhaps Harry unconsciously wants his worst fears realized.) Why is the money laid out on a table in the Director's office, when earlier it had been offered in an envelope? and so forth. David Denby offered the best explanation for this reaction:

Murder mysteries are often full of such loopholes, but we generally don't notice them—the pacing is too fast. *The Conversation*'s slow, repetitive, accumulative method forces us to review what we know, like a detective building a case, and the narrative sloppiness becomes irritating.[8]

Another, more niggling problem with the plot is its manipulation of the audience. Through the first half of the film we are made to feel Harry is a low, contemptible human being. When his conscience is finally aroused in the second half of the film, he unsuccessfully attempts to find a course of action. Along the way, we find that the beautiful people, the supposed innocents, are actually treacherous and that our empathy with them, like Harry's was misplaced. The one character in the film with any sense of morality or conscience is Harry. However, the film is so set on violating our expectations, proving the subjectivity of perception, in effect cheating us, that we are never made to see Harry's moral development in a positive light. Any final solution to the problem of electronic surveillance in our society will require people who deal with it morally and conscientiously. Harry's struggle with an emerging conscience, however, seems more like a paranoid tic than a desirable response to the moral quagmire surrounding him. Harry never truly becomes a tragic figure. Coppola later sensed a problem with the film and told *City Magazine* that it "made people feel crummy" because "in the end the guy didn't breakout." As a result, Coppola said he was "looking at a lot of Frank Capra these days."[9] However, it is not just a question of happy versus sad endings. Shakespeare's Hamlet also does not "break out," but the play does not leave us feeling "crummy." The problem is that Harry's attempts at "breaking out" are never shown to be noble. Through the course of the narrative Harry becomes more pathetic than tragic.

## Art Imitates Life

This perspective may have emerged from too much fidelity to Harry's real-life model, Bernard Spindel, which is worth exploring. A fascinating account of Spindel's life is contained in Jim Hougan's 1978 book, *Spooks*, which is a broad survey of undercover espionage in America. Hougan mentions Coppola's film in the following passage:

Bernard R. Spindel is a legend within the spook's milieu, a wireman of unequaled genius. He was, by all accounts, the Nikola Tesla of electronic eavesdropping, an inventor whose seemingly magical breadboards and conceptual leaps revolutionized the state of the art—time and again. Had Spindel devoted his talents to more banal technologies, it's likely that he'd be alive and prosperous today. Instead, he was obsessed with intrigue, and like the wireman in Francis Ford Coppola's *The Conversation*, he approached his work with the reverent intensity and painful doubts of a man imprisoned by his craft. He died in 1971.[10]

Reading the passage, one immediately thinks of Harry Caul refusing to show Bernard Moran his inventions, from which Moran claims as partners they could make a fortune selling to the "catalogue suckers." Spindel died in 1971 after spending time in prison for what many believe was a trumped-up charge. Spindel had been arrested and indicted 207 times. Hougan writes: "The *only* conviction he suffered in all his forty-seven years was the one alleging that he *intended* to provide information that *others intended to use* in the commission of a crime. It's obvious that someone wanted Spindel badly."[11] The speculation is that the Justice Department was after Spindel for among other things being a thorn in Robert Kennedy's paw both in his assistance to Jimmy Hoffa and some alleged tapes he had of Marilyn Monroe and John Kennedy. Hougan writes that the ironic thing about Spindel's conviction was that Spindel was "responsible for eliminating more bugs and wiretaps than anyone in history." Spindel had spearheaded a *Serpico*-like crackdown on New York police officers who were doing bugging in their spare time for blackmail; he was frequently paid by clients worried about surveillance to "de-bug" their living areas. In 1968, a year before his conviction, Spindel published an incredibly self-righteous book about wiretapping, criticizing existing laws and absolving himself of guilt in the development of the profession. Hougan's mention of "intrigue" partly refers to some double-dealings Spindel had with the dictator, Trujillo, of the

Dominican Republic, which ended with Trujillo's putting Spindel on his "death list" of people he would pay to have assassinated. Spindel's personal idiosyncrasies closely match Harry Caul in many ways. Spindel's wife never knew who he worked for: he refused to tell her any of his secrets, reasoning that she was safer that way. Spindel was obsessed with being sure no one else was bugging him, and he was a stickler for ensuring that his operations were carried out in what he deemed a professional manner. Spindel's death in prison was a pathetic end for a man of such eccentric talents.

Hougan's book could almost be considered supplemental to understanding some of the finer details of *The Conversation*. The technology displayed in the film seems outlandish; for instance, the "harmonica bug" which Moran demonstrates. But Hougan offers exact descriptions of the same technology and how it operates. As was noted before, Coppola kept up on the latest developments in the field. The wiretappers' convention that Harry attends in the film was an actual one, according to Coppola, shot just before such conventions become illegal.

Beyond the content and subject matter of *The Conversation*, the stylistic and formal qualities of the film are also fundamental to the film's meaning and impact. Personnel decisions in the production of the film indicate Coppola had a firm conception of the visual style he wanted for the film. Coppola began the film with the well-known cinematographer/director Haskell Wexler, whose *Medium Cool* shared with *The Conversation* a thematic concern with professional detachment in the face of ethical questions. *Medium Cool* featured a news cameraman who tries to remain objectively aloof from the political events of the 1968 Democratic convention but gradually is drawn into involvement. The film juxtaposed conventional Hollywood narrative development of the story of the cameraman with cinema verité scenes of the cameraman actually involved in the convention's riots. Given Wexler's cinema verité experience, it seems surprising that after shooting began, Coppola fired Wexler, allegedly because he refused to work in low light situations.[12] Coppola replaced him with Bill Butler, his cinematographer from *The Rain People*, a film that relied far more on improvisation than well planned shooting situations. Although *The Conversation* seems a controlled, intimate character study, two of the major scenes, the opening bugging of Union Square and the buggers' conventions, rely on live locations, and no sets were built for the film.

*The Conversation* and *One from the Heart* feature Coppola's most expressive use of the moving camera and zoom lens. With *One from the Heart* the moving camera tied more into the overall visual lavishness of the film; dreamy swoops of the camera over the Las Vegas set enhanced the overall feel of the fantasy life the film examined. In *The Conversation*, the moving camera is much more obtrusive and noticeable, almost demanding judgment about its use. This begins with the film's opening shot, a three minute zoom from a long shot of Union Square to a long lens close-up of various characters walking about the square. It is an ostentatious shot and most commonly explained as putting us in the voyeuristic perspective of the buggers, as we are often throughout the film.

However, Robert Kolker fruitfully extends the interpretation of the shot: "It is a shot that seems to reveal something to us, but never does, for this is a film in which nothing is revealed, save for the frightened soul of an individual who traps himself by his own blindness and fear."[13] In positing that "nothing is revealed," Kolker is referring to the stylistically unconventional way the camera is often handled in the film: "The camera acts as a barrier between us and the events and the central character, refusing to reveal what we want to see or think we ought to see, revealing instead only the phenomenon and problem of observing." The problem of observing in Harry's case is that although he is attracted to that act as a way of hiding himself or remaining inviolate, the more he watches the more he becomes vulnerable on two levels: the first, his own guilt about what he is watching, which increases his subjectivity; the second, that his employers will watch him all the more closely.

Thus the long zoom has a double edge: it seems to be from Harry's perspective, hidden, faraway, zeroing in on the unsuspecting couple. But then as it reaches close-up level the view seems to wander, seemingly searching for details, and then settles on Harry. Harry's presence puts the shot in the third person perspective, and Kolker argues that we become "the buggers of film fiction, which is made for our gaze, but pretends ignorance of it." Kolker goes on: "The result is a simultaneously twice-viewed film: we are involved in the life of a fictional surveillance man and in our surveillance of the fiction." Kolker, to my mind, ultimately never makes clear the implications of this "complex of first and third-person perspectives" although certainly he lays the groundwork.

The long zoom shot and other stylistic uses of the camera are signals, alerting us to view the narrative with a detached, almost Brechtian distance. A three minute zoom calls attention to itself, and announces, not unlike Godard's exaggerated double 360° pans in *Weekend*, that we will not be allowed the passive, anonymous effacement of consciousness and merger with the narrative that is the goal of standard Hollywood camera style. This detachment is even more pronounced in the scenes in Harry's apartment wherein the camera sweeps by Harry as if it were a grocery store surveillance camera, or Harry walks completely in and out of the frame while our perspective remains fixed. Even the most unsophisticated film viewer should be uncomfortable here by the marked departure from traditional narrative film composition. That discomfort and self-consciousness we feel about what we are viewing is important because it becomes a corollary with Harry's own vague discomfort with his voyeurism; this occurs without making us identify with him through conventional events in the narrative or character psychology. Thus Harry as a fictional character is free to be eccentric, paranoid, miserly, and small. He is not an unrealistic Everyman serving as our tour guide through a predatory world of murder and corruption (which is more the approach of a film such as *Three Days of the Condor*).

In terms of Coppola's visual conceptualization of the film, one image—in its resonances, its ability to define the entire film—stands with Coppola's most imaginative visual concepts and that image is the backed-up toilet that overflows with blood. Harry has been snooping around a hotel bathroom for evidence of a murder. Noticing bubbles in the toilet, he flushes it. Rags used to clean up the murder scene cause blood to spew out onto the floor, much to Harry's horror. This scene prompted David Thomson to write that the film was "the best sign yet of a capacity for feverish psychological imagery that Coppola usually keeps under lock and key."[14] Thomson calls the bloody toilet "a menstrual holocaust for a frigid man." On a more obvious level the image crystallizes the moment when all Harry's fears about the morality of his occupation come to the fore, a return of the repressed. David Denby commented: "It is one of the most grimly satisfying scenes in recent movies, a true horror epiphany. And at that moment our feelings are finally resolved into outright sympathy. Harry has been punished enough."[15]

The image had been set up by another striking image moments earlier. In order to hear what is going on in the room next door, Harry drills a hole through the bathroom wall and flushes the toilet to cover the noise of the drill. The image of a grown man squatting on the floor next to a toilet with earphones defines forever the debasement of Harry's profession. The final images of the film are no less compelling: Harry destroys his apartment looking for a "bug." In the final shot the camera sweeps by him, again like a surveillance camera, as he sits in the rubbish filled corner playing his saxophone. The demolished apartment has become an "objective correlative" to Harry's battered consciousness.

Coppola's sense of Eisensteinian counterpoint is once again present in *The Conversation.* Midway through the film, he cuts directly from a close-up of a priest in a confessional to a security monitor at the wiretappers' convention. The oft-repeated conversation itself is used in a series of juxtapositions wherein the words of the taped conversation become ironic commentary on the images we see. For instance, Harry listens to the tape while Meredith prepares to have sex with him. The lines "A lot of fun you are, you're supposed to tease me," "Does it bother you, walking around in circles," or "There he is, half-dead on a park bench" take on new meaning in this context. In another scene, immediately following Harry's break-up with Amy, we cut to Harry alone on the subway. The lights momentarily go out, and we cut to a tender shot of the couple, showing Harry's thoughts. The editing establishes that the fantasy of Ann has taken the place of the reality of Amy for Harry. Some of this editing may be attributed to Walter

Murch, but the theoretical background is consistent with Coppola's previous work.

The acting in the film deserves note. Gene Hackman played against his movie star persona of virile, "tough guy," as established in *The French Connection*, and won critical raves. Coppola commented that at first Hackman resisted Coppola's efforts to deglamorize him, but eventually went along with it, cutting his hair and transforming himself into a "nudnick."[16] The decision to make Hackman go against type is key to the believability of Harry, as the repressive part of Harry's personality correlates with the suppression of Hackman's more usual macho persona. That there is a submerged power also makes believable Harry's preeminence in his profession.

Two of the character actors' performances are especially convincing. In comparing the 1972 script to the final film, it is clear that Allen Garfield added an edge to the Bernard Moran character that makes him one gigantic raw nerve. John Cazle as Stanley is also very compelling. Combined with his other roles as Fredo Corleone and as an important character in *Dog Day Afternoon* and *The Deer Hunter*, Cazale defined the frustrated, small man bordering on neurosis living in a world of bigger men.

In critical writing about *The Conversation*, much has been made of Coppola's apparent tradeoffs in making *The Godfather* for *The Conversation*, which was extrapolated to entertainment making possible art, profit making possible integrity. One senses that some of *The Conversation*'s praise could be attributed to the critical establishment's own self-imposed guilt: here was the American *art* film, the absence of which they so often lamented. Appreciating it was a duty, which might explain the reviews that lauded the film and then listed its flaws. That *The Conversation* represents what American cinema *ought* to be doing was perhaps no better underscored than in a Roger Ebert and Gene Siskel "Sneak Previews" show several years ago. The two Chicago critics compiled a short list of the films they would most like revived at local theaters. *The Conversation* dutifully appeared. Its failure at the box office is now taken as a nagging reminder of the shortcomings of the American moviegoing audience: their failure to appreciate and patronize films which are "Art."

Pauline Kael blames the public's reaction on the Philistine movie executives in this rather interesting diatribe:

With their overweening campaign budgets for *The Great Gatsby* and *Chinatown*, the Paramount executives didn't even take a full-page ad in the *Times* to announce that *The Conversation* had won the Grand Prize at Cannes. They didn't plan on *The Conversation* being a success, and nothing now is going to make them help it become one. *Gatsby* and *Chinatown* were their pictures, but *The Conversation* was Francis Ford Coppola's, and they're incensed at his being in a position (after directing *The Godfather*) to do what he wanted to do; they're *hurt* that he flouts their authority, working out of San Francisco instead of Los Angeles. And they don't really have any respect for *The Conversation*, because it's an idea film. . . . Maybe the reason the promotion people didn't try to exploit the Watergate tie-in was that they suspected the picture might also be saying something about movie companies.[17]

However, it should be added to Kael's accusations that Coppola, through-out his career, has shown a prodigious ability to generate interest and pub-licity for films on his own efforts regardless of the movie executives' disposition toward his films. Somewhere amid Coppola's rush to get *God-father II* off the ground, his efforts to become a force in the San Francisco community with publishing and artistic ventures, and his preparation for *Apocalypse Now*, *The Conversation* unhappily was shunted aside. The film, in retrospect, seems in a mode toward which Coppola shows no sign of returning. This is sad in that of Coppola's entire canon it seems his most uncompromised film in terms of displaying originality, vision, and matu-rity. Steven Spielberg and George Lucas are routinely castigated for not following their blockbuster hits with smaller, more personal and challenging works, works like *The Conversation*. They perhaps understand Coppola's ambivalence about his effort in that direction and likewise understand the imperative larger in Hollywood than critical raves, which is financial suc-cess.

## NOTES

1. Coppola told Brian DePalma: "When I was a kid about 13 or 14 I wasn't much of a hotshot, but there was a tremendous sense of power in putting micro-phones around to hear other people. There was a sense of being important and superior because I could tap a phone and no one knew. I even had a plan to put microphones in the radiators of all the rooms in the house so that I could tune in on what I was going to get for Christmas. And I would think that those kind of people, the unappreciated school weirdos, might turn into something like Harry." Brian DePalma, "The Making of *The Conversation*, an Interview with Francis Ford Coppola," *Filmmakers Newsletter* (May 1974), 34.

2. *Life*, May 20, 1966.

3. Coppola has said there were many influences on *The Conversation*. Perhaps one that has not been accounted for up until this time was a rather unmemorable British espionage/romance film titled *Sebastian*, which premiered in New York, January 24, 1968. There are some striking similarities to *The Conversation*. The film centers around a priggish, closed individual, played by Dirk Bogarde, who is the head of a government decoding unit. Like Harry, he is an expert in the field, and like Harry he places more emphasis on doing his job proficiently than in examining the ethics of the people he serves; in fact one of his underlings tells another that they only break the codes, they never read them. Just as Harry is involved with two women, one of whom betrays him, so is Sebastian. One is a communist undercover agent who puts LSD in his wine. The other is played by Susannah York. She comes to work for Sebastian, falls in love with him, and leaves him temporarily after he treats her rather shabbily when she inadvertantly declares her love for him in front of the other office girls. There is a happy ending: she has a child by him and the sound of the child's rattle prompts him to break a Russian code. At one

point in *Sebastian*, the Susannah York character, intent on changing Bogarde's outlook toward life, tears down his ugly wallpaper. When she does this she discovers a "bug," which prompts Bogarde to make a scene at his office that leads to his resignation. When breaking the final code, which is sent by Russian satellite, Bogarde uses reworkings of the sound through tape recorder manipulation, much like Harry unscrambles his initial melange of sound. Given the release date, there is every chance that the screenwriters of *Sebastian* were influenced by *Blow-up* as well.

4. Stephen Farber, "A Nightmare World with No Secrets," *New York Times*, May 12, 1974, p. 1.

5. David Denby, "Stolen Privacy: Coppola's *The Conversation*," *Sight and Sound*, 43 (Summer 1974), 131.

6. Michael Pye and Lynda Myles, *The Movie Brats* (New York: Holt, Rinehart and Winston, 1979), 99.

7. Going against the norm, David Denby found this one of the more inspired scenes in the film and wrote: "Coppola has a savagely good time with Harry's surveillance colleagues. Boastful, frenetic, absurdly aggressive, these American go-getters can't stop competing for a moment, not even at a party, and so they begin showing off and playing dirty tricks on one another. Their viciousness while 're-laxing,' more revealing than any amount of overt skullduggery, suggests that they are successful precisely because they don't give a damn who they hurt or how much. The code of 'professionalism' provides an apparent morality, a blinding justification for any act; they have no idea, not even a suspicion, that they are evil men. The surveillance experts are hideously funny and also tragic; looking at them it's hard for an American not to think of soldiers testing weapons in Vietnam and other examples of professionals run amuck." Denby, p. 132.

8. Denby, p. 133.

9. Hal Aigner and Michael Goodwin, "The Bearded Immigrant from Tinsel Town," *City Magazine* (San Francisco), June 12, 1974, p. 41.

10. Jim Hougan, *Spooks* (New York: Bantam, 1979), 83–84.

11. Hougan, p. 87.

12. Coppola told Aigner and Goodwin: "Haskell is a friend of mine, and a very complicated, talented guy, but the relationship was just not working out in a way I was comfortable with. He didn't like certain locations, said they were impossible to light, impossible to shoot. One of them was the Director's office—remember that strange office where Bobby Duvall is? Haskell vetoed that, and we were shooting it somewhere else; it was tense, and I was having to make the movie differently than I wanted to, so . . . I fired Haskell. I didn't want to make anything of it, and then someone came for an interview; I was very late, and so the guy invented a lot of stuff about why I fired Haskell. Haskell read it, got very upset, and wrote a lot of stuff. Basically, he's a talented photographer, but he didn't make me feel comfortable." Aigner and Goodwin, p. 36.

13. Robert Kolker, *A Cinema of Loneliness* (New York: Oxford University Press, 1980), 194.

14. David Thomson, *Overexposures* (New York: William Morrow, 1981), 301.

15. David Denby, p. 133.

16. Aigner and Goodwin, p. 34.

17. Pauline Kael, *Reeling* (Boston: Little, Brown and Co., 1976), 314.

# 6

## Renewal in Revision

### Godfather II

In Robert DeNiro's first extended scene as young Vito Corleone in *Godfather II* (1974), a very subtle moment of filmic self-reflexivity puts a perspective on Coppola's function in participating in a sequel to *The Godfather*, the greatest financial success to that time. Young Vito and his friend Genco go to a neighborhood music hall to see Genco's girl friend, who is one of the players. The music and drama presented is a popularized version of opera. The topical subject matter, the scope of the production, the working class audience, and the hall size are reminiscent of the English vaudeville of that period (circa 1917), reminding us that opera to Italians has always cut across class distinctions, a popular art form much like film today. The little skit being played on the stage, "Senza Mamma," is about an immigrant who has left his mother in the old country to come to New York. It was written by one of Coppola's ancestors and was popular during that era. The immigrant is unhappy with his wife and not adjusted to America. The Statue of Liberty, seen often through the *Godfather* saga, is here painted on the backdrop. A letter comes from Italy telling him his mother is dead. He produces a revolver to shoot himself and launches into an aria about how he loved his mother. The skit mirrors the childhood memories of the taciturn Vito (shown in previous scenes): his mother was killed by a Mafia chieftain when she pleaded to have Vito saved; the child Vito's entry into the U.S.A. was not a happy one, as he was quarantined for smallpox and his surname was changed by an indifferent immigration official.

The melodramatic qualities of the skit, however, shift from the stage into the audience. A large dark figure rises, blocking our view of the stage.

Genco swears at him. He turns: It is Fanucci, the alleged neighborhood Black Hand terrorist. Genco apologizes and Fanucci departs. Genco tells Vito to come backstage to meet his girl friend. As they enter the dressing room unnoticed by the inhabitants, they come upon Fanucci threatening the girl friend in order to extort money from her father. Vito watches the action with the same impassive countenance with which he watched the opera. The parallel seems intentional on Coppola's part, because he stages Fanucci's extortion with the same flamboyant, dramatic gestures of the opera. Fanucci holds a knife to the girl's throat, a tableau reminiscent of a D. W. Griffith silent melodrama.

The pronounced stylization of this scene, and the manner in which it parallels the stage opera melodrama forms a "self-reflexive" commentary on the artificiality of the film melodrama in general. The scene neatly doubles the larger narrative questions of the Little Italy episodes. When confronted with the hardships of the immigrant life, does the immigrant passively resign himself to the hardship, as do Genco and the character the opera singer portrays, or does he take action, as Vito finally does by killing Fanucci. The "either/or" nature of the question is a condition of melodrama; realistically life has more options. But beyond the narrative questions, this scene also suggests a consideration of Coppola's authorial position in attempting a sequel to *The Godfather*, one of the most popular film melodramas of all time. In the discussion of *The Godfather*, it was apparent that the main narrative actions and the melodramatic elements were all from Puzo's novel. Coppola's contributions lay predominately in the non-narrative area, in the evocation of the Italian-American experience and the family relationships, in the film's texture, and in certain nuances of characterization. Not bound by the novel in Part II, Coppola had a narrative carte blanche so to speak. One might have expected that the non-narrative aspects of Part I noted above would be even more manifest in Part II. Indeed, the opera scene described above was not in the novel; Coppola was so enamored by this addition that he tried to get Luciano Pavarotti to play one of the performers.[1] Showing and exploring how Italians loved opera in the immigrant setting was just one of the many details that attracted Coppola to the project of the sequel. It seems, however, that once into the project Coppola had to pare his "non-narrative" interests down in order to provide the strong narrative that would guarantee an expensive Hollywood film's acceptance at the box office. Perhaps this explains why the opera scene has the feel of parody about it. As Coppola explained his position:

My heart was really in the Little Italy sequences, in the old streets of New York, the music, all that turn-of-the-century atmosphere. I had great scenes in the script that we couldn't include in the movie: There was one where Enrico Caruso showed up in the neighborhood and sang *Over There* to get guys to enlist for World War One; I had scenes of Italians building the subways, of young Vito courting his girl and joining his friends for music and mandolins and wine. . . . But it all got too long and too expensive.[2]

It may be that to explore the area really of interest to him (i.e., the texture of the life of his immigrant forefathers), Coppola should have utilized a more documentary mode, wherein "atmosphere" was not subservient to narrative. But for such an experiment, would anyone have funded the re-creation of the streets of 1917 New York on the scale realized for *Godfather II*? The film cost $12–13 million in 1974.

However, there were more motivations for Coppola to do a sequel than the desire to re-create and explore life in Little Italy from the time his ancestors arrived. Paramount was pressuring him to make the film, because sequels as a rule gross two-thirds as much as the original. Since the original *Godfather* had grossed over $200 million, much was potentially at stake, enough that Charles Bludhorn (the Chairman of Gulf & Western, which owns Paramount) personally asked Coppola to do the sequel, explaining "you can't give up the formula for Coca-Cola,"[3] and offering him $500,000 plus a hefty share of the profits.

A half million of his *Godfather* profits had been garnisheed by Warner Brothers for the failure of American Zoetrope. Reports are that Coppola made $6–10 million on that film with his profit participation, and he rationalized that he could make enough on the sequel so that he would never again have to make a film he did not want to make.[4] Because of the success of *The Godfather*, Paramount arranged financing and distribution for *The Conversation*, although it was not a good commercial prospect. Coppola reasoned that there could be more of the same following *Godfather II*. Other nonpecuniary considerations included: Coppola's concern that audiences did not perceive Michael to be the monster that Coppola intended him to be at the end of the first film (they applauded his shutting the door on Kay); Coppola's interest in making a seven-hour movie out of both parts; the challenge of making something more than the average sequel and more than what critics expected; and perhaps the abstract notion that, from a moral point of view, he had not completed the structure begun in Part I:

I felt that *Godfather* had never finished; morally, I believed that the Family would be destroyed, and it would be like a kind of Gotterdammerung. I thought it would be interesting to juxtapose the decline of the Family with the ascension of the Family; to show that as the young Vito Corleone is building this thing out of America, his son is presiding over its destruction.[5]

This melange of motivation somehow produced one of the most challenging, complex narrative structures of mainstream commercial cinema. Late in the editing process Coppola decided to break with linear chronology and structure his film in terms of jumps back and forth in time between two proceeding plotlines: the rise of young Vito Corleone as a don and the spiritual decline of his son, don Michael. Dazzling contrasts result as we are forced to consider the interrelations between the two narratives in tandem. The scheme also forces the average viewer to do much more "work" in terms of keeping the two complicated narratives in order, making this film much more of an intellectual exercise than the viscerally exciting *The Godfather.*

The veneer of seriousness and moral purpose about the whole enterprise surely contributed to the film's Best Picture Academy Award and Coppola's Best Director award, as well as more reviews portraying Coppola as a director who combined "Art" with commerce. Actually, although the film was a commercial success, it grossed closer to one-third of the *The Godfather*'s take, still a formidable amount, but considerably less than the conventional two-thirds Paramount expected. *Godfather II*'s 3 ½ hour length was challenging and the film did not supply some of the emotional attractions of its predecessor. While film historians credit this film as the beginning of the modern sequel phenomenon, it had none of the phenomenal success of the first *Godfather.*

Some critics portray *Godfather II* as an object lesson in how to combine moral seriousness with relative commercial success. However, at the outset some of the assumptions about the "depth" of the work need examination. Is it an optimistic, utopian streak in Coppola that made him think that immoral empires such as the Corleones' are necessarily destroyed? And why, both in terms of his above quotation and in terms of his shaping of the narrative, did he see Vito's earliest actions so positively? Perhaps it is a truism that organizations built with the best of intentions often become too big and too perverted to serve their original aims. Nonetheless, in the case of Vito Corleone's crime Family, which was founded through robbery and murder, immorality was a factor from the beginning. Except for two scenes of gruesome, violent revenge, Coppola essentially portrays young Vito as a modern day saint and absolves him of blame for the eventual failure of his Family. Was it Coppola's romanticized view of the pre-modern American past, his innate skepticism about things that become too large, his over-fondness for his own immigrant past, or his need to create a hero for this $13 million story that produced this lionization of young Vito at the expense of his more conscience-ridden son, Michael?

A plot outline should suggest where the emphasis is thrown. The following outline is organized around the jumps back and forth in time, and the film's running time is charted to suggest how the individual sections are weighted. The young Vito section is essentially drawn from Puzo's novel—a section not treated in the original film—and the Michael section constitutes an original screenplay that Coppola and Puzo developed:

1) (10 minutes)  Vito as a boy. His mother, brother, and father are killed in a vendetta, and he escapes from Sicily. He arrives in New York and is confined at Ellis Island because of smallpox.

2)  (33 minutes)   Anthony Corleone's first communion in 1958 at Lake Tahoe, Nevada. During the celebration, Senator Geary attempts to "squeeze" Michael on a liquor license for a casino. The Family's warmth, ethnicity, and closeness is diminished, upon which a Capo from New York, Frankie Pentangeli comments. Someone within the organization attempts to assassinate Michael and fails. After turning all power over to Tom Hagen and preparing to leave, Michael is offered help by his young son.

3)  (16 minutes)   Young Vito and his family. Vito goes to a local music hall and encounters Fanucci, a feared gangster. Vito loses his grocery store job because of Fanucci. Young Clemenza "gives" Vito a rug in Vito's first participation in a crime.

4)  (50 minutes)   Michael takes a train to Miami to meet with the Jewish gangster, Hyman Roth, and plan a deal with the Cuban government. Michael goes to New York and tells Pentangeli that Roth was behind the assassination attempt. Unknown to Michael, we find out Fredo was duped into helping Johnny Ola, Roth's assistant, in the attempt. Roth's affiliates, the Rosato brothers, attempt the murder of Pentangeli. Senator Geary is blackmailed into Michael's employ. Michael goes to Cuba to arrange the business deal with Roth. He discovers Fredo's treachery, and his assassination attempt on Roth fails. He returns to Nevada and is informed that Kay had a "miscarriage."

5)  (16 minutes)   Vito watches Fredo's "cure" performed by old immigrant women. Vito consolidates a gang and takes charge after murdering Fanucci. Vito tells Michael he loves him very much.

6)  (6 minutes)   Michael returns to Tahoe in the snow. The senate crime committee questions Willie Cicci about the Corleone organization. Michael asks his mother if one can lose his family while being strong for them.

7)  (8 minutes)   Cut to Vito getting oranges. He is now a man of respect. A comic section about a greedy landlord who is intimidated by Vito establishes Vito as a Robin Hood figure.

8)  (23 minutes)   Michael testifies at the crime hearings. Frankie Pentangeli turns up alive and will testify against Michael. Frankie's brother is flown in from Sicily, which causes Frankie to observe "omerta" and save Michael. Kay tells Michael she had an abortion and wants to leave him.

9)  (7 minutes)   Vito and his family return to Sicily. Vito kills his father's murderer, a decrepit old man. Vito goes to church with his family, then departs Sicily.

10)  (21 minutes)   Mama Corleone's funeral brings Connie and Fredo back to Tahoe for a reconciliation. Michael coldly shuts the door on Kay, who has visited her children. Michael initiates the final series of killings, which include Fredo and Roth, and Pentangeli's suicide.

11)  (4 minutes)   Flashback to the family gathering on father's birthday in 1941.

12)  Brief cut of Michael in Sicily with his father.

13)  Shot of Michael alone and in half-shadow.

The effect of juxtaposing the two time periods rather than telling the story in chronological progression is to make us feel that Vito's business and his family have become perverted and inhuman under MIchael's leadership. Visually, Coppola juxtaposes the warm interiors and the red glow of the "Vito" sequences with the cold blues and the snow of the "Michael" sequences. We see scenes of affection between Vito and his family, whereas Michael hits his wife at one point and has only one scene of interaction with his son. The only comic scene in the film comes when Vito does a good deed for an old woman harassed by her Calabrese landlord. Michael's section is dour, serious, and depressing. Vito is portrayed as a man forced into violent actions to sustain his family. Michael is a cold autocrat trying to protect his power while losing his family through insensitivity.

Not only is Michael's section juxtaposed with Vito's, but it is also juxtaposed with our memory of the first *Godfather* film. This is set up by similarities in narrative events between *The Godfather* and the Michael sections of *Godfather II*. Both films begin with religious celebrations, in the first case a wedding, in the second a first communion. Both sequences feature bright outdoor action contrasted through cuts with the dark inner sanctums in which the respective dons conduct business. However, Don Vito's business is a series of favors he does for dependents. Michael's "business" consists of a WASPish senator who tells him he does not like people with "oily hair," his dissipated sister asking for money to marry a fortune hunter, and a representative from another gangster who is doing business with Michael. Sicilian justice is not being meted out in the manner of Don Vito. Furthermore, the communion celebration is in sharp contrast to the earlier wedding by its being stripped of ethnicity. Whereas Connie's wedding relied heavily on ethnic flavor, for instance the mother singing "Che La Luna," the father dancing with the bride, and so forth, the first communion is noticeably non-Italian. A blond boys' choir sings "Mr. Wonderful" to Michael. Frankie Pentangeli is surprised to find that the musicians know no Italian music and that Michael drinks champagne instead of red wine. Fredo is married to a vulgar blond who cheats in front of him and Connie is engaged to another blond played by Troy Donahue (an actor who was the WASP teenage heartthrob of the 1950s). In the first film, contrasted with Michael's stoicism, we had the robust lifeforce of James Caan's Sonny and the enigmatic paternalism of Brando's Vito. In the second film we feature Tom Hagen, a shell of his former self, Fredo, who cannot control his wife's drunken sexual advances to another man, and Connie, who is more interested in asking Michael for more money than in seeing her children. The mystique of the Corleone family unity is gone, and with it some of our vicarious enjoyment in its celebration.

Other parallels in the action of the two films point to the degeneration of Michael and the Corleones. Whereas Vito in the first films terrorized Jack Woltz by placing a dead horsehead in his bed, in part II, Michael even more cold-heartedly has a dead prostitute placed in the bed of Senator Geary. While both films end in a series of killings, the series in *Godfather II* includes two characters we are fond of: Fredo and Frankie Pentangeli. In both films Michael symbolically closes a door on Kay. However, we feel the pain even more in *Godfather II* because he shuts the door on her in order to keep her from her children, not merely to keep her out of the dirty aspects of the Family business, as in Part I. Thus there is a double juxtaposition at work in *Godfather* : the juxtaposition of the rise of Vito versus the increasing alienation of Michael within the film; and outside of the film the juxtaposition and reference to events in Part I, against which the parallel events of Part II seem far more degenerate.

The structuring suggests Coppola's penchant for Eisensteinian montage of collision. Coppola later spoke of showing *The Godfather* and *Godfather II* together to produce a "synergy." In light of the suggestion in Chapter 4 that *The Godfather* was more Puzo's film and *Godfather II* more Coppola's, and that in general the Puzo worldview was more benign whereas Coppola's is more angry and judgmental, we should consider the Coppola/Puzo interaction on this script, again officially listed as a collaboration and an adaptation from Puzo's novel. Puzo's interviews following the film suggest a certain disaffection from the project, as in the following:

I would have showed Michael at the height of his power, everybody around him. Everybody loves him, his wife comes back, his children come back. Everything is great with him. He's the only one who knows what's happening to him. That's a different concept. I would not have visualized it the way Francis did. But I can't quarrel with it because it succeeded with the audience. I would have done it differently. It was too pointed a moral. It was almost like saying, "Look, we want to show you that we don't think the Mafia are good guys. This is how bad they are, and this is what evil leads to." It was too much on the nose, too blatant. I think they should have been more subtle about it.[6]

Puzo's conception of the ending is novelistic: juxtaposing the inner state of the protagonist with the differing outward appearance, a subtlety that is more difficult to achieve in the film medium. It also has a cynical tinge and does not really advance the conception much from the first film, essentially still plumbing the vision of the original novel. Coppola, as we have seen, very clearly wanted *Godfather II* to go beyond the first film. However, moving from concept to execution proved demanding of Coppola's time and energies. Coppola was wrapping up the post-production on *The Conversation*, eventually leaving the fine tuning to Walter Murch and:

I looked at the calendar and realized that I had three months to write a 200-page script for *Godfather II*—and I didn't even have a hint of what it was about. I was in a desperate situation. I'd go upstairs and write and write, write on the blackboard, until somehow I finished the script three days before we were gonna start.[7]

In contrast to Coppola's version, which has him burning the midnight oil alone, Puzo claimed that the two worked together in the same fashion as they did on *Godfather I*:

He rewrote me, and I rewrote him. That's the way it worked. Same thing on *Godfather II*. I did the first draft, he did the second draft, then we'd get together, and I'd do the third draft. I think it worked fairly well. The only time we had a conference was over Al Pacino. I didn't want him to slap his wife. I said "That's crazy. If he's a big Mafia leader, he doesn't have to beat up his wife. Why are you having him do that?" He said that Al Pacino wanted to slap her.[8]

Coppola was later quite complimentary about Pacino's contributions to the scripting process. Pacino's desire that Michael have more shades of grey in his character provoked a last-minute re-write just prior to rehearsals. Puzo also suffered a heart attack during this period, which prevented him from novelizing any of the sequel. In the new material not drawn from the original novel, Puzo's influence most clearly hangs over the section dealing with the Senate investigation of the Corleones. One of the funnier scenes in the film occurs as Senate investigators try to interrogate Willie Cicci using words such as "behest," "buffer" and so forth, while he responds in Mafia jargon using expressions such as "push the button," "soldiers," and so on. Puzo had written that one of the most interesting things that came out of his research into the Valachi hearings was the difficulty the investigators had in communicating with the witnesses. At the conclusion of this sequence, which relies on the Sicilian code of *omerta*, or silence in the face of authorities, we once again empathize with the Corleones and hope they defeat their enemies. The scene's style and resolution would seem to be Puzo's. The crime committee investigation of Michael is closely modeled on the Kefauver investigation of organized crime in the 1950s. Perhaps the key fictional change is that Michael refuses to plead the Fifth Amendment because of his wife, a constraint that did not worry the real Mafiosos.

Amid the usual puffery of a studio press package, one rather interesting item was a press release on Debbie Fine, who was hired as the research coordinator on the project and who spent two years collecting information mostly in the areas of modern organized crime, corporate activity in Cuba, and immigration practices at Ellis Island in the early 1900s. Fine has an M.A. in library science and had worked on other films. She remarked: "I don't know if I'll ever get an assignment like this again. Many filmmakers want research done merely to verify or contradict something they've already decided. Or, they ignore what you give them. Francis Coppola, on the other hand, has a way of absorbing everything that comes his way. He has a great sense of history and respect for detail. I realize that audiences don't see details the way we do but I do believe they are nevertheless affected by the cumulative result."[9] Fine's remarks suggest an openness about Coppola's receptivity to research, but also that it was Coppola, not Puzo, most responsible for introducing the new narrative concerns to the *Godfather* saga.

Coppola's sensibility in sifting through these details of historical research for revealing moments seems reminiscent of his own spadework on George Patton for that striking conception. The inspired scene where gangsters and corporate heads cut up a birthday cake with a map of Cuba emblazoned in the icing is a cinematic flourish analogous to Coppola's image of George Patton standing in front of a huge American flag. In the *Godfather II* research, the most interesting historical personality to emerge was Meyer Lansky, a notorious Jewish gangster who became the basis for Lee Strasberg's Hyman Roth in the film. The brilliant touch of having the enormously wealthy Roth living in an extremely small Florida home was suggested by Lansky's lifestyle and not the result of either screenwriter's imagination. Another scene that fuses a striking visual conceit with a historical context is the scene when the corporate heads pass a solid gold telephone around a table, which unsubtly exposes their real interest at the meeting.

Perhaps related to some of this research, Coppola in interviews of this period begins to emerge as politically more sophisticated. In an interesting exchange he chided a *Playboy* magazine interviewer for not being aware of CIA activity in Chile and corporate assassinations in this country.[10] He began professing an admiration for Castro, which is also reflected in the rather scathing view of Batista's Cuba that the film carries. At the same time, he confessed: "Politically no one knows what I am, including me."[11] While making a film concerned with the corrupt political repression in Batista's Cuba, he was shooting in the Dominican Republic, an island heavily owned by the multinational Gulf & Western (also the owner of Paramount pictures), and ruled by another corrupt regime. Charles Bludhorn, the chairman, told Coppola not to worry when extended rain set the production back; it was good for the sugar crop owned by the multinational. In later years Coppola would ruminate about setting up a communications empire in Belize, free of U.S. control, a philosophy sounding not dissimilar to Hyman Roth's.[12] Although *Godfather II* sets out to expose Michael Corleone as the ultimate corporate monster, as David Thomson observes: "the making of alliances, the application of pressure and whispering of conspiracy have an erotic luster that shines out of the siesta gloom."[13] Our fascination often outweighs the condemnation of corporate practice contained in the film.

In the last several scenes of *Godfather II* the metaphor of "Michael is America" or the practices of the Corleones as a metaphor for modern corporate America, became more literal. Rather than suggesting that crime families have similarities to American corporations in their ruthlessness, their profit motive, their clandestine nature, the film begins to suggest the crime families are a vital component of recent American history. Tom Hagen tells Michael that Hyman Roth cannot be assassinated while entering an airport filled with federal agents. Michael coolly responds: "I'm surprised at you, Tom. If history has taught us anything, it is that anyone can be gotten to." The obvious reference here is to the Kennedy assassination and the conspiracy theories that Kennedy was "hit" either because of Robert Kennedy's pursuit of Jimmy Hoffa and the Mafia or because of Kennedy's own alleged desire to assassinate Castro. The association is cemented when Roth is gunned down in a scene that seems staged intentionally to recall Jack Ruby's murder of Lee Harvey Oswald.

Although the glimpses of the Mafia in its relation to modern American corporate practice forms an interesting and revealing subtext to *Godfather II*, there is also a questionable romanticization of the historical roots of modern American crime. This becomes clear as we look at the film's relation to Puzo's original novel. Both the novel and the first film open in late summer, 1945. In the novel, following the sections on the murder of Sollozzo and on Johnny Fontane, Puzo provided a thirty-two page description of how Vito came to his present power. This section had to be scrapped due to length considerations in the first film, but forms the basis for the narrative elements of the "Vito" section in *Godfather II*. It is surprising, however, that given the fact that Coppola was spending much film time on a small section of the novel, he chose to ignore some key points Puzo was making in his narrative. In the chapter on *The Godfather*, it was noted that Puzo described Vito's initial unscrupulous business tactics: the violent elimination of honest competition in the olive oil business. In addition to this, Puzo described how Vito made a fortune during Prohibition by using his delivery trucks to run liquor illegally. After Prohibition, to continue his high profits, Vito overthrows another mob leader and annexes his gambling operations. In contrast to Puzo, Coppola in *both* films never shows us how Vito made his fortune. Puzo made it very clear that there was a link between how the children eventually turned out and what their father did. In Puzo's thirty-two page explication, there is a description of how Sonny is arrested for a petty robbery. Vito angrily begins to chastise Sonny, who in turn defiantly reveals that he saw his father kill Fanucci. Sonny then announces that he intends to enter the family business.[14]

Thus, the film's view that Vito was a Robin Hood, while Michael is simply a failed individual who cannot measure up to his father and succumbs to the temptations of power, is not really present in Puzo's novel. Puzo did write the scene in which Vito altruistically helps a widow keep her apartment, but that was just one aspect of his complex portrayal. The film's conception of Vito as a sort of immigrant-American entrepreneur with a good idea that was destroyed by the corporate mentality was one that Coppola brought to the film. Coppola's sentimentalized view of history was also reflected in an ongoing project, the film *Tucker*, which at one point was to be the film that followed *Godfather II*.[15] Perhaps in *Godfather II*

Coppola was inappropriately soldering the theme of American ingenuity and productivity smothered by corporatism to the rise of American crime.

Against the romanticization of Vito, however, we have the filmic rendition of Vito's brutal and shocking murders of Fanucci and Don Ciccio. We are not presented something in the fashion of Gary Cooper shooting men in black hats and casually walking away; Vito disembowels Don Ciccio, a decrepit old man who seems hardly worth revenge, and coolly and methodically splatters Fanucci's brain on the wall. Although within the narrative the revenge is motivated, the graphic quality of the murders chastens empathy and reminds us that this is a man who is not an ordinary do-gooder.

The murders are effective in eliminating some of the sainthood that accrues to a killer in this narrative, but had Coppola really wanted to "finish" morally with the Corleones, he could have suggested, as Puzo did, that, in the way of the Corleones' rise to success, there were some "pain-in-the-ass-innocent-bystanders," bystanders we might identify as being like ourselves.

Someone who did "read" the text of *Godfather II* in an extremely interesting and provocative way was John Hess, whose "*Godfather II*: A Deal Coppola Couldn't Refuse," is one of the most cogent Marxist essays on any big-budget, Hollywood film. Hess's basic premise is that: "*Godfather II* works out on the level of human relations Marx's insight that capitalism, even at its best, must destroy human life and associations to exist . . . this contradiction is most clearly visible in American gangsterdom, the perfect microcosm of American capitalism."[16] Hess divides the human relations into four categories: church, family, ethnicity, and friendship between men, and then shows how the values associated with each are progressively broken down by the needs of "business," or capitalism within the text. On a narrative level these contentions are easily supported: we see terrible deeds committed during religious ceremonies, Michael is losing his family and ethnicity, and he tells Tom that he cannot trust his subordinates because their relations are based upon business. Hess feels what really separates *Godfather II* from a typical dynasty film showing how money perverts human relations—he mentions *The Magnificent Ambersons*, *Written on the Wind*, and *Giant*—is the juxtaposition of time periods within the film which sets up an historical analysis of the current condition of Michael's family. Hess does not attribute conscious intention, but notes that Latin American political directors: "have used disjunctions in time as a distancing device to help them analyze rather than simply create the filmic fantasy into which an audience is drawn unthinkingly."[17] Thus, although I suggested earlier that the Vito sequences were over-romanticized for no good purpose, Hess feels: "The sentimentality is there, but only to set up the audience for the demolition of the sentiments in the following sequence."[18] Hess finds much order and coherence to Coppola's critique of capitalist society, even though Hess feels Coppola is limited in his lack of a fully articulated Marxist orientation to film. Thus Hess finds the ultimate contradiction and irony of the film that: "Few films have used such extensive means ($13 million) and created such beautiful images in order to show the corruption and perversion of the system which supplied those means."[19]

Extending and commenting directly on that same irony, Robert Kolker in his book *A Cinema of Loneliness* suggests that Coppola is "the great sleight-of-hand artist in American film of the seventies—and the great subversive." Noting that Coppola has in the past structured *Patton* so that it could be read two ways: as either pro-war or anti-war, depending on the viewer's inclinations, Kolker suggested the same strategy could be going on with *Godfather II*. If we see the film as an indictment of modern corporate capitalism, Michael's adventures in Cuba could be seen as presenting an alternative: people willing to die for freedom and the expulsion of the corrupt Batista regime. If, however, the audience starts with the premise that the Cuban revolution was a failure in American foreign policy, the following interpretation becomes possible:

Michael is still a figure of some nobility, even of pathos, then it is quite possible to see the episode not in political and social terms but as part of Michael's personal downfall, the concatenation of events partly of his own making, partly resulting from situations outside his control, that make him a sad, lonely, rich man.[20]

Kolker suggests that it is possible that the only way criticism of the American capitalistic system can be made in American feature films is in this ambiguous fashion. Both Hess and Kolker approach Coppola's film with a perspective of alternative film practices—Hess, Latin American political films, and Kolker, European art films, especially the New Wave. However, the distinctiveness of *Godfather II*'s accomplishment only fully emerges when we consider it relative to other Hollywood products. George Lucas, a paragon of Hollywood success, looked at Coppola's footage and told him: "Francis, you have two movies. Throw one away, it doesn't work."[21] Needless to say, Lucas's work since the Coppola-produced *American Graffiti* has been quite conservative. If we think of a filmmaker who is more daring, it is difficult to imagine Sergio Leone's long version of *Once Upon A Time in America* without the relative success of *Godfather II* as a precedent. Not many other filmmakers working in the Hollywood industry have matched Coppola's ambition to push the limits of feature film's form; sometimes that ambition seems an overreach. However, at this point in Coppola's career, the overreach was still financially viable. *Godfather II* is ambitious, it tries our patience, it asks us to consider the political underpinning of American culture, its heroes are problematic in terms of our identification with them. Yet this is all done under the umbrella of a tre-

mendous curiosity in the ticket-buying public based on the fond remembrance of *The Godfather*. With Coppola's commercial name-power floundering
in the 1980s, the prospect of Coppola using a *Godfather III* as license for
further experimentation does not seem as outlandish as it did in the 1970s
before *One from the Heart*. Paramount has a script for *Godfather III* written
by Dean Riesner and covering Anthony Corleone's exploits in Cuba in the
1960s. Reportedly, John Travolta was temporarily interested in doing the
film with Sylvester Stallone directing. At the time of this writing, there is
talk of Puzo scripting a Part III. Coppola's public rhetoric has been that his
participation on another *Godfather* film would be a sellout of his artistic
ambitions.

The pressure the requirements of a multi-million dollar feature film put
on the creative process are vividly illustrated by the post-production struggle
*Godfather II* went through. Christmas is notoriously a time when box office
receipts soar, as people have more time for attending movies. A popular
film may double during the holidays what it would do if it opened in
February. Early in the production process of *Godfather II*, Paramount slated
that film for holiday release in 1974. Additionally, it would be premiered
in time for Academy Award consideration in March of 1975; delaying that
consideration a year would be delaying the return on the investment. However, Coppola's efforts to finish *The Conversation*, his lack of time in the
writing process, and the sheer magnitude of *Godfather II*'s production requirements slowed its completion beyond the earlier projected date. Consequently there was a frantic rush to get it edited in time for the holiday
opening. Several journalist/critics—Stephen Farber, Jay Cocks, and John
Carroll—were in attendance at this process and paint a picture of round-
the-clock work, frantic second-guessing, and a feeling that there would be
flaws that a few months more work would have alleviated.[22]

Farber, who was probably most familiar with Coppola's other work, had
the unusual opportunity to view three separate cuts of the film in the weeks
prior to its release. An earlier cut, unseen by Farber, had run four hours
and 45 minutes. By the time Farber got to the film it was running at its
eventual three hour and 20 minute time. However, with the extra material
available, whole scenes and subplots were shuffled in and out of the ongoing
narrative shaping. A long section where Michael's first $2 million payment
is stolen by Roth, a scene where Hagen chases down Kay in New England
and has an emotional confrontation, and a scene where Al Neri leads a
strongarm takeover of the Tropicana casino—all were casualties in the par-
ing down to a running time satisfactory to exhibitors. In particular, Farber
was unhappy with the final sequence of events with the Senate investigation
of the Corleones. In one cut, Fredo's confession to Michael of his treachery
and the reasons for it is followed by Michael's asking his mother if one can
lose their family, then followed by the Senate investigation. However, to
enhance the surprise of Frankie Pentangeli's testimony against Michael,

Fredo's scene was sandwiched in the middle of the investigation, and Farber felt it did not retain its emotional force, urgency, and climax, instead functioning as a distraction to our interest in the outcome of the investigation. Farber was convinced that had Coppola taken more time he would have restored the scenes to the original order. Farber mused about the pressures of the release date: "A truism about the movie business may be worth repeating: Artistic considerations are secondary to the demands of the marketplace. Even a director of Coppola's stature must finally submit to the commercial realities."[23]

It may be that time and financial pressures also had to do with some more troubling narrative problems that call to mind *The Big Sleep*, which probably had the most convoluted plot of any film in the Hollywood studio era. With that film's release, attentive critics noticed that one of the murders was never explained, and wondered who did it. When the writers and the director were asked about this, they could offer no explanation; the complications of the plot had been created for their own sake, not with logical explanations in mind. It almost seems the same circumstances were at work in the Frankie Pentangeli story in *Godfather II*.

The character of Frankie Pentangeli was added to the narrative at the last minute when Richard Castellano would not come to contract to play Clemenza again. Thus we learn that Clemenza has mysteriously died and that Pentangeli, his successor, suspects foul play. That point is never cleared up or referred to again.[24] Pentangeli early on has difficulties seeing Michael, gets drunk at dinner, and spills wine on the tablecloth. The close-ups around the table suggest an omen in the act of spilling wine. After Pentangeli finally complains to Michael about his problems with the Rosato brothers and leaves, one of Michael's henchmen asks whether they should let him go back to New York. Michael sinisterly replies: "Let him go back. I've already made my plans. The old man had too much to drink tonight." From this, the obvious assumption is that Michael intends to kill Pentangeli. Immediately following comes the assassination attempt on Michael. Michael then goes to Cuba and tells Roth that Pentangeli was behind the assassination attempt. He ends the conversation with "Then you agree, Pentangeli is a dead man?" Roth responds: "Small potatoes." Following this scene, Michael goes to his former home in New York where Pentangeli lives. He screams at Pentangeli about the assassination attempt and then changes tone to say Hyman Roth was behind the attempt, but that Pentangeli should keep peace with the Roth-backed Rosato brothers. We are prepared to take Michael at his word until, at Pentangeli's summit with the Rosatos, an assassin begins to garrote Pentangeli, saying "Greetings from Michael Corleone." The murder is foiled by the entrance of a patrolman. Pentangeli is then taken by the police to testify against Michael in the crime investigation. On hearing that Pentangeli is dead (he is not) Michael asks Roth who gave the go-ahead on the murder, saying he did not. Roth gives Michael a lecture about never asking about things that do not affect business and makes a veiled threat in reference to Michael's own order for Moe Greene's assassination (seen in the first film). From this we are apparently supposed to deduce not only that Roth had the attempted murder of Pentangeli intentionally flubbed so that Pentangeli would think that Michael was behind it, but also that Michael had wanted his own men to think he was going to assassinate Pentangeli earlier at Tahoe, hoping that a traitor would inform Roth of this.

The plot is so convoluted that it is difficult to imagine many viewers comprehending it on first experience. It seems safe to assume that the rush in the composition process accounted for some of the confusion, but it also seems that if Puzo, with his experience as a crafter of hard-driving narrative, had had more say about the final results, much of this might have been cleared up. It is reminiscent of some of the convolutions of *The Conversation*'s plot. Another approach could suggest that the confusion was well motivated. The narration toys with our sympathy with Michael, first presenting him as unsympathetic by his rejection of the likeable Pentangeli, then rescuing him from this charge by making the murder attempt a strategy of the villainous Roth. Finally, the murder of Fredo settles the issue of Michael's cold-bloodedness, but our interest in Michael has been maintained on a teeter-totter throughout.[25]

Rather than nit-picking further, let us switch attention to a few of the scenes that give considerable power to the film. Perhaps the most fully realized scene is the flashback that occurs (as Michael's recollection) when Michael hears the shot and knows that Fredo's murder has been carried out. The flashback is to a scene that occurred shortly after Michael had enlisted in the Marines in 1941. It is another family dinner table scene, similar to the one Coppola added in Part I in which Carlo was upbraided for talking business at the table. In this brief new scene, James Caan's Sonny again presides, injecting a dash of warmth and energy into this sullen film. There is horseplay among all the brothers except Michael. Sonny finds out Michael has enlisted and explodes at him in his characteristically brutal, hot-headed manner. Tom coolly explains, to Michael's resentment, that he and Vito had made other plans for Michael. Vito enters off-stage and everyone but Michael runs out to greet him. Michael is left alone, characteristically brooding. That Michael, having just ordered Fredo's murder should think of another time when he was totally separated from his family is appropriate. The melancholic tone of the scene underscores that Michael was always a loner, that he always had a different relationship with his father. Our understanding of Michael's personality has changed from *The Godfather* to *Godfather II*. Whereas in *The Godfather* we saw Michael's joining the Marines positively, a patriotism tinged with a certain existential desire for freedom from his family, by this point in *Godfather II* the action is to be interpreted as a basic expression of his inability to feel the family warmth and love that ultimately excused Vito. Michael killed for his country in the South Pacific and later killed for the corporation that had once been a family enterprise. As a pathetic character never quite able to grasp a basic humanity, a love for those nearest to him, Michael's real forebears are Dostoevsky's Underground Man or Charles Foster Kane. He is not simply a failed individual.

Another powerful scene that suggests Michael's downfall in a way not approached in Part I occurs when Kay reveals her abortion. Michael seems to snap, and violates the Old World Italian tradition of treating women as sacred and strikes Kay. We hear their arguing in the hall in a shot of the two stoic children. Kay proclaims "This Sicilian thing must end." The scene is a departure from the novel, wherein women seem incapable of any kind of action or judgment. In tone, it is a companion to Coppola's *The Rain People*, which is about a woman whose unexpected pregnancy leads her to question her marriage and run away to find herself. It is also a jolt from the otherwise convincing period realism of *Godfather II*, as abortion is more an issue of the 1970s and seems too contemporary an alternative for Kay in the 1950s. The scene's creative lineage is mixed. Earlier, it was mentioned how Puzo felt the scene was implausible and claimed it was Al Pacino's idea to have Michael strike Kay. The decision to have Kay opt for an abortion came from Talia Shire's suggestion. The original plan was to have Kay bear the third child and then leave. Shire claimed that Francis, out of gratitude for the suggestion, wrote her the scene where she begs Michael to forgive Fredo.[26]

Such behind-the-scenes creative bartering makes one approach the question of personal artistic vision with trepidation. Nonetheless, the following observations by David Denby suggest a thematic preoccupation in Coppola's work that seems borne out in this particular film:

Coppola's personality (sad word) emerges in the way he chooses to reveal his characters. For instance, he has a genius for noisy, shallow, self-propelling types— the American as an untrammeled egotist, powerful and infantile at the same time. He appears to love their theatrical energy and flash, and his sense of how such people behave in social situations is so accurate that he can do very funny scenes without a trace of caricature.[27]

Denby specifically writes about the wiretappers' convention in *The Conversation* as an example, but the description seems highly appropriate for *Godfather II*'s Fanucci. Fanucci, though not so much an "American egotist" (he is more Old World), certainly fits with other characters Coppola has shown insight into: George Patton, Clemenza and Sonny, Tom Buchanan in the Coppola-scripted *The Great Gatsby*, and Robert Duvall's Colonel Kilgore in *Apocalypse Now*. A number of visual and stylistic flourishes separate the Fanucci character from the rest of the cast. First, there is his visual appearance: the florid clothing, and a cape and curled moustache that make him look like a nineteenth century melodramatic villain. As the religious procession marches one way down the street, Fanucci moves against the grain, acting as the lord of this territory, and visually in contrast with it. The actor, Gaston Moschin, who Coppola had to convey instructions to in Italian, manifests a certain unbashed self-involvement. Fanucci wanders about the Holy Celebration making comments to no one in particular, for instance, "This is much too violent for me" as he walks away from a puppet show. As an arch-villain for Vito to oppose, he is established very well, although our desire to see him vanquished is thrown back at us somewhat when Vito, in an almost sadistic fashion, places a pistol in Fanucci's mouth and fires into his brain. In like fashion, Senator Geary in the Michael section makes a strong impression as a villain who embodies the worst stereotypes about crooked politicians. The actor, G. D. Spradlin, had in fact at one point been a politician. Both characters are set up as strong adversaries for the Corleones, but in tone they seem far more severe than the villains of Puzo's original novel.

From the production accounts, it seems clear that even more than in *The Godfather*, Coppola was the dominant force in *Godfather II*'s overall structure. This time there was no wrangling over casting, no stipulations made about what he could and could not do; the Paramount executives were convinced he had an innate commercial sense and whatever decisions he made would pay off for them. The major conceptual decisions about the film were all Coppola's: that the film would tell two stories and eventually jump back and forth in time, that Michael would not die but be presented as a spiritually destroyed man, that the film would re-create the immigrant experience, and so forth. We have seen the usual creative collaboration in the production background, but all things considered the appellation "a film by Francis Coppola" seems correct in this case. Coppola has called it a "$12 million personal film."[28]

Where those "personal" concerns are in a vast sweeping epic of change in America, of America's role in the Third World, of the historical development of modern American crime, of the Italian-American immigrant past, is difficult to locate. Puzo had written a mythic story of a king and three sons that happened to be set at the end of World War II. Coppola expanded that time context and made it more intrinsic to the tragic downfall of the protagonist Michael. Michael *is* America, or at least an aspect of it. If capitalistic power has corrupted America in the post-World War II domestic and international arenas, then certainly Michael mirrors the lack of humanity in that corruption. Michael's final inability to separate business from his personal family life chillingly suggests a perversion and invasion of modern life on every level by the American corporate ethic. This seems to be Coppola's "personal" statement, and it is a compelling one. *Godfather II* may reveal a certain ideological fuzziness in its ambivalent deification of Vito, but there is a clarity in the indictment of modern corporate America in the Michael saga that suggests Coppola the artist had matured and would be working at a new level in the future. *Apocalypse Now*, the next text, also demanded an epic scale in its treatment of an historic American moment. The evidence suggests that *Apocalypse Now* demanded a "personal" vision as well.

## NOTES

1. Bob Mottley, "Two 'Godfathers' are better than one?" *New Times*, 2 (May 3, 1974), 58.

2. William Murray, "*Playboy* Interview: Francis Ford Coppola," *Playboy*, July 1975, p. 62.

3. Mottley, p. 57.

4. Many things motivated this decision and in different interviews Coppola has given different explanations for his decision to do the sequel. To Marjorie Rosen, he said, "I really had made so much money on *The Godfather*, it was irrelevant for me to do a film for any other reason than because I wanted to do it." Marjorie Rosen, "Francis Ford Coppola," *Film Comment*, 10 (July/August, 1974), 45.

5. Hal Aigner and Michael Goodwin, "The Bearded Immigrant from Tinsel Town," *City Magazine* (San Francisco), June 12–25, 1974, p. 36.

6. Mario Puzo, "Dialogue on Film," *American Film* (May 1979), 44.

7. Aigner and Goodwin, p. 40.

8. Puzo, p. 42.

9. From the Paramount Pictures press kit: "Research for *The Godfather, Part II* Becomes an Epic Job," pp. 6–7.

10. A transcription of the exchange with Murray: "*Playboy*: As far as we know, A.T.&T. hasn't killed anyone in pursuit of its business. *Coppola*: Who says? Who says? *Playboy*: Have you got something on A.T.&T.? *Coppola* : A.T.&T. I don't know about, but I.T.T. in Chile? I wouldn't bet my life that it hadn't. And it's not just business. How about the Yablonski murders in the coal miners' union. That was just the union equivalent of a Mafia hit. How about politics? Assassination of a President is the quickest way to bring about lasting and enormous social change. What's the difference between the United States putting a guy like Trujillo in power so our companies can operate in the Dominican Republic, and the Mafia's handing the Boston territory to one of its *capos*? Then, after twenty years, either guy gets a little uppity and either organization feels free to knock him off." Murray, p. 58.

11. Murray, p. 68.

12. Coppola did an exploratory visit there in 1981. See Todd McCarthy, "Coppola Scouts Belize As Future Site of Electronic Wonder Studio," *Variety* (December 16, 1981), 5, 23. Coppola discusses it further in David Thomson and Lucy Gray, "Idols of the King," *Film Comment*, 19, 5 (Sept./Oct. 1983), 69, 70.

13. David Thomson, *Overexposures* (New York: Morrow, 1981), 312.

14. Mario Puzo, *The Godfather* (New York: G. P. Putnam, 1969), 218. Puzo was upset about the line about lawyers not appearing in the first film.

15. Susan Braudy, "Francis Coppola: A Profile," *Atlantic*, August 1976, p. 73.

16. John Hess, "*Godfather II*: A Deal Coppola Couldn't Refuse," in *Movies and Methods*, Bill Nichols, ed. (Berkeley: University of California Press, 1976), 89. The essay originally appeared in *Jump Cut*.

17. Hess, 83.

18. Hess, 82.

19. Hess, 85.

20. Robert Kolker, *A Cinema of Loneliness* (New York: Oxford, 1980), 191.

21. Jon Carroll, "New York Intelligencer," *New York*, November 11, 1974, p. 98.

22. Carroll, noted above; Stephen Farber, "L.A. Journal," *Film Comment* (March/April 1975), 2+; and Jay Cocks, "Outs," *Take One* (December 1974), 36.

23. Farber, p. 62.

24. In a copy of the screenplay dated September 23, 1973, Pentangeli claims that anxiety about the activity of the Rosato brothers caused Clemenza's heart attack. The line does not appear in the final film.

25. In regard to a second confusing scene, a number of critics have faulted the logic of Michael's bodyguard's failed assassination attempt on Hyman Roth. Why do a group of marching soldiers leave the New Year's party and inexplicably arrive at the hospital just in time to save Roth's life? Chance? No solution has been offered. One solution would be that since Michael had told Fredo that Roth would try to assassinate him (another question: how does Michael know this?), Fredo has warned Michael's enemies. This seems borne out by Michael's nervous watching of Fredo's every movement at the party. It may be that manipulation of our character identification prevailed over logical narrative motivation in Coppola's final editing. Without Fredo's culpability established, he seems more pathetic and Michael seems more ruthless in later having Fredo killed. If we are completely aware that Fredo spoiled Michael's attempt to eliminate Roth, then there seems more justification for Michael's later elimination of Fredo. Given these twists and turns, it is not surprising that some of our interest in *Godfather II*, as in a mystery story, lies in simply deducing the reasons for what happens.

26. Stephen Farber and Marc Green, *Hollywood Dynasties* (New York: Fawcett, 1985), 357–358.

27. David Denby, "The Two Godfathers," *The Partisan Review*, 43, no. 1 (1976), 118.

28. From the Rosen interview cited above, p. 45: "I didn't like what was then a script called *Death of Michael Corleone*. What they were essentially saying to me was that they'd let me do anything I wanted. I began to think of letting *The Godfather* format subsidize me in doing something more ambitious in the sequel than they wanted. It was then I made my bargain with them to let me bring back all the original actors that were relevant to my story that I hadn't figured out yet. If it could be a real continuation as though it were really part of the first film and be called *The Godfather*, and if I could have total control over it, I would do it. They said yes and therefore, *Godfather II* falls more in the category of a personal film, although it cost twelve million dollars, than the first one. I have to make it relevant or tie it into the first film, but it's very ambitious on other levels."

# 7

# Going up the River

## *Apocalypse Now*

In the film world, 1974 was the year of Coppola. In the spring *The Conversation* was released to some of the best reviews of Coppola's career. Although the film never caught on with the public, reviewers hailed it as a prescient view of the Nixon/Watergate era and marveled that the director/screenwriter could go from the highly commercial *The Godfather* to this smaller, less compromising view of America. *The Great Gatsby*, based on another Coppola screenplay, came out in the summer of 1974 with much fanfare, although it was a disappointment critically and commercially. Finally, in a 1974 Christmas release, *Godfather II* appeared to more than moderate critical and commercial success. It seemed as if Coppola would be a director who would subsidize smaller, personal "art films" with larger, less personal blockbusters. The following spring, the 1974 Academy Awards were dominated by Coppola: *The Conversation* was nominated for Best Picture, *Godfather II* won Best Picture, and Coppola won for Best Director and Best Screenplay. With screenwriting Oscars for *Patton* (1970) and *The Godfather* (1972), Coppola had a total of five Oscars. Such fame, respect from his colleagues, and a successful box-office track record meant that Coppola had a degree of creative autonomy rare in Hollywood. Any reasonable project he suggested would get made, and the parameters of what was "reasonable" were probably wider than for any other director working.

However, in 1975, Coppola's career took an unexpected turn. With the huge profits from the *Godfather* films, Coppola invested heavily around the San Francisco area: real estate, a theater, and *City Magazine*, an unprofitable monthly devoted to the concerns of San Francisco. With the acquisition of

"The Little Fox" theater, Coppola announced plans to make a legitimate theater district out of what had previously been a strip joint area; he would use the theater to direct plays and form a repertory company.[1] With *City Magazine* he would chronicle the advance of the San Francisco cultural community with top-notch journalism. It seemed that being a filmmaker was no longer enough for Coppola, he would now be a leading citizen in the community, "Citizen Coppola" if you will. Further parallels to *Citizen Kane* suggested themselves when Coppola came to the *City* office daily for six months. The circulation began to rise, but so did the production costs attendant to changes Coppola implemented, such as hiring the eccentric Warren Hinkle, a former *Ramparts* editor. *City* became even more of a losing proposition. In addition, Coppola was not welcomed by the San Francisco establishment, who regarded him as sort of a Hollywood carpetbagger.

When the fictional Kane failed in his attempt to make the people love him in an election, Jed Leland observed that maybe he would "lord it over the monkeys." *City Magazine* failed within two years and Coppola was hurt by San Francisco's reaction to him: he left San Francisco for the Philippines to begin the *Apocalypse Now* project, and, ironically, in one of the closing scenes a number of monkeys are shown walking on an empty patrol boat (ostensibly a reference to Herzog's *Aguirre: Wrath of God*). Coppola was lording it over more than the monkeys, however, as the production swelled out of control. Eventually the twelve million dollar film became a thirty-one million dollar film. Eventually what was to have been a "quickie" action-film transformed into a masterwork oozing with profundity. Coppola later commented that there was a certain inevitability about the *Apocalypse* experience, that had he started out to make a film about Mickey Mouse it would have ended the same way. Apparently, however cynical or commercial his original intentions might have been, Coppola eventually felt compelled to make the film his magnum opus, a film that was wide-reaching in its vision of contemporary America's capacity for war. Finally, it was also a personal exploration of the director's own tendencies toward the excessive and his relation to the central character, Kurtz.

Why Coppola, of all directors, felt a compulsion to deliver a "statement" on the Vietnam War is interesting. In pre–1974 interviews and film work, Coppola had never shown even a passing interest in the Vietnam War. He once remarked that he had no idea why he was not drafted. In his screen-writing work on *Patton*, which occurred in the mid–1960s as the controversy about the war began to mount, he consciously attempted to adopt a position toward the main character that would appeal to doves and hawks alike, more concerned with his own success than with his personal opinion about war. With the formation of American Zoetrope in 1968–69, Coppola and George Lucas were listening on a regular basis to Vietnam war stories told by John Milius. Milius was living the war vicariously by pumping returning veterans for tales of what was transpiring overseas. Coppola later remarked: "I knew very little about the war, truly. But I heard these things that sounded almost like fantasy and I listened very intently."[2] Not only did Coppola listen, but he made the crucial suggestion that Milius and Lucas write up the stories with Conrad's *Heart of Darkness* as the underlying structural agent. Then, while negotiating for Lucas' *THX–1138* with Warner Brothers, he tossed *Apocalypse Now* into the deal and got Milius $15,000– 25,000 to write the screenplay that Lucas would direct in 16mm and Coppola would produce. Lucas at the time called it a super-John Wayne movie and predicted it would be: "taking the American dream, the two-fisted, two- gunned tough killer everyone grows up on and saying that all the guys in America and Vietnam are just like that."[3] Coppola observed at the time: "An amazing screenplay called *Apocalypse Now*, part zany comedy, part terrifying psychedelic horror." Milius recalled the genesis of the script in interesting detail in 1982:

The original started at cinema school. George Lucas and I were great connoisseurs of the Vietnam War. Of course, we hadn't lost it then so it was a little easier to be interested. As a matter of fact, I wanted to go to Vietnam but I had asthma, couldn't get in anything. I was the only person I knew who wanted to go in the Army. George and I would talk about the battles all the time and what a great movie it would make. I had the title to call it, *Apocalypse Now*, because all these hippies at the time had these buttons that said "Nirvana Now," and I loved the idea of a guy having a button with a mushroom cloud on it that said "Apocalypse Now," you know, let's bring it on, full nuke. Ever hear that Randy Newman song "Let's Drop the Big One Now?" That's the spirit that it started in right there.[4]

From this description, we can isolate three basic reasons for Milius' desire to write this screenplay: 1) the Vietnam War was an appropriately cinematic subject; 2) Milius loved the idea of combat and was unhappy at not being able to participate; and 3) Milius felt anger and disdain toward the pacifists, who were the dominant voice of the youth culture at the time. These three elements all figure prominently in the original screenplay, which is widely available in bootleg form.[5] The unabashed love for war in the screenplay was notorious enough in Hollywood that it paved the way for Milius's becoming one of the highest paid screenwriters in the early 1970s, with *Dirty Harry*, *Magnum Force*, *The Life and Times of Judge Roy Bean*, *Jeremiah Johnson*, and *Dillinger* some of the more representative examples of the highly eccentric Milius touch. The more recent *Uncommon Valor* (Milius produced) and *Red Dawn* (Milius directed) are quite close in tone to Milius's original draft of *Apocalypse Now*.

Despite the notoriety of the script, Warner Brothers was afraid to make *Apocalypse Now*, probably guessing that the militant, rightwing tone would not sit well with the anti-militarist younger audience. With the withdrawal of Warner Brothers' support for American Zoetrope, precipitated by their extreme dislike of Lucas' *THX–1138*, Coppola was deep in debt and not in a position to produce *any* film, including his own *The Conversation*, which was in development. Later, with his large profit returns from *The Godfather*, Coppola quickly bought back both *The Conversation* and *Apocalypse Now* scripts from Warners and shot the former. Following the success of *Godfather II*, Coppola decided to revive *Apocalypse Now*. By this time, Lucas had had an enormous success with the Coppola-produced *American Graffiti* and was beginning work on *Star Wars* (1977). Milius had commitments as well. Rather than wait, Coppola decided to direct the film himself. Dale Pollock's *Skywalking* reports that Lucas is quite bitter both that Coppola offered a low salary to him to direct and that Coppola would not wait for him. Milius rewrote the script a few more times for Coppola and was initially upset about Coppola's efforts to "liberalize" the story, at one point calling him the "Bay area Mussolini"[6]; but he now seems quite proud of the eventual film.

In light of how far Coppola eventually departed from Milius' original screenplay and of Coppola's initial apathy or lack of an opinion on the Vietnam War, it is curious what Coppola's intentions were throughout this process. I do not want to argue that intentions should be used to interpret what is finally up on the screen, but the production process of *Apocalypse Now* was dramatic and has become well-known enough to invite its own acts of interpretation. We all shared more or less in its ongoing myth. Two alternative interpretations seem to present themselves: One is that the film was a consciousness-raising experience for Coppola, in that through the course of the filming he developed antipathy toward the ideas that had seduced him back in 1969. The other is that in a move similar to his conceptualization of *Patton*, Coppola cynically decided that a pro-American-involvement-in-Vietnam film would not play in the late 1970s.

Perhaps the key goes back to the earlier described attempts to become more than a filmmaker around the San Francisco area. A change had occurred in Coppola's conception of himself. He was no longer an artist interested in creativity for creativity's sake. The acclaim of *The Godfather* films and *The Conversation* consistently portrayed him as an artist with an insightful, epic vision of the contemporary American experience. If that was to be his status, what could be more fitting than to be the first major American feature filmmaker to deliver a post mortem on the Vietnam War? One of the reasons he did not wait for Lucas was that he wanted to complete the film by 1976, the American bicentennial year. This motivation was combined with Coppola's opinion that Lucas and Milius had a sure-fire commercial touch, that he could explore his attitude toward the Vietnam War with that "built-in" commercial sensibility protecting him from absorbing any heavy losses in the process.[7] What was to result, however, was one of the most dramatic and dangerous film productions of the modern era, a film that threatened to abolish the good standing Coppola had earned in 1974 and finally, if the hyperbole about the production is to be believed, also threatened Coppola's sanity.

Authors might be divided into three categories: those that write imaginatively from personal experience, those that write imaginatively with material based on research, and those that do both. Coppola as an auteur has straddled the three categories. *You're a Big Boy Now* and *The Rain People* included loose autobiographical aspects that could be classified as coming from personal experience. His most successful previous films combined personal experience and research: *The Godfathers* and *The Conversation*. With *Apocalypse Now* he set out to make a film entirely from research materials—even the Milius inspirations involved a degree of research. Coppola had not been involved in the Vietnam War and consequently hired as technical assistants a number of veterans for accuracy. But the film metamorphosized into a personal experience and vision in and of itself. Coppola later talked about the film "making itself," but it would seem more precise to say that the adversity Coppola suffered on the production forced an empathy with the material that dissolved some of his former apathy and naiveté.

Much has been made of how the production of the film came to mirror American involvement in the war. Such characterization trivializes the experience of the millions of Vietnamese and Americans who fought there. But to continue with an examination of how the production process became a myth, I will detail those comparisons. The parallel most often mentioned between the production and America's involvement in the Vietnam War is the miscalculation about the size of the commitment and the unexpected escalation of cost. The original conception of the film in 1969 was rather daring in that it would be shot in 16mm with a budget of about $1.5 million, this to approximate the look of the television footage coming back from the war. In 1975, when Coppola was to direct, the budget was upgraded to $12 million. However, after the difficulties in finding stars who would commit themselves to the jungle for four months of location work; after a typhoon hit the production; after Martin Sheen suffered a heart attack; after there were difficulties with Marlon Brando and Harvey Keitel (the original Willard); after difficulties getting the proper military equipment for the production; and after Coppola's conceptual difficulties with the ending, the budget had swelled to $31 million. In an attempt to retain control of the film, Coppola reportedly had mortgaged all his assets, and if the film failed commercially, he was faced with personal financial ruin.

If waste and excess characterized American involvement in Vietnam, so too did it Coppola's production. Well into the production, Coppola began having all kinds of luxuries shipped into the Philippines. His wife, back in San Francisco, became alarmed, as this passage from her *Notes* indicates:

I sent a telex to Francis telling him that because I loved him, I would tell him what no one else was willing to say, that he was setting up his own Vietnam with his supply lines of wine and steaks and air conditioners. Creating the very situation he went there to expose. That with his staff of hundreds of people carrying out his every request, he was turning into Kurtz—going too far.[8]

After the film opened, *Saturday Night Live* did a parody wherein Martin Sheen was an assassin hired by a film company to go up river and stop the excesses of a film director gone mad. Perhaps not so humorous was the effect the production had on the local populace:

Pagsanjan, the sleepy river town north of Manila where the *Apocalypse* crew had its headquarters, had been accustomed to an average wage of less than $2 a day. But for nine months, the movie company pumped $100,000 a week there. As a result, the robbing of local coconut plantations stopped, rents for homes shot up astronomically, and every night the high-school principal, Ricardo Fabella, went from bar to bar in his jeep urging the Filippino film workers not to waste their windfall wages on liquor and women. "Our people have lost their sense of values," he said. "Everything I've taught them they've forgotten."[9]

In paying the Marcos government for use of its military equipment, Coppola was supporting a government possibly more repressive than the South Vietnamese government of Diem. At one point during the shooting, the Filippino helicopters had to be called off the set to fight insurgents several hundred miles away. The government supplied Coppola with personal bodyguards in case the insurgents developed hostile ideas about the famous American director.

Coppola himself saw parallels between the production and the American war effort and did much to foster the analogy, as evidenced by his remarks to the press conference at the Cannes Film Festival where the film eventually shared the Grand Prix with *The Tin Drum*:

My film is not a movie; it's not about Vietnam. It *is* Vietnam. It's what it was really like; it was crazy. The way we made it was very much like the way the Americans were in Vietnam. We were in the jungle, there were too many of us, we had access to too much money, too much equipment; and little by little, we went insane. I think you can see it in the film. As it goes up the river, you can see the photography going a little crazy, and the directors and the actors going a little crazy. After a while, I realized I was a little frightened, because I was getting deeper in debt and no longer recognized the kind of movie I was making. I thought I was making a kind of war film, and it was no longer a war film. Then, as Marlon (as Kurtz) says, "it struck me like a diamond bullet in my head" that I wasn't making the film. The film was making itself; the jungle was making the film, and all I did was do my best.[10]

To another interviewer, Coppola commented: "as the experience of filming went on, I became more interested in the way the color of the smoke would blow in the wind than I was in the story. And that's what it was like for the people in Vietnam."[11] Perhaps the deep involvement Coppola came to have with the material does much to explain the difficulties he had in finding a satisfying conclusion for the film. To find a truthful ending to the film he would have to confront whatever personal changes he had gone through in the making of the film.

The final moral of this story is that Hollywood-in-the-Philippines is not Vietnam. Interested in part in all the gossip and drama that surrounded the production, worldwide audiences paid $200 million to view the film. If Coppola went through moral anguish with the rigors of *Apocalypse Now*, he was eventually well paid for his nightmares. The ending of America's involvement in Vietnam was without rewards, and whether *Apocalypse Now* confronts the scars left from that tragedy will be one of the focal points for the following discussion.

Summarizing the narrative of *Apocalypse Now* will not give much insight into the real success of the film. It is in the narrative of the film that Coppola had his greatest difficulties. The greatest success of *Apocalypse Now* is in its visual texture, the total immersion the viewer feels into the look and sensations of the Vietnam War. Whether it is in a jungle where the vegetation dwarfs the characters, a combat trench where black soldiers fight for a country that has denied them equality, or in a combat landing zone where an ox is elevated by a helicopter while soldiers conduct a mass, the strongest and most consistent vision of the film is in the control of the imagery. Coppola's maturity and craft as a filmmaker, his personal commitment of spending months in the jungle, and his strong visual conception of the film are the focus behind the considerable accomplishment of *Apocalypse Now*. However, although Coppola began his career as a screenwriter, it is in the narrative areas that the film is weakest: fluctuating conception of character psychology and uncertainty about plot direction and resolution are the main failings. As will be developed, Coppola's ambivalent attitude toward the John Milius screenplay as a point of departure and his last minute attempts to rectify his misgivings have much to do with the shortcomings. To give a sense of the film's real power, the following plot summary will attempt to give consideration to the visual texture of the film as well as the main narrative line.

*Apocalypse Now* open with a nightmare. Willard, asleep in a Saigon hotel room, dreams of helicopters dropping napalm in the jungle; the whirling of the overhead fan in his room melds into an image of helicopter blades. Images of flame, helicopters, and the jungle gradually dissolve together with an upside-down shot of Willard's (Martin Sheen's) head, suggesting the inescapability of the horror the character has experienced. Although at the beginning of the film, Jim Morrison on the soundtrack sings "This is the end, beautiful friend, the end." Through the course of the film Willard exudes the cool appearance of a trained assassin. However, this opening scene and the following scene, wherein he drunkenly smashes his hand in a mirror, suggest a troubled and painful conscience for Willard, a conscience that should undercut the macho posturing of the rest of the film.

Following the establishment scene, Willard is taken to a headquarters to be briefed for his mission. The scene features the most extensive use of extreme close-ups of any Coppola film. The technique both understates the material excess of the general's quarters and establishes Willard's alienation from the high command (two-shots are rare). Willard is told of a renegade American officer in Cambodia whom he must "terminate with extreme prejudice," a CIA term meaning political assassination. It is explained that Willard will go up-river by PBR boat so as not to call attention to his mission. In juxtaposition to the claustrophobia of the command headquarters, Willard is then ferried by helicopter through the wide-open spaces of the countryside to the delta where the crew of the boat wait for him. There we meet the "rock and rollers with one foot in the grave" (Clean, Chef, and Lance) and the boat captain, Chief, who immediately gives a veiled threat to Willard about exposing the crew to unnecessary danger.

The crew dances and waterskis to rock music, thus establishing the dissolution of discipline and purpose aboard the boat in contrast to Willard's methodical dedication to his duty. Going up the river, Willard begins reviewing Kurtz's career and developing a psychological attraction to the concept of a man who had reached his limit.

As the mission proceeds we meet the 1st Air Cavalry and Colonel Bill Kilgore (Robert Duvall); they are mopping up from a helicopter assault on a Vietnamese village. Handheld cameras and wind and noise from the helicopters give a sense of being right in the middle of the confusion. Coppola himself appears in a cameo as a television director asking the participants to not look at the camera (as Joris Ivens did in his documentary work in China). Kilgore dispenses "Death from Above," playing cards on the enemy bodies. During a raucous beach party following the mop-up, Willard arranges for Kilgore to escort them to the mouth of the river. Kilgore becomes excited when he hears that although the area is controlled by a Viet Cong base, it is good for surfing. In perhaps the most visually exciting scene of the film, the helicopters attack the base while playing Wagner's "Ride of the Valkyries" on their loudspeakers. Fast-cutting and rapid traveling shots dominate the visual approach to the attack. After the attack, Kilgore orders his aides to surf while shells are still exploding. To make the beach safe he calls in an air strike, and proclaims the now-famous, "I love the smell of napalm in the morning." Willard departs.

After an encounter with a tiger in the jungle, the crew comes into Hau Phat, a supply depot where a Playmate USO show is about to take place. The decor of phallic rockets and lights gives the feel of a science fiction war. The incredible array of commodities at the outpost emphasizes Milius' pun in the name (Hau Phat/How fat). The Playmates drive the crowd of

GIs to a frenzy and they storm the moat around the stage. Amid smoke bombs and riot control police, the Playmates escape.

As the boat moves up the river, the crew becomes increasingly undisciplined. To reassert his authority, Chief orders a routine boat search of a Vietnamese sampan. Nerves on edge, Clean panics and begins machinegunning the peasants after a young woman innocently chases Chef (we will return to this later). In a chilling finish, Willard methodically murders a wounded survivor so the mission is not held up. Following this, the crew arrives at the Dong Lo Bridge. Machine gun fire, cursing, screams, eerie music, and explosions dominate the soundtrack, and blurred visuals, flashing lights and phantasmagoric colors dominate the imagery, giving a surreal quality to the scene. Lance is doing acid, and several soft focus shots suggest his perspective. In a trench Willard encounters several black machine-gunners who dispense with a Viet Cong on the perimeter by calling a zen-grenade specialist named Roach in to do his specialty. Willard discovers there is no commanding officer and departs. The scene has a nightmarish quality. As Willard asks who is in command, his face bobs in and out of shadow, later to be repeated as a motif when we meet Kurtz.

The next day in a sun-drenched scene, which seems to connote safety after the previous night, a sudden ambush kills Clean as the men are reading mail. Not long after this the boat heads into a fog. When they emerge, Kurtz's Montagnards "attack" with play arrows to scare the crew. As Chief loses his temper at Willard, a spear hits him in the chest and kills him. After a "burial at sea," the crew comes into the Kurtz compound, an Angkor Vat style collection of temples. A group of Montagnards painted in white and standing on canoes watch the entrance. Willard meets a freaked-out photojournalist (played by Dennis Hopper), a Kurtz sychophant. Amid severed heads, smoke, hanging bodies, and a generally primitive setting, Willard comes to Kurtz. In a shadowy den that "smells of death," Kurtz's head darts in and out of the light, as he quizzes Willard about his background and mission. After Kurtz tells Willard he is an "errand boy sent by grocery clerks," Willard is placed in a bamboo cage. As it gets dark, an extreme low-angle shot of Kurtz's legs approaching establishes a menace that is confirmed when he drops Chef's head in Willard's lap. Having been thus exposed to Kurtz's psychological terror, Willard is allowed to listen to Kurtz recite poetry in the temple. Willard realizes Kurtz is sick and wants to die in a way appropriate to his position. In a disturbing montage, Willard hacks Kurtz to death, and the same is intercut with the natives ritualistically slaughtering an ox. The natives put down their weapons for Willard, the new king. The Cannes Film Festival prize-winning release ended with Willard poised at the temple, weighing whether to continue Kurtz's methods or to leave. The 70mm U.S. release print and subsequent video cassette copies ended with Willard taking Lance away on the boat and switching off a radio call asking for coordinates. The 35mm version ended with explosions in the Kurtz compound; it is unclear whether they are from an air strike or whether Willard ordered it. I personally do not find the last two endings radically different.

The key structural concept behind *Apocalypse Now*, borrowed from Joseph Conrad's novella, *Heart of Darkness*, is the idea of a journey up a primitive river as a metaphor for an excursion into the darkest parts of man's being; this plan was in the Milius screenplay from the beginning in 1969. However, Milius used the structure loosely and to a different purpose than did Conrad. In both works, a narrator details his contact with primitive, violent aspects of human behavior. Conrad's narrator comes to an unsettling truth about man: that his manners, his civilization, his ethics, are a very basic attempt to deny and hide the truth about his innate darkness: "The mind of man is capable of anything—because everything is in it, all the past as well as all the future."[12] However Milius' narrator in the original 1969 screenplay, quite different from the film's later narration written by Michael Herr, embraces the horror, and more specifically advocates it as the final solution for winning the Vietnam War. Conrad's Marlowe feels sympathetic and attracted to Kurtz, but he never steps over the line into savagery as Kurtz has done. Milius' original Willard is never critical of Kurtz, and the unspoken message of the work is that the war cannot be won without Kurtzes, although Milius' Willard never quite goes to the extremes that Kurtz has. In the final film, Coppola's Willard tells Kurtz that he can "see no method" to Kurtz's operation, but his cold-blooded shooting of the wounded Vietnamese woman seems a Kurtzian action.

Conrad's *Heart of Darkness* was not without its topical references, based on an actual journey Conrad took in the Belgian Congo. The story takes place in the early 1890s when the European powers were colonizing Africa and greedily stealing that continent's natural resources: "The conquest of the earth, which mostly means the taking it away from those who have a different complexion or slightly flatter noses than ourselves, it is not a very pretty thing when you look into it too much" (p. 69). In the heart of Africa: "The word 'ivory' rang in the air, was whispered, was sighed. You would think they were praying to it. A taint of imbecile rapacity blew through it all, like a whiff from some corpse. By Jove! I've never seen anything so unreal in my life" (p. 89). While Conrad's narrator feels a sympathy for the African natives as victims, he sees them as inferior primitives without much hope for becoming civilized. Similarly, Milius' and Coppola's Willard is preoccupied with winning a war and shows little concern for the people on whose behalf the war was supposedly fought. This lack of clarity of purpose has much to do with the hollowness of accomplishment. When Willard completes his mission: what has been gained?

Coppola later claimed he relied on *Heart of Darkness* more closely than did Milius, at one point intending to change the title to Conrad's title.[13]

However, a number of the elements Coppola deleted from Milius' screen-play were directly inspired by the novel. Milius framed the story with Willard on a boat in Washington's Potomac, telling the story to a female journalist; this followed Conrad's framing of Marlowe on a boat on the Thames recalling his journey to find Kurtz. The framing emphasized that the respective rivers were once like the primitive river that leads to Kurtz, that the thriving civilization on their banks only obscured the fact, never eradicated it, and a dark cloud line hovering on the background meta-phorically suggested in both the novel and screenplay the omnipresence of the primitive elements of man's consciousness. Coppola toyed with the idea of shooting the story as a flashback from the Saigon hotel room scene, Willard waiting for debriefing, but ultimately decided on a linear time narrative with a voice-over that functions more as an interpreter of the narrative than as a re-teller. The Michael Herr narration stresses more of a disgust and alienation from the proceedings, in contrast to the relish Milius' narrator exudes for the violent aspects of the story.

Some of the other Milius borrowings from Conrad were as follows: in the original script a Montagnard interpreter comes along on the voyage. He is portrayed as something of a mascot who does not help in any way and cowers in fear every time the boat is attacked. Nearing the Kurtz compound he inexplicably attempts to escape, and Willard orders Lance to machine-gun him. Because the Montagnard is the only Vietnamese character in the script, the interpretation comes across as racist. As a device it seems suggested by the cannibals that accompany Marlowe in Conrad's story. However, Marlowe comes to see them as no worse than the ridiculous, greedy white "pilgrims" who accompany him. Milius, apparently, could never bring himself to a similar conclusion. Coppola did well to eliminate this plot element, as there was never an effective point behind it. The glimpses of Vietnamese washing clothes while buffeted by waves from Lance's water skiing (reminiscent of Flaherty's *Louisiana Story*) or stoically watching the decadent USO show from behind a barbed wire fence, eco-nomically and effectively added a counterpoint to the American madness on display. The film does not pretend to understand the Vietnamese ex-perience, but it does passingly acknowledge the carnage we wreaked upon the people.

Milius' ending was actually more similar to Conrad's novella than Cop-pola's eventual ending. As in the Conrad version, Kurtz is dying from wounds suffered in a recent battle when Willard arrives. In both the Conrad and Milius endings there is an exciting scene in which Kurtz is extracted from the compound while the horde is poised to attack. Milius, however, could not let this potential violence escape, and further down the river the horde catches up with the boat and has a climactic fire-fight, ending with the arrival of American helicopters, at which the surviving Willard and Chief maniacally shoot their guns. Had Coppola followed this version, he easily could have avoided the criticism that his eventual ending was a visceral letdown in relation to the tone of the rest of the film, but any philosophical conclusions would be overwhelmed by the predominating action.

Eleanor Coppola's *Notes* details how Coppola vacillated on how to end the film even as he was filming the final scenes. Much of the difficulty stemmed from Marlon Brando's reluctance to play the part according to Coppola's original intentions and from the short duration of time (ten days) Brando was on the set. In Coppola's December 3, 1975, draft of the script, the ending was terrifying and violent, more in keeping with the Do Long Bridge sequence's tone. The Kurtz of this draft was much more threatening and self-possessed, at one point personally shooting a Vietnamese merely to dramatize a point to Willard. Furthermore, Kurtz was injecting himself with morphine to ease the pain of a horrible wound and doing acid to prepare himself for a final cataclysmic fire-fight with approaching NVC regulars. Willard is mesmerized by this Kurtz and fights alongside him with a sense of purpose. The emphasis was again on the psychedelic, awe-inspiring war, with little of the pagan elements of the final film in evidence.

Milius also had some Conradian touches in the initial script that Coppola did borrow. The lack of commanding officers at the Do Long Bridge mirrors the deterioration evidenced in the up-river colonial outposts that Marlowe encounters. The tail of a B–52 sticking surreally out of the water matches some rotting hulks of machinery Marlowe sees on the edge of the jungle (which suggest the jungle can overwhelm anything man can make). Approaching the river, Marlowe sees a French frigate firing senselessly into the jungle, which in a sense matches Kilgore (Wyatt Kharnage in the original script) calling in napalm on unseen enemy gunners. In both the screenplay and film, as the boat approaches the Kurtz area, natives shoot sticks and twigs at the boat to scare the crew, which parallels action in Conrad's story. Coppola retrieved the idea of a spear killing the helmsman, which Milius deleted from his version of this scene. The Milius script retained more of the idea of Kurtz as a greedy man, substituting opium for ivory, as in the following passage:

*Willard (V.O.)*: He tried to tell me what he'd done—about participating in unspeakable atrocities and how he organized the tribes and executed those who opposed him—He told of raiding the Golden Triangle for opium—tens of millions of dollars worth. He had plans—he wanted a kingdom—Kurtz wanted to be king.[14]

In both the 1975 script and the final film, Coppola made Kurtz a more personally threatening character, not as physically emaciated as Conrad's Kurtz, and de-emphasized his greed. While the megalomaniacal demagoguery is still very present, it now seems that Kurtz is using his power to explore ideological aims. Willard's remark to Kurtz that he could see no method to Kurtz's actions, not present in the earlier drafts and borrowed from Conrad, signals a distance between Willard and Kurtz. While Willard is throughout the film fascinated and attracted to Kurtz, this final skepticism toward Kurtz's methods makes logical Willard's dropping the machete and leaving at the end of the film; he has not embraced the Kurtz philosophy, just as Conrad's Marlowe never embraced it. Coppola toward the end of the post-production wanted to end with Willard at the top of the temple, unsure whether to leave or stay, but Coppola, I think wisely, listened to his subordinates and left the ending as we now know it. While many found the last half hour of the film boring and pretentious, it does set a tone of meditation and reflection rather than of visceral catharsis in the manner of Milius' original screenplay.

The tone of Milius' screenplay was less reflective; in fact it evokes more of a comic book or "B" movie approach to the violent and sexual aspects of the characters. Some reviewers of the film claimed we do not really believe in Kurtz's power in the film because we never see him in action. In the original screenplay, prior to the beginning of Willard's narration, Milius presents a scene in which Kurtz's men ambush a North Vietnamese contingent. Consider the way the engagement begins:

The North Vietnamese approach. TRUCK WITH them as they pass and FOL-LOW on the leading few as they edge around a bend in the deep tangled jungle. Suddenly, directly in front, about ten feet away, a large man steps out clad in rags and bushes and holding a 12-gauge automatic shotgun casually at his side. The two leading N.V.A. SOLDIERS freeze momentarily. The huge AMERICAN smiles laconically—they start to bring up their guns—he is quicker—blasting out FIVE SHOTS that rip through the men. By the second shot the whole jungle blazes with AUTOMATIC FIRE.[15]

Milius frequently gives the direction that men are to smile while they fire their weapons, weapons he describes with great relish. The passage quoted above very blatantly evokes the Western gunfighter, quick on the draw, unafraid, proficient, and taller than his adversaries. Milius was reflecting his own tastes as a connoisseur of violent action films. In the 1975 version of the above passage, Coppola made one small but important alteration. The staging directions said that the men should fire at the camera, meaning us, rather than at the North Vietnamese, which signals the strains of American guilt evident in the final film but never evident in Milius's original conception.

Coppola restricted the unadulterated love of war and killing mostly to the Kilgore character, or caricature, and distanced it through the absurdist elements of the performance. Violence as handled by Coppola is nonetheless much more disturbing—for example, in the sampan scene. Coppola's dislike of using violence to excite the audience in *The Godfather* was discussed in an earlier chapter, and Andrew Sarris perceptively spotted the inclination when reviewing *Apocalypse Now*:

A severed human head seems to echo the chopped horse head in *The Godfather*. But Coppola's deepest instincts now, more than ever, seem to lie in evading violence rather than exploiting it. Gifted barbarians like Mario Puzo and John Milius rhapsodize about violence for its own sake, and Coppola is dragged, inwardly screaming, into these projects, because his own survival as a filmmaker is involved.[16]

Even in the helicopter assault scene, where Coppola wanted to give the audience the visceral feel of a combat assault, he made us pause in any vicarious enjoyment of the spectacle by cutting away to a tranquil shot of Vietnamese school children dressed in white, or providing a shot in which an American soldier hysterically and futilely screams that he will not get out of a helicopter and is shoved out into the attack. Such reflective counterpoints to the action would not have been tolerated in the Milius version of the attack, which features Kilgore pulling out a big-game hunting rifle to shoot down a Vietnamese peasant.

It would be naive to deny that some soldiers enjoyed the Vietnam violence, and any veteran will recall knowing men who thrived on the war situation. The Milius screenplay reflected some of the more barbaric habits of some of our troops in wearing strings of ears cut off from the enemy or scalps draped on their weapons. Coppola eschewed this as perhaps too exaggerated or atypical. However, Coppola's handling of Milius's Do Long Bridge scene demonstrates his interest in some of the more desperate violence of the war.

Milius provided the Do Long Bridge scene as a short sketch demonstrating the extreme danger confronting the Americans in advanced positions and the age-old wartime disregard for foot soldiers by generals. Americans fight to hold a bridge site just so the American generals can tell the press the bridge remains open, in spite of the fact that it is destroyed every night by the Viet Cong. Willard tries in vain to find any commanding officer in an advance trench. There, in a very haunting scene, he encounters a gunner trying to eliminate some Viet Cong near a barbed wire barrier. Frustrated, the gunner calls for "the Roach," a deathly figure who has been sleeping amid the commotion, and who seems to be the final solution. Roach methodically prepares a grenade launcher, dispatches the enemy with one deadly shot, curses, and goes back to sleep. This basic sketch was in the Milius screenplay, but Coppola made all the characters in the trench blacks, thus recalling the fact that forty percent of the front line troops in Vietnam were black, mostly from the American ghettos. They are listening to Jimi Hendrix, the black psychedelic guitarist who in his own inimitable way was the poet of violence of the Vietnam era. As Willard approaches, the black gunner is screaming at the Viet Cong things like "You think you bad, huh, niggah?" The idea of American blacks calling Vietnamese "niggers" has a sobering effect, and perhaps unintentionally recalls Conrad's term for the inhabitants of the Congo. On realizing Willard is an officer, the gunner abruptly switches into standard, white English. The switch brilliantly underlines the necessity for black soldiers for both affecting a violent, primitive demeanor and also being able to survive in the white man's army. In the Milius screenplay, Roach wears a helmet with "God Bless Dow" inscribed on it and carries a paisley-decorated gun; Coppola instead dresses him like an African warrior, complete with beads and war paint; Roach's countenance suggests someone who has been killing for a long time and never can really go back to civilization. He also seems drugged, which reflected a means commonly used by American soldiers for dealing with the terror of this particular war. Coppola adds this exchange: Willard asks Roach, "Soldier, do you know who's in command here?" Roach responds, "Yeah," and trudges away. The exchange eerily suggests that something other than military discipline is in charge of this particular situation. In the Coppola version we are not so much in awe of the proficiency of this deathly specialist, but rather in horror at the desperate circumstances in which war can place men. The overall treatment of the scene suggests just how much nuance and characterization Coppola added to the script in the performance process.

Christopher Sharrett used the trench scene as an interesting demonstration of how the film reflects the overall disintegration of values embodied by the Vietnam War. Sharrett is particularly insightful on the importance of rock music both to the actual war and to Coppola's film. Noting the Jimi Hendrix number played in the trench, the Doors' songs used in the opening and the closing, "Satisfaction" during the water-skiing sequence, and the hard-rock number "Suzie Q" during the USO show, Sharrett observed:

As Michael Herr suggests, rock became a kind of snyesthesia that found the Romantic relationship between sexual impulses and the death wish, Freud's Eros-Thantos construct. In *Apocalypse Now* Coppola uses rock to annotate the futility and suicidal aspect of the war in a classically eschatological sense ("The End") as well as to show how rock music actually provided a lift, a morale boost that substituted for patriotic or martial music popular in armed conflicts of the past (music had some significance for Hitler and German troops in World War Two).[17]

The weight of Sharrett's analysis of the film suggests a probing, critical relationship to the popular culture icons on display in *Apocalypse Now*. The tone of Milius' original screenplay is more that of reveling in pop culture than examining it. Milius also injected a large dose of sexual content into his war story, most of which Coppola deleted. In the 1969 script, several times the crew members of the PBR sit around discussing past affairs they had with prostitutes or other men's wives; these scenes are sandwiched between the action and establish a certain camaraderie aboard the boat. More outlandish are two extended Milius scenes that Coppola shot and then left out of the final print. In the first, the boat is damaged and the crew pulls into a French rubber plantation for repairs. Some of the history of Vietnam is reflected in the fact that the colonial family has been living there and fighting off communists for years. However, a beautiful French woman seduces Willard and then the following morning informs him that her family has taken half the boat's supplies "on his orders." If they resist, the Americans will be killed. The crew is understandably upset with Willard over his seemingly selfish action, but later he receives an opportunity to make amends. Coming upon a downed helicopter in an area near the front, Willard discovers the Playboy playmates, who have run out of gas after leaving their USO show. Willard arranges to give them enough gas to leave if they have sex with each of the crew members. Morale is restored. Milius's fantasies about sex seem in line with his fantasies about violence; clearly for Milius war is a place where dreams come true. Although Coppola shot these scenes, somewhere along the line he realized they did not fit with his conception of the film.

The one bit of sexual business that Coppola did retain from the Milius script is the Playboy Playmate show at Hau Phat, which is a stunning piece of work. This sequence and the helicopter assault for the surfing beach sequence are the only two sequences in the film which appear substantially as Milius wrote them. In the first, a group of about one thousand men anxiously await a USO show. The Playmates arrive in a helicopter on a landing pad with a moat around it. A hard rock song, "Suzie Q" is played on the loudspeakers. The Playmates are dressed in skimpy Western costumes, and they begin dancing erotically with guns. At one point the lead Playmate is carried toward the men on a large platter, as if she is to be served to them. The men are driven into a frenzy by their taunting and they rush the stage. The sequence cogently underlines Willard's remarks about the absurdity of our involvement in the war: we tried to remain as comfortable as possible by not denying the soldiers the pleasures they were accustomed to having back home, which only made them more unhappy. Coppola added a coda to the action, a shot of Vietnamese stoically watching the American insanity through the barbed wire with Willard's comment: "Charlie's idea of R&R was a dead rat and cold rice. He had only two ways home, death or victory."

Milius would probably agree with Coppola's added coda, as criticism of American involvement in Vietnam is implicit in the first draft as well. In both interviews and in films such as *Red Dawn*, Milius has shown a curious admiration for anti-U.S. insurgents such as the Vietnamese, Castro's Cubans, and the Sandinistas. Milius felt we should not have become involved in Vietnam, because as General MacArthur observed, a major Asian land war is unwinnable, but: "Once we were there we should have fought a proper military action, rather than hamstringing ourselves with that government. If you're going to fight a war, you don't food around."[18] To Milius, how one fights the war is much more important than whether the war is for a worthwhile cause. Coppola's vision of the film, though less militaristic, never really cements the connection between the waste and inefficiency the film criticizes and the lack of morality behind the war effort. Instead there seems to be an almost intentional open-endedness. We can make the connection on our own or we can refuse to see it; perhaps, as with *Patton*, Coppola was again shaping the narrative so that both hawks and doves could enjoy the film. This perspective also informs the surfing beach sequence.

Like the Playmate sequence, the surfing beach sequence also appeared substantially as Milius wrote it. The antics of Kilgore have been criticized by veterans as being too absurd, too unrealistic and a distortion of how Americans conducted themselves in Vietnam.[19] Milius, however, claims he based it on an actual American commander, substituting the passion for surfing for a passion for marijuana:

Everybody likes the helicopter scenes. It got a lot of laughs, like *Dr. Strangelove*. That's based on a colonel who, instead of surfing, liked dope. He could still operate as a pilot, but he was fascinated by marijuana. He would fly special missions to Cambodia to get a better grade of red. He used to drop "Death from Above" flags. He was going mad. He never actually got there because he was wiped out by typhoid.[20]

The passion for surfing reflects the preoccupation of Milius's younger years and was dealt with more thoroughly in *Big Wednesday*. Its appearance here has a 1960s resonance, since during that time the "Beach Boys" made surfing a part of young America's consciousness. Robert Duvall gave Kilgore a larger–than–life flamboyancy, and many reviewers compared him to George C. Scott's Buck Turgidson (*Dr. Strangelove*). His "I love the smell of napalm in the morning" parodies the war lover in a way that is consistent with both Coppola's and Milius' vision; Coppola's view that war is crazy, and Milius' vision that war demands total effort.

Another example of this double structuring of meaning in the text is the classical music being played by the helicopters' loudspeakers: Wagner's "Ride of the Valkyries." This was Milius' idea, perhaps inspired by the Ku Klux Klan's attack on the blacks set to the same music in D. W. Griffith's *Birth of a Nation* or by Guido's harem fantasy scene in Fellini's *8 1/2*. In conception, one wonders whether Milius saw the use of Wagner as ironic. However Coppola, in the staging of the scene, left no question about the irony of glorious, Teutonic operatic music playing while whites kill non-whites. The key cut in facilitating the ironic point of view is to the shot of Vietnamese school children dressed in white just before the violence begins. Thus later, when a Vietnamese woman, apparently one of the teachers, tosses a grenade in a helicopter picking up American wounded, we can feel the irony when Kilgore calls her a "savage," orders his pilot to "put a skid

up her ass," and guns her down. Of course if someone does not care about
the school children, the irony is lost. The ultra-rightwing, war-loving *Soldier of Fortune* magazine commented about the cut to the school house: "The
Russians must have loved that Coppola-inspired scene."[21] But the writer
was admiring of the technical prowess of the scene: "You'll feel like you
were right back in 'Nam on the way into a hot L.Z."[22]

Perhaps part of the reason the film succeeded commercially was that it
depicted the sensations of war in a way that the curious liberal could accept,
whereas those inclined to enjoy the violence for its own sake were able to
ignore the sentiments not appealing to their political viewpoint. As Paul
Coates commented: "Criticizing America, the film implicates itself in the
critique. It is anything but complacent."[23] A student has told me he almost
enlisted in the Marines after seeing the film. However, Coppola did take
one important step toward eliminating the possibility of enjoying the idea
of Americans fighting on someone else's soil. Very late in the production,
perhaps reflecting an evolving consciousness on Coppola's part, Coppola
wrote and added the puppy–sampan scene, a scene that is deeply disturbing
and difficult to read as anything but an indictment of American involvement
in Vietnam.

The build-up to this scene was very effective. As Willard and his crew
advance farther up the river they become more on edge. The crew begins
to smoke more pot and discipline begins to break down. Chief, realizing
this, sees a Vietnamese sampan and, against Willard's wishes, orders a
routine search in an attempt to buttress his sagging control over the crew.
Chef, complaining about the pointlessness of the search all the while, reluctantly goes through the stores of the sampan. A girl runs to protect a
basket in which she has hidden her dog, and Clean, thinking she is running
for arms, begins machine-gunning the peasants. The climax of the scene
comes after they realize that the girl is still alive, though very badly
wounded. Chief orders the crew to take her to a hospital, but Willard
ruthlessly shoots her in the chest and orders the mission to go on. Whatever
the rationale of his action, it assaults the sensibilities of the viewer and
should destroy at least temporarily any sense of vicarious identification with
the adventurers going up the river to complete a mission. Coppola had
taken the film in another direction.

The scene ostensibly recalls the My Lai massacre, which represented a
key moment in the solidification of the anti-war sentiment in the United
States (particularly in the middle-class sector of the population). In the same
fashion, the puppy–sampan scene is the moment when our horror about
this war as embodied in the film is strongest; the later goings-on at the
Kurtz compound have none of the realism or immediacy of this scene.[24]

The puppy-sampan scene was shot in April of 1977, near the end of the
production. As early as a 1976 interview, Milius felt Coppola was changing

the tone of the original script as evidenced by the following bitter remarks about Coppola's rewriting:

Basically he wanted to ruin it, liberalize it, and turn it into *Hair*. He sees himself as a great humanitarian, an enlightened soul who will tell you such wonderful things as he does at the end of *Godfather II*—that crime doesn't pay.... We may come up with some great statement at the end of *Apocalypse Now* to the effect that war is hell.... Francis Coppola has this compelling desire to save humanity when the man is a raving fascist, the Bay Area Mussolini.[25]

Besides the "liberalizing" tone that the puppy–sampan scene sets the scene also destroys a certain amount of character empathy, which would normally go with a classical Hollywood narrative. After we see Willard's actions, how can we identify with a cold-blooded killer? On the voice-over Willard announces: "Those boys were never going to look at me the same again, but I knew one or two things about Kurtz that weren't in the dossier." The implication is that Willard has joined Kurtz now as an enlightened warrior who sees through the "bullshit of Vietnam" and is able to take appropriate action. Yet we may not be so ready to join these supermen in their disturbing vision. Our disaffection from the main characters and the increasingly abstract quality of the narrative in the second half of the film takes on a modernist tinge. The surreal, hallucinogenic, nightmarish aspect of the narrative's images becomes more important. We are far from the iconoclastic "action-pic" envisioned in 1969 at the American Zoetrope hothouse.

The Willard character may have been affected by the difficulty which Coppola had in casting an actor for the role. Coppola felt he needed a star persona in Willard's role to compensate for the lack of characterization in the original Milius screenplay. He originally hired Harvey Keitel for the role, after frustration about not being able to hire Robert Redford, Steve McQueen, Al Pacino, Marlon Brando, Gene Hackman, or James Caan had prompted him literally to throw his five Oscars out the window in a moment of anger. Keitel's film persona had been that of explosive emotional violence and a series of tics that call attention to his volatility, in, say, *The Duellists* or *Bad Timing*. Coppola went to the Philippines with Keitel and fired him several weeks into the production, apparently a result of a personality clash and a feeling that Keitel was not right for the part. Thus Martin Sheen, whose best previous work was in *Badlands*, was a last minute, fortuitous replacement after Coppola bumped into him in an airport lounge. Sheen, however, had not established a strong, independent, leading–man persona; Coppola would have to supply the depth of the character himself.

Eleanor Coppola relates how one night, troubled about the direction the film was going, Francis had a dream. In it, he was doing the character of Willard wrong. A Green Beret advisor told him that these types of soldiers were vain, so he would have Sheen look in the mirror and admire himself and Sheen would turn into Willard. Later, following the instincts suggested in the dream, Coppola got Sheen drunk for two days, isolated him, and then in an improvisational style asked Sheen to play different characters. Then:

Francis asked him to go to the mirror and look at himself and admire his beautiful hair, his mouth. Marty began this incredible scene. He hit the mirror with his fist. Maybe he didn't mean to. Perhaps he overshot a judo stance. His hand started bleeding. Francis said his impulse was to cut the scene and call the nurse, but Marty was doing the scene. He had gotten to the place where some part of him and Willard had merged. Francis had a moment of not wanting to be a vampire, sucking Marty's blood for the camera, and not wanting to turn off the camera when Marty was Willard. He left it running. He talked Marty through the scene. Two cameras were going. I was outside in the street shooting. When I went back to the set, Enrico, Vittorio and the people who had been inside during the scene were coming out, visibly shaken. Silent and disturbed, emotionally affected by the power of Marty/ Willard baring his guts in the room.[26]

One thinks of D. W. Griffith placing Lillian Gish on an actual ice floe in blizzard conditions for the climactic scene in *Way Down East*. Directors of spectacles at some point seem to become jaded about conventional play-acting and feel the need to manufacture images of real, unfeigned human emotions. Of course, Coppola *was* being the cinematic vampire, as the scene was out of control and far from Coppola's intentions: smashing one's fist at one's image in a mirror is a far cry from vainly admiring that image. (Sheen later commented that it was his decision to continue the scene.) Sheen, with that blow, had taken Willard in a wholly different direction from that suggested in either the original Milius screenplay or by Coppola himself.

But what is the new direction in which this action takes the character? In the scene, Willard, naked, alone, drunk, wallowing in apparent self-loathing, seems a pathetic figure. In terms of character psychology, it is difficult to reconcile this Willard with the Willard who casually places a gun at the head of a wounded Vietnamese woman and fires. To prevent the easy generalization that Willard was another Vietnam veteran mentally suffering for his sins, Coppola patched on a running narration, written by Michael Herr, which serves to explain Willard, if he can be explained. The narration does flesh out both Willard's reaction to the war and his fascination with Kurtz, something the original screenplay failed to do.

The real dilemma of the mirror smashing scene is that it suggests two contradictory personalities for Willard. The Willard who reacts with horror and self-loathing to his deeds is more of an Everyman, embodying a more universal attitude toward war. This attitude is against the Kurtzian, en-lightened warrior approach to war. From the standpoint of the latter, Coppola was right in his initial perception of the scene: if Willard as a special forces agent was capable of political assassinations and later would go up river to kill another American, then he might very well look in the mirror and be proud and vain in the manner of the Green Beret of Coppola's dream. The Green Beret mentality, with which the Milius screenplay is enamored, is born of an arrogance, a self-image that does not allow one to wallow, even momentarily, in self-pity as Willard does. A telling sign of the difficulties with the contradictory impulses toward Willard is that the mirror smashing scene was shot four months into the production, just before the crew began work on the Do Long Bridge sequence and well after the helicopter assault filming. Much of the film was shot with no knowledge that this aspect of Willard's character would be revealed. So it seems Coppola was going two directions with Willard: one toward a Willard who hates himself, and because of this hatred has the necessary moral sensibility to end what Kurtz has started, to call in the air strike, and to take Lance home; another toward the Willard as Kurtz, Willard the unscrupulous warrior who can murder a wounded Vietnamese woman to avoid an impediment to his mission, Willard who may succeed Kurtz as the ruler of the kingdom.

Willard's split personality and the process of discovery it seems to indicate, was created during the production; this fact is closely related to Coppola's difficulties in ending the film. As Eleanor Coppola's book details, Coppola decided he would not retain the Milius *Gotterdammerung* ending. In the middle of production, he frantically tried to come up with a new ending before Brando arrived for the three-week period during which the ending would be shot. Brando arrived, overweight, and without having read *Heart of Darkness* as Coppola had asked him to do. The production shut down while Coppola and Brando had a marathon talk session over how they would end the film. They decided to improvise the ending, and Storaro suggested the lighting techniques that dominated the mood of the Brando scenes. Thus, in heavy chiaroscuro lighting that emphasizes only portions of Brando's physique, ten minutes is spent on the mad ravings of Kurtz/Brando. The most quoted rumination in the critical reaction to this sequence is the one in which Kurtz explains that he developed his conception of moral terror after inoculating children in a Vietnamese village and later finding out that the Viet Cong had hacked off their arms. He concludes that with an army of men able to commit such atrocities he could win the war, that what defeats us is the judgment of our actions. The explanation is seductive, but of course totally lacks any rationale for why we should want to win the war at such a price. In the Kurtzian vision, winning the war is an end in itself.

Perhaps partially as a result of a distracting fascination with Brando's salary and with the difficulties detailed by Eleanor Coppola's book, critics reacted extremely negatively to Brando's portion of the film. Many treated it as if it had taken up the last third of the film, instead of the ten minutes of film time actually occupied by Brando's ruminations. However, as we do spend much of the film waiting to meet Kurtz, his scenes need to be strong in conception, which isn't suggested by Coppola's description of his interaction with Brando:

Marlon's first idea—which almost made me vomit—was to play Kurtz as a Daniel Berrigan: in black pajamas, in VC clothes. It would be all about the *guilt* (Kurtz) felt at what we'd done. I said, "Hey Marlon, I may not know everything about this movie—but one thing I know, it's not about is 'our guilt'!" Yet Marlon has one of the finest minds around: thinking is what he does. To sit and talk with him about life and death—he'll think about that stuff all day long.

Finally, he shaved his head—and that did it. We'd go for it—we'd get there. That terrible face. I think it's wonderful that in this movie, the terrifying moment is that image: just his face.[27]

Unfortunately, that face was not viewed by critics or audiences with horror; instead, the fact that this famous, rich actor had shaved his head in the manner of Telly Savalas was viewed with curiosity. In this instance the film was a victim of its own publicity and the use of the star persona. Perhaps Coppola's horror at this face, and it may be shared by some knowledgeable filmgoers, is that one of the most handsome faces in the American cinema had degenerated into this bloated, bald caricature; like Kurtz's degeneration, Brando the actor had lost one of the most impressive physiques in cinema. What was needed, however, was an actor who seemed totally at one with the surroundings. Brando does convey a sense of personal menace, particularly when he drops Chef's head into Willard's lap, but he does not convey the sense that he has been leading this tribe on combat missions. Time pressures may have prevented Coppola from integrating Brando into the surroundings, but cinema is inclined toward the explicit; to be convincing one has to show things, not speak of them in the past tense.

The nature of the different endings that Coppola eventually used has nothing to do with the Kurtz character and everything to do with the Willard character. In each ending Kurtz is killed ritualistically in the temple. As was discussed earlier, the earliest ending used at Cannes and the early previews had Willard leaving the temple, and standing and looking at the horde, who drop their arms; Kurtz's green face is superimposed with "The horror, the horror." The question of whether Willard would replace Kurtz or leave remains unresolved. The second ending, which appeared on the 70mm prints in the large cities and the later videotape copies, had Willard leaving with Lance in the boat. The boat's radio asks for instructions and Willard just shuts it off, leaving Kurtz's empire intact. The third ending, used for the 35mm prints, goes one step further; Kurtz's temple is destroyed by napalm while the credits are rolling; it is unclear whether Willard had anything to do with the destruction.

In one of the best interviews ever done with Coppola, Greil Marcus of *Rolling Stone* probed Coppola's attitude toward the different endings. Marcus discovered that Coppola actually preferred the first ending, but had discarded it because his many advisors, as well as computer printouts, concurred that Willard should leave the compound.[28] Coppola had distributed lengthy questionnaires at previews asking the viewers to help him end the film by telling him what they thought should happen to the characters.[29] (Even President Carter was asked to fill one out.) People tend to like happy endings, or at the very least narrative tensions neatly resolved. His advisors probably realized the economic danger of choosing a disturbing ending for a $31 million film. Coppola also had problems ending the three previous films he had completed before *Apocalypse Now*, and one wonders if the audience poll constituted some sort of escape from the responsibilities of finding an ending for his material. He explained his preference for the unpopular ending:

*Marcus*: I'm stunned. In your mind, the movie still ends with Willard on the steps of the temple.

*Coppola*: I felt that in the end, the movie was always about choice. He was deciding, he was evaluating the mission. The tone of it was, well, this guy is American, can I kill him? He's looking at the USO almost as though he's saying, "Is it appropriate?" In the light of guys up there getting shot? Is this all right? Is this correct? All the way through. So I thought the film should end with a choice, which was: "Should I be Kurtz? Or should I be Willard?" But I think what happened is that it was abrupt, that maybe I didn't have enough material to really extend it, as I would have had I known that was where the movie was going to end. And maybe his going down, and taking Lance by the hand, getting in the boat and going—

It's not the same, though. At the end, when the face comes on and you hear, "The horror, the horror," that's an echo of a warning rather than a real choice. Oh, fuck.

*Marcus*: You didn't want to deal with this again?

*Coppola*: Oh, it's not that. But the ending of this movie has tortured me for five fucking years. I know this ending is a more popular ending, but *that* was *my* ending. But I can't fool around. If the picture doesn't get some form of popular support—I mean, the first couple of weeks it'll do very well, but if it doesn't begin to attract people . . . although I think it will.

This goddamm *Apocalypse* . . . ah, it's a lot of money. It's going to be done, though. It'll be interesting to see.[30]

How do we judge this "auteur" who at this crucial moment of his most ambitious film lets financial pressures decide how his film will end? Perhaps this finally is the greatest, and most honest, example of how the Hollywood auteur is a creature of compromise. Even in this film that is so spectacular in its accomplishments, and this film which goes so much further than any comparable effort, a film that surely will influence how Americans think about Vietnam for years to come, the final decision is not how to best fit an ending to the material but how to live to fight another day.

Once the film was assured of paying off its debts, perhaps Coppola felt it was, in the final sense, completed; now it had ended happily. In the final part of the Marcus interview, several months after the initial questioning about Coppola's ending, Marcus asked him if he was more reconciled with the ending than he had been before. Coppola responded that he now had no regrets, that he changed his mind when he saw the film with the music added and now liked the more sentimental ending. He felt too much had been made of the ending, and that he would never put an inappropriate ending on one of his films.[31]

The problem is that what Coppola, or anyone else, thinks is appropriate may change, as Marcus' interviews seem to indicate. Going back to Coppola's original remarks about the ending, some of the problem may be in his conception that the film was about "choice." Many things about the nature of the film suggest that Willard has to go back to civilization, not stand on the steps and deliberate. First, there is Conrad's model; the essential structure of juxtaposing Kurtz to a narrator depends on the fact that one comes back, while the other does not. Secondly, the title *Apocalypse Now* suggests a cataclysm of destruction followed by revelation and cleansing; only if Willard puts the temple and Kurtz behind him can those notions come into play. (It is questionable whether his leaving as depicted in the final ending really suggests that the experience has been put behind him.) If Kurtz is madness and evil, what revelation comes from Willard succumbing to it as well? The only logic in this would be that in his actions at the sampan he has already become Kurtz; but all sense of contrast would be lost. Finally, if the film is an allegory for American involvement in Vietnam, the fact is we came back. Whether we learned anything can only be judged by our actions in the future.

One other key influence on *Apocalypse Now*'s controversial ending was Sir James Frazer's classic study of primitive rites and rituals, *The Golden Bough*, particularly a section on the replacement of weak kings. Frazer detailed how many primitive cultures had practices of violently killing a sick king because weak kings supposedly made the crops falter. The Kurtz compound is in Cambodia and in a coincidence Frazer actually mentions that region: "The mystic kings of Fire and Water in Cambodia are not allowed to die a natural death. Hence, when one of them is seriously ill and the elders think that he cannot recover, they stab him to death."[32] This becomes another explanation of Coppola's ending. The primitive tribe worships Kurtz as a god, he is ailing, so his death comes according to primitive practices: Willard slashes him to death and replaces him.

Coppola made a questionable judgment, however, in providing a pan over a new-looking copy of Frazer's book and Jesse Weston's *From Ritual to Romance* in the Kurtz compound. Reviewers howled about Coppola's pseudo-intellectualism,[33] since few viewers would be familiar with these works and recognize their significance. This, and Brando's slurred reading of T. S. Eliot's "The Hollow Men" seemed attempts to dress up a muddied conclusion.

In the conclusion of the film, more dominating than the literary motifs, is Coppola's graphic intercutting of Kurtz's people sacrificing a steer with Willard's murder of Kurtz. Stylistically, the intercutting recalled Eisenstein's finale in *Strike*, where slaughtered workers were juxtaposed with the slaughter of an ox, and Coppola's baptism/execution montage in *The Godfather*. It gives the proper tone and texture of primitiveness to the actions of Willard. Coppola repeated this stylistic device with the juxtaposition of Dutch Schultz's murder with tap dancing at the end of *The Cotton Club*.

A final note about the conclusion of *Apocalypse Now*: just prior to the murder at the temple there is a shot of Willard's head in camouflage slowly rising out of the river; it seems to steam as it rises. It is a striking shot that suggests that the ensuing action comes straight out of a dark, primitive unconscious. It is interesting that the same image was in the Milius screenplay, but employed to a different effect. In the screenplay's first scene, when Kurtz's soldiers ambush a Vietnamese patrol, they rise out of the swamp as if they were one with it. How much more effective is the image in Coppola's version, coming at the end, when we really have seen a regression to the primitive and we have some idea of the causes of that regression.

Much of the success of *Apocalypse Now* can be attributed to Coppola's efforts in the first two-thirds of the film to make the view of the war more macrocosmic than the bloodlust celebration of Vietnamese combat that the Milius screenplay represented. Coppola's method in this endeavor was described in the following exchange at the Cannes press conference:

*Questioner*: Why didn't you include any of the political history of Vietnam?

*Coppola*: When I started this film I said to myself that I must assume it's the only one that will be made. At that time I was one of the more successful film directors in America and I couldn't get anyone to let me do it. Nor would the war department help—and how could you make a film about Vietnam without helicopters and machinery, which the Department of Defense controls? So I made a list of all the things you would have to touch on to make an honest film about Vietnam, and there were 200 things. Like the use of drugs, the fact that black soldiers were up at the front line, the fact that American officers lived in affluence and played golf, that American soldiers there were very young, 17 and 18. And my list went on, thing after thing. I tried as well as I could to get as many of those things into the film. For those of you who choose to see the film again, you will see that every inch of it is packed with some other point.[34]

Many other filmmakers have managed to make films about Vietnam without Defense Department assistance. It is curious that Coppola would have expected the Defense Department to assist in a film that was eventually so critical of our war effort.[35] In any case, the list of "200 things" demonstrates a certain conscientiousness and a desire for authenticity on Coppola's part. As an artist he had evolved from the desperate filmmaker who took a job directing a film that glorified the Mafia because he needed the money to the artist convinced of the power of his medium and concerned about its ability to create distortions in the public's conception of the subject matter. The "200 things" *are* very prevalent in the film; often they are subjects needing attention from the American public and contribute to the power of the film. For instance, at several points Chief makes a veiled threat to Willard about going past the Do Long Bridge. If one is aware of the Vietnam War phenomenon of "fragging" (some officers would be afraid to take their men into a dangerous area for fear of later having a grenade rolled into their tent), the scene takes on an added resonance. Likewise, the breaking down of discipline among servicemen throughout the film seems to suggest larger problems about our involvement in Vietnam. Details like the row of motorcycles for sale in an advance supply depot have their own way of raising questions about how our war effort was conducted.

Coppola hired many of the actors on seven-year contracts with the idea of developing a repertory company around them and using them in other films and in plays he would direct in the San Francisco area.[36] The idea of contract players is a throwback to the Hollywood studio system, which Coppola has come increasingly to see as a model of filmmaking efficiency. His rearward view to old Hollywood contract players puts a final perspective on this film. It is doubtful that a film like *Apocalypse Now* could have been made in the old Hollywood. Such risks as are the fibre of *Apocalypse Now*— and the flaws—were not permitted in the studio system. The degree of personal risk Coppola took with this film cannot be minimized. In an attempt to maintain control over the production, he mortgaged his house, his future earnings on the *Godfather* films, and he sold foreign distribution rights. His personal life and his problems with the film were placed in the public eye with the publication of his wife's book, *Notes*—perhaps one more attempt to drum up interest in an expensive film. But no film was made after world War II or the Korean War that approached the scope, the critique, the nuances, the overwhelming qualities of *Apocalypse Now*, nor the eccentric personal vision, even though it is sometimes compromised. While certainly independent, less commercially successful filmmakers have put everything on the line for some vision they wanted to convey, it is difficult to think of a successful director in the Hollywood context who has so risked that success as Coppola did with this film.

Coppola took vivid images and situations from the Milius screenplay, a metaphysical conceit from Conrad, and advice and data from sources as diverse as Sir James Frazer, computer printouts, and Vietnam veterans; through all this there is still a steady exposition of the filmmaker's craft and vision and finally a power in the experience of the film. In his ability to bankroll an enormously expensive production about a controversial subject the studios did not want to touch, to overcome a number of setbacks with typhoons, difficult actors, and so forth, and to risk his own financial welfare in the endeavor, we have an idea of the courage and stamina of the man.[37] Although this sounds like an argument for a Romantic artist with an irrepressible personal will, it is important to note that the current system of Hollywood film uses such a myth first as a means of product differentiation (See the film that threatened Coppola's sanity!), and second as a cautionary tale of what the ordinary director should not do: only crazy men would spend this much money. Be that as it may, *Apocalypse Now* does reveal much about this country's involvement in Vietnam, and it reveals it with powerful visual imagery that suggests Coppola had a distinct vision of the subject. In the years since the controversy of its initial release, *Apocalypse Now* has become the starting point for any discussion of popular film and the Vietnam War.

## NOTES

1. A very interesting article about this period of Coppola's career is Joseph McBride's, "Coppola, Inc.," *American Film* (November 1975), 14–15. McBride quotes Fred Roos: "Sometimes we who are working on films would like more of his time. I worry about it. We wonder why the hell he's spending so much time on the magazine. But we have to defer to his instincts—he's been right so often."

2. Tony Crawley, "Apocalypse Then, Now and Forever," *Cinema 80* (London: Colibri, 1980), 58.

3. Crawley, p. 58.

4. John Gallagher, "John Milius," *Films in Review*, 32, no. 6 (June/July, 1982), 360.

5. Seven or eight reviewers have mentioned reading the screenplay before the film came out. The most extended commentary on the relation of the screenplay to the final film is: Brooks Riley, "*Heart* Transplant," *Film Comment*, 15, no. 5 (Sept./Oct. 1979), 26–27.

6. Richard Thompson, "John Milius Interviewed," *Film Comment* (July/August 1976), p. 15.

7. Audie Bock observed: "In *Apocalypse Now*, according to Lucas, Coppola saw another potential supergrosser. He was encouraged by his sense that Lucas had a commercial nose, and the project, after all, had originated partly with Lucas. Coppola began to insist that it had to be made. But the film that Lucas and Milius, and their producer Gary Kurtz, had envisioned as a low-budget, documentary-style, 16mm quickie took an entirely new shape in Coppola's hands." "Zoetrope and *Apocalypse Now*," *American Film* (September 1979), 60.

8. Eleanor Coppola, *Notes* (New York: Simon and Schuster, 1979), 177.

9. Maureen Orth, "Watching the Apocalypse," *Newsweek*, June 13, 1977, p. 63.

10. G. Roy Levin, "Francis Coppola Discusses *Apocalypse Now*," *Millimeter*, 7, no. 7 (October 1979), 137–38.

11. Fred Robbins, "Interview: Francis Coppola," *Genesis*, April 1980, p. 97.

12. Joseph Conrad, *Heart of Darkness* (New York: Signet, 1950), 106. All further references to Conrad will have page numbers in the text.

13. Dale Pollock, "An Archival Detailing of UA's *Apocalypse Now* Since 1967 Start," *Variety*, May 23, 1979, p. 5.

14. John Milius, *Apocalypse Now*, unpublished screenplay, p. 146.

15. Ibid., p. 2.

16. Andrew Sarris, "Heart of Coldness," *Village Voice*, August 27, 1979, p. 45.

17. Christopher Sharrett, "Operation Mind Control: *Apocalypse Now*, and the Search for Clarity," *Journal of Popular Film* (August 1, 1980), 38.

18. Tom Seligson, "The Macho World of John Milius," *Penthouse* (publication data unavailable), p. 95.

19. Tony Bliss commented: "And so, they surf as the battle rages. (We did a lot of surfing in 'Nam during firefights, didn't we?)" Tony Bliss, "*Apocalypse Now*: Bonanza or Bomb?" *Soldier of Fortune*, February 1980, p. 59.

20. Dave Zurawik, "John Milius: The Writer as Warrior," *Detroit Free Press*, October 12, 1979, p. 5b.

21. Bliss, p. 58.

22. Ibid., p. 59.

23. Paul Coates, *The Story of Lost Reflections* (London: Verso, 1985), 108.

24. Andrew Sarris offered a different interpretation of this scene, as follows: "Certainly, even John Wayne at his most bathetic as a director would have hesitated to show a young girl shot down as she tries to save her puppy. Coppola is made of sterner stuff in *Apocalypse Now*. The girl is shot down trying to save her puppy, but everything is all right because she is shot down by an American soldier. For Coppola as for many other filmmakers in recent years, anti-Americanism has become the last refuge of banality." Sarris, p. 45.

25. Thompson, p. 15.

26. Eleanor Coppola, p. 104.

27. Greil Marcus, "Journey up the River," *Rolling Stone*, November 1, 1979, p. 54.

28. Marcus, p. 56.

29. David Denby, who irritated Coppola by reviewing the preview, commented: "On the way in, we were handed a peculiar document, a four-page questionnaire sealed with tape. It was like going back to school. Some of us waited for the bell to sound so we could begin work. On the cover, a flattering letter from Coppola told us that the questionnaire was 'my invitation to you to help me finish the film.' He was like a politician making his appeal directly to the people—his saviors, and also potentially, his enemies." "8 1/2 Now: Coppola's Apocalypse," *New York*, May 28, 1979, p. 102.

30. Marcus, p. 56.

31. Marcus, p. 57.

32. Sir James George Frazer, *The Golden Bough* (New York: Macmillan, 1951), 310.

33. Stanley Kauffmann commented: "The Kurtz is just a literature-lacquered version of the arch-villain *Superman* or the James Bond scripts; a mastermind who has seen through the spurious niceties of human behavior . . . Kurtz's quotations from Conrad and from Eliot (who quoted Conrad) are glib attempts to enlarge him. His own dialogue is larded with what I'd call soundtrack profundities, 'You have

the right to kill me,' he tells Willard. 'You have no right to judge me,' " "Coppola's War," *The New Republic*, September 15, 1979, p. 25.

34. Levin, p. 146.

35. A very good account of the wrangling with the Defense Department is in Lawrence Suid, "Hollywood and Vietnam," *Film Comment* (October 1979), 20–25.

36. Pollock, p. 5.

37. As late as August 1986, Zoetrope Studios and United Artists Corp. were still wrangling in court as to whether the *Apocalypse Now* debt had been totally paid off. See "Coppola, Zoetrope Say They're Relieved of 'Apocalypse' Debt," *Variety*, August 6, 1986, p. 7.

# 8
## Between Epics

### Style Pieces

Jean Renoir once commented that he made only one movie in his career, but that he made the same movie repeatedly. That comment rings true because it describes so well the consistency of style and vision throughout his many films. While there are different periods in Renoir's work, the same preoccupations, the same approach to the world, manifests itself over and over again. Likewise, most of the "pantheon" directors—Eisenstein, Hitchcock, Bergman, Lang and so forth—exhibit a similar consistency of style and worldview. This consistency made easier the work of the auteur critic who looked through the aggregate of a director's films for the repetitions that proved intention, the nuances and deviations that proved the formal consistency, thus allowing a greater appreciation of the director's craft than an examination of any single film.

But what of Coppola? The post-*Apocalypse Now* period of his career has produced three films, the subject of this chapter, which vary tremendously in content, form, and the director's intentions. The first, *One from the Heart* (1982), is a hybrid between a lavish Stanley Donen-style musical and a naturalistic romantic melodrama. The second, *The Outsiders* (1983), is a teenage tearjerker that seems influenced by the James Dean, *Rebel Without a Cause*-style films in the 1950s. The third, *Rumble Fish* (1983), is *film noir* á la Camus, with a dash of German Expressionism. Coppola's experimentation and inconsistency with these three films follow the pattern of the rest of his career. The leaps from *Finian's Rainbow* (1968) to *The Rain People* (1969) to *The Godfather* (1972) are just as striking. Although Coppola with *Godfather II* is sometimes blamed for initiating the sequel craze of the last decade, no other sequel stands in such contrast to its predecessor as does *Godfather II* to *The Godfather*. Coppola seems temperamentally unable to repeat himself, as the three films discussed in this chapter dramatically demonstrate.

The real consistency, and possibly the real significance of Coppola's work, is to be found in the overall dynamic of Coppola's relationship with the filmmaking industry and its product. Repeatedly, Coppola's films challenge conventional notions of what film *is* by presenting a more revolutionary approach to what films *could* be. *One from the Heart* and *Rumble Fish* stand as very bold experiments and are difficult to place within a convention operating in contemporary film. But even with the most commercial projects—*The Godfather, Godfather II, Apocalypse Now, The Outsiders*—where a conventional approach would seem mandated, Coppola felt compelled to push the limits, to approach the films a bit differently, to take gambles. A decision to make a somber, operatic gangster film, or a surreal, hallucinatory war film, is a challenge to the industry's conventions, and the success of a good many of those gambles is the basis of Coppola's reputation. Coppola has never rested on his laurels; he continually sets out new challenges.

With the triumvirate of *One from the Heart, The Outsiders*, and *Rumble Fish*, however, the gambles failed in both the commercial reception and in the critical reaction. *The Outsiders* made some money on the strength of Matt Dillon and an all-beefcake cast, as well as S. E. Hinton's appeal, but came nowhere near offsetting the financial disaster of *One from the Heart*, which cost $27 million to make and grossed less than $2 million, causing the demise of Coppola's privately owned studio. *Rumble Fish* had a relatively modest budget but lost money. All three films received critical drubbings, the worst of Coppola's career. The title of one review of *Rumble Fish* asked "Where, oh where has once-great Coppola gone?"[1]

It is the reception of these three films that I want to take on as the main theme of this chapter. Coppola's name as a marketing tool was certainly operable long before this period in his career, probably as early as *The Conversation*, and is dramatically in evidence with *Apocalypse Now*. However, by 1982 the expectations and drama that had accrued to the appellation "a film by Francis Ford Coppola" threatened to warp the reception of any film carrying that distinction. Just as with Woody Allen's *Interiors*, one wonders how different the reaction to these films would be with another director's name attached. There is a double edge here: the films could not be financed without the power built upon that name recognition. In any case, expectations about any film by Coppola, pre-release publicity and production accounts, and the much bandied about costs of films directed by Coppola create a climate where it is difficult to evaluate the films themselves objectively. In regard to *One from the Heart* and *Rumble Fish*, I will offer an alternative interpretation to the mainstream critical line that they are generally overwrought style pieces devoid of content. To the contrary,

I find they contain interesting thematic material. *The Outsiders* is far less compelling and perhaps more deserving of its critical shelling, but the three films together raise questions about how we apprehend director cinema in an age when the media are so conscious of its appeal.

It may be that in the future, Coppola's reputation will be based on his epic spectaculars. The triumvirate under discussion here may come to be seen as Coppola's self-indulgent experiments between the more commanding and massive *Apocalypse Now* and *Cotton Club*. A parallel might be drawn with D. W. Griffith's career. Griffith is best known for the epics *Birth of a Nation* and *Intolerance*, whereas cineastes knowledgeable about Griffith's entire canon might argue that smaller films such as *Way Down East*, *Broken Blossoms*, and *True Heart Susie* are, in their well-executed lyricism, more representative of the real scope of Griffith's artistic vision. In like fashion, *One from the Heart*, *The Outsiders*, and *Rumble Fish*, to varying degrees, may define a Coppola worldview more precisely than *The Godfather*, *Apocalypse Now*, and *The Cotton Club*.

Some of the critical misapprehension of this trio of films could be attributable to intriguing journalistic accounts of *One from the Heart*'s production and ballyhoo connected with Coppola's plans for Omni-Zoetrope studios. The most obvious hook was that Coppola, fresh from the trauma of dealing with typhoons and a runaway production in the Philippines with *Apocalypse Now*, had retreated to expensive tinkering in the controlled studio environment of the sound stage. *One from the Heart* featured a $4.5 million recreation of the streets of Las Vegas. The set was called a "Las Vegas of the mind." Furthermore, Coppola directed much of the action from an off-stage trailer equipped with video monitors. His instructions were piped to the stage via loudspeakers, prompting a *Life* magazine writer to make an analogy to the Wizard of Oz.[2] Every minute detail of the lavish production was carefully planned and orchestrated through extensive rehearsal and pre-visualization using sophisticated video playback systems.

Ironically, this unusual approach to filmmaking came from the same filmmaker who had successfully insisted on location shooting in Sicily for *The Godfather* against the wishes of the Paramount studio heads, who had given New York a new cinematic look with *You're a Big Boy Now*, and who had gone on the road in search of a film with *The Rain People*. The desire for more controlled locations seems linked with Coppola's frequent nostalgic mention (in interviews of this period) of the bygone studio system. Always one to try turning dreams into reality, Coppola began signing actors to long-term contracts reminiscent of the studio years—perhaps a reaction to his difficulties in securing a lead actor willing to brave months of location work in the Philippines for *Apocalypse Now*. Thus, although Coppola returned to location work with *The Outsiders* and *Rumble Fish*, in the studio tradition the crew and many of the actors worked on both films.

If there is any major similarity between the epic *Apocalypse Now* and

Coppola's three subsequent films, it is in the movement away from nar-
rative-dominated films toward films concentrating more on mood, ambiance, character relationships, and visual texture. Coppola said of *Apocalypse
Now*: "It didn't really have a story. It was more of a case of a film trying
to be what it was about . . . it was trying to be that state of moral warfare,
and you were supposed to look at it and become involved in that conflict."[3]
In like fashion, *One from the Heart*'s lavish visual style in treating seemingly
small characters was the perfect evocation of how we are sometimes un-
satisfied by mundane reality and taunted by a vision of a more perfect,
dream reality. The lyrical, but overwrought visuals of *The Outsiders* evoked
the exaggerated desperation of the teenage years, unleavened by adult experience. The more somber compositions and black and white photography
of *Rumble Fish* connoted an adult look back at the teenage experience, despite
Coppola's ill-advised proclamations that it was to be an "art film for teenagers." Just as Coppola's subject matter seems diverse, so too do the stylistic
approaches he adopts, but the overall point of view that the visual look of
film be intrinsic to the experience of the film is consistent.

### One from the Heart

The critical reaction to *One from the Heart* was of derision unequalled in
Coppola's career. So let us begin the discussion of *One from the Heart* with
a fairly typical pan of the film by one of the nation's leading critics, Vincent
Canby of the *New York Times*, who was commenting on the film's scrim
light effects:

The trouble is not that the device calls attention to itself rather than the characters,
which it does, but that Hank and Frannie have no internal feelings worth italicizing
in the first place. They are vacuous blobs of flesh. They are so ill-defined they are
less than ordinary. They are the creations of someone condescending to ordinary
America, someone who, at this point, doesn't seem to have much idea of what
ordinary America is all about.[4]

What I would like to argue is that rather than "condescending to ordinary
America," *One from the Heart* is one of the few recent films vitally concerned
with some of the real dilemmas of "ordinary America" in its 1982 socio-
cultural and economic context, although concerned in an allusive way. *One
from the Heart*'s veneer of lavish, glimmering visuals and ostentatious but
well-executed camera style, combined with the pre-publicity controversy
surrounding Coppola's attempts to keep his studio afloat, distracted most
critics from what closer analysis will find to be an extremely unusual and
provocative look at the quality of American life after the "Me Decade."
Although the majority of critics followed Canby's line that the film was
style without substance, two critics, Sheila Benson and Carrie Rickey, of-

fered interpretations that can form the foundation of a better understanding of *One from the Heart*'s allusiveness and singularity. Both critics saw the film as predicated on post-modernist skepticism of deep, complex meaning, as well as the embrace of the superficial. Benson called the film a "work of constant astonishment" and felt it came "from the same artistic impulses that inspire airbrush art, three-dimensional popup greeting cards and the delicately beautiful new neon that illuminates L.A. shops. It is post-Warhol, where everything is 'pretty,' all slickness and sleekness, and it cherishes its surfaces even more because of the hollowness they cover."[5] The film lends itself easily to such an interpretation, as we will see, but from the auteurist perspective Coppola's career has been much more pre-Warhol modernist than post-modernist. Coppola's formative influences were artists such as Goethe, Gide, Antonioni, Hesse; his work as a whole shows little affinity with the more hip David Byrne, David Lynch, or Jonathan Demme. Is *One from the Heart*, then, an aberration?

Carrie Rickey's interpretation brings us closer to something we can reconcile with Coppola's other work. Noting the influence of drama theorist Bertolt Brecht, art director Van Nest Polgase, and architect Robert Venturi, she felt the project was endowed with:

1. theatrical distanciation, establishing the dialectic between the "real" and the "staged";

2. the oxymoronic aesthetic of Theatrical Realism, the visual counterpart to Brechtian drama, calling attention to its ersatzness while at the same time producing the psychological effect of "realism."

3. the ontological preference for "messy vitality over obvious unity" (Venturi).[6]

Such an interpretation is congruent with Benson's, but Rickey goes further to situate the film within the musical genre in its exploration of sex and romance via the sublimation of music and dance. She finds the moral ethos ultimately rather conventional. The surface glitter becomes equated with the erotic freedom which the main characters finally renounce. Rickey concludes: "Ultimately Coppola is interested in titillation, not consummation; he dazzles viewers with sets and sex, teasing instead of delivering." Such a view is not so out of line with Coppola's other work, say, the moralist and defender of family virtue in *The Rain People*, or the two *Godfather* movies.

Rickey compares the film to Disneyland; you experience the thrills of Pirates of the Caribbean, but you end up back on Main Street. However, I feel the film has more substance; Rickey and Benson never light upon the film's cultural critique. *One from the Heart*'s relation to post-modernism may be a coincidence of Coppola's interest in Japanese Kabuki as a way of interpreting the American experience. Note Coppola's description of the project's germination:

I thought, what would happen if you just took the story—a guy, a girl, another guy, another girl (as simple as it could be, dumbbell but sweet)—and set it in Las Vegas? And I'm walking down the Ginza—the Ginza's in the heart of Tokyo, and it looks just like Las Vegas—thinking that Las Vegas was the last frontier of America. When they ran out of land, they built Las Vegas, and it was built on those notions of life and chance—which, to me, are sort of like love. You know how things come together when what you're interested in and emotionally attached to, just by accident, kind of hits a resounding thing in you? So I said, why don't I take the dough (they were offering me a lot of money) and do *One from the Heart*, except *not* set it in Chicago and *not* make it like one of those films that they make a series out of— relationship films—but make it like a kind of Kabuki play set in Last Vegas! That way I'd get all that money, I'd be able to keep Zoetrope going, and I'd get to learn how to use this style in a movie.[7]

It is important to note from this passage that Coppola is not interested in Las Vegas as a metaphor for superficial appearances, but rather as a cultural myth. Coppola's awareness of the mythic potential of Las Vegas dates back to his research for the *Godfather* movies, in which the Corleones move west to Last Vegas after they find gangland opportunities constricted in the East. From a certain perspective *Godfather II* is a burlesque of the traditional Western's myth of Easterners going west to make a fresh start. Ultimately the frontier myth in *Godfather II* is a bankrupt one.

From *Godfather II* to *One from the Heart*, Coppola moved from larger-than-life mythic figures in the Corleones to more mimetic characters in Hank and Frannie, the protagonists of *One from the Heart*, who on their own level have found life in Las Vegas less than ideal. Frannie (Teri Garr) comments: "Life has to be more than this. If this is it, it's not enough." Hank (Frederick Forrest) comments: "You know what's wrong with America don't you? It's the light. There's no more secret. It's phoney bullshit. Nothin's real." Hank and Frannie have less background characterization than the Corleones, and as such stand symbolically for average Americans, aware that somehow the dream is not working, but not capable of answering why. Hank's intuitive observation about the deceptive qualities of superficial lighting is as close as Hank and Frannie come to any real understanding of their dilemma. They do not have the moments of insight and revelations that mythic characters like the Corleones have. They are more naturalistic, which runs counter to the lavish, fantasy look of the film.

Hank owns a junkyard and Frannie works in a travel agency, and they squabble about whether they go out to dinner too often. But they have not succumbed to Las Vegas' chief attraction, gambling. Unhappy with their lifestyle, they seek new lovers, not slot machines. A conventional film set in Las Vegas might make their reunion hinge on whether one of them won at a high stakes crap game. This film, however, avoids the notion that money is the balm to spiritual discomfort. Hank and Frannie simply want to understand each other and be happy; they are not seeking the "big score." In this

sense, *One from the Heart* is a truly optimistic film, in that with the reconciliation at the end of the film, the characters have accomplished just that goal.
As Rickey pointed out, this is a rather conventional, moralistic ending.

Still, the ethics of the film have a double edge. The road to Hank and Frannie's eventual reconciliation is paved by their sexual adventures: he with a
circus girl, she with a Latin singer/waiter. On one level the film's ending
suggests that acting out one's sexual fantasies destroys some of their potency
and makes it easier to reconcile oneself to mundane reality. As Hank remarks
of an earlier affair: "Aw, that was nothing. Just a little something." The notion that one is the wiser for investigating one's fantasies has become quite
current, if a spate of recent pop songs about the subject is any indication. The
film wants to revel in its promiscuity even as it ultimately censures it.

That the film self-consciously intends itself as a commentary on American
sexual mores in the 1980s is indicated by the fact that most of it takes place
on the Fourth of July, Hank and Frannie's fifth anniversary. Iconically, at
the travel agency where Frannie works, she replaces a model of the Statue
of Liberty with a poster of Bora Bora; symbolically the old values of personal
freedom have been replaced with the new values of self-indulgence. This
is furthered in the dialogue, when Hank bitterly remarks about Frannie
leaving him: "My folks were always fighting, but they knew they loved
each other and they were together. But nowadays you just move on, ain't
nobody committed to nothing but having a good time." At one point during
the production Coppola intended to underscore the commentary on American values by premiering the film on the Fourth of July. Production delays
made that impossible.

On one level the film endorses the new morality it reflects: in the narrative
Hank and Frannie's relationship seems better after their promiscuous adventures. But in terms of the deeper structure of the film, the new values
and the new morality constitute a morass of emptiness. Coppola's selection
of Tom Waits and Crystal Gayle to do the soundtrack would be the first
indication of that point of view: their country/blues style is born of quiet
desperation and is probably more popular with divorced people than with
teenagers. It suits the lifestyles of Hank and Frannie, who are frustrated
with coming up short of the American dream. The music is anything but
post-Warhol and begins to undermine Benson's critique that the film revels
in surfaces.

When reviewers wrote about the camera style of the film, the adjective
"empty" came up frequently.[8] However, the style reflects artificiality with
the purpose of commenting on a dimension of the characters' lifestyles; not
in the sense of style-for-style's sake. Hank and Frannie live in a world of
empty messages, of travel posters that suggest a better life, of neon signs
that shed light but illuminate nothing. Hank works in a junkyard called
"Reality Wrecking" where the same signs are discarded like disposable
plates. Hank's new-found lover, Leila, is trying to run *away* from the circus

rather than to it. Frannie's new-found lover, Ray, tells her he is a singer, but he is really a waiter. Nothing seems to be real, and the camera style is the perfect evocation of surface deception. The long takes and elaborate tracking movements pointedly remind the viewer that what is on display is contrivance. Rather than cut from a scene of Hank to a scene of Frannie, Coppola used a scrim-light effect where the foreground darkens as the background lights up and the camera dollies forward. The theatrical element and the artificial sets are thus emphasized, but more important is our awareness of the illusion, just as on some level we are aware that we are never in the *real* Las Vegas. Style in *One from the Heart* is not simply to be admired; it is contrapuntal commentary on the film's substance.

Thus the movie is a search for what is "from the heart," what is real beneath a surface of deception. The key plot point in the narrative, then, is when Hank asks Frannie what is wrong with their relationship. She replies: "You never sing to me," which Ray, who will accompany her to Bora Bora, does. Hank chases her to the airport and in front of a crowd of people sings in a raspy, off-key voice, "You are my Sunshine." Frannie ultimately comes back to him because of this extremely corny, but touching moment, which demonstrates that it is the intention rather than the packaging that counts. In fact, most people cannot sing beautifully in the same way people on television and film do. *One from the Heart* is about being reconciled to a substantive, real life rather than the fantasy life the mass media would have people think they should be living, a life filled with Bora Boras. We live in an age when Americans are slowly and uncomfortably realizing that contrary to the cherished American dream of children living a better life than their parents, new economic realities may bring just the opposite. The American dream is tarnished, and Hank and Frannie are the embodiment of a resultant dissatisfaction that no amount of flashy surfaces will alleviate.

That Hank and Frannie's relationship is the one *real* value in their lives is underscored by the acting style and dialogue of the opening portion of the film. A long scene at Hank and Frannie's partly furnished house is set up by Frannie abruptly leaving the glitter and music of Las Vegas and trudging up the steps of her apartment with groceries falling out of the bags she carries. On the soundtrack Crystal Gayle sings "I'm sick and tired of picking up after you." As the scene continues, and Hank and Frannie meet at home, naturalistic acting and dialogue predominate. Frannie, walking toward the bathroom, unglamorously "moons" the camera. Hank and Frannie have a rather mundane fight and begin to make up. Before they can make love Frannie has to run upstairs to put her diaphragm in, while the camera holds for a long time on Hank trying to make the light from a cheap lamp romantic. They comment on each other's appearance: Frannie no longer shaves her legs, Hank has gained weight and looks like an "egg." (Frederick Forrest gained 30 pounds for the role.) That the emphasis here is on kitchen-sink realism in a film that opens with stylized camera movements reminiscent of some of the special effects in *Citizen Kane* may initially be disconcerting. However, the contrast is appropriate because the film ultimately shows Hank and Frannie's relationship to be the one real and solid element in their otherwise superficial existence.

With these dialectical contrasts, *One from the Heart* is a striking film; it welds an unusual formal style to allusive social commentary. Jonathan Cott in *Rolling Stone* wrote: "In *One from the Heart*, Coppola has created his most graceful, most inventive and wisest work, gently and beautifully reminding us that, in the words of Thoreau, 'our truest life is when we are in dreams awake.' "[9] Cott was one of the few exceptions to the overwhelming critical view that there was little to recommend *One from the Heart*. Some of the dismissals almost seemed gleeful, which leads one to speculate that the advance publicity about the film and Coppola's efforts toward being a "mini" mogul might have adversely affected critical opinion. There is also the possibility of violated expectations with a director whose name is built upon epic spectaculars. Whatever the factors affecting *One from the Heart*'s critical disfavor, the ticket-going public did not rescue the film. *One from the Heart* opened in eight selected cities, did poorly, and failed to "break wide," industry jargon for opening in all cities across the country.

### The Commercial Context

Insight into why *One from the Heart* failed to find an audience, and, in the larger sense, into the complicated financial system under which Coppola is now operating, was provided by Lillian Ross' excellent "Some Figures on a Fantasy."[10] Ross is often cited for having written the definitive behind-the-scenes film book with her *Picture*, which was the story of John Huston's ill-fated *The Red Badge of Courage*. The *New Yorker* magazine commissioned her to write a similar, shorter account of *One from the Heart*, and the result is one of the most fascinating production accounts of Coppola's career, even though the piece basically covers only the period from post-production to when Coppola pulled the film out of general distribution. At the beginning of Ross' account is Coppola's remark to her: "The adventure of *One from the Heart* was simply my trying to own the rights to my movies."

With *Apocalypse Now* Coppola had sold foreign distribution rights as well as mortgaging other films' earning potential and his personal property in order to own the copyright of that film. The film's commercial success paid off all the loans to the point that a $4 million sale to cable television, a $1.1 million sale to Japanese television, and a $10 million sale to American television were essentially gravy for Coppola's company. All future profits from the film are Coppola's, rather than going to a distributor or a studio. The same approach was tried with *One from the Heart* to a much different result. Because of the spectacular financial failure of that film, Coppola essentially lost the Hollywood General Studio. He had bought the oldtime studio for $7.2 million, renovated much of it, mortgaged it against the earnings of *One from the Heart*, and eventually sold it for $18 million. Coppola told Ross: "I believe that an artist has a right to own what he creates, but I can't get my hands on the capital that I need to do the creating. I was running a movie studio that had no money."

The high stakes of the film's success necessitated very careful attention to arrangements made with distributors. Initially, MGM had brought the script to Coppola's attention. As costs escalated, MGM dropped out and a favorable deal was struck with Paramount. Bad blood developed between Coppola's Zoetrope and Paramount when disagreements came up concerning how much "completion money" Paramount was liable for after cost overruns set back the premiere. Further complications developed when Paramount prematurely screened a rough cut to exhibitors who leaked word to the press that the film was a disaster. Coppola, without notifying Paramount, audaciously arranged two sneak previews of the film at the 5,000 seat Radio City Music Hall in order to "let the people decide what to do with the film." Response to the media event was mixed and Paramount dropped out of their distribution arrangement, which had called for them to deliver 600 prints to the theatres with a $4 million advertising blitz, on February 10, 1982. Coppola briefly toyed with the idea of releasing the film himself, but soon settled with Columbia, who in one week put together an advertising approach and marketing strategy for the film and opened it in eight cities. The first week's business was very poor, and Columbia immediately engaged Patrick Caddell and the Cambridge Survey Research Group to find out how to change the advertising approach. They recommended a campaign that would incorporate: "1. Coppola. 2. An innovative film which only he can do, which he always does. 3. A love story or romance captured in an extraordinary atmosphere of fantasy-photography, scenery, lighting, and music."[11] However, the subsequent attempts to change the image of the film failed, and Zoetrope decided to take the loss and keep the film out of wide release. Zoetrope president Robert Spiotta told Ross:

We made a lot of mistakes. We should have had trailers in the theatres at least two months before release. We did not. The publicity was not right. We had no time for research. We should have had the attention of the public on the film, not on Zoetrope, not on Francis and the financial problems. We didn't bring the music out as an album before the picture was released. In retrospect, the ad campaign was all wrong. After the Music Hall previews, we went on the wrong assumption that we had to get the picture out in a hurry. We should have waited.[12]

Spiotta, Caddell, and Columbia all seemed to fail to understand one very basic thematic issue about the film, which is that *One from the Heart* is not a "boy gets girl" fantasy romance. In terms of its relation to the fantasy musicals of the classical period, *One from the Heart* would have more in common with *Barkley's of Broadway*, wherein Astaire and Rogers begin the movie married, briefly stray, and come back together, than to *Top Hat* or the other films wherein the main drive of the film is our identification with Astaire's search for the perfect partner. The thrust of *One from the Heart* is to *undercut* the fantasy romance contained in Hank chasing Leila and Frannie being chased by Ray, not to make it our main concern. It would seem obvious that if one identifies with the fantasy/love-chase aspect of the film, one feels cheated at the end when Hank and Frannie reunite. One would ask why the dream lovers were abandoned and whether this film preferred mediocrity to excitement. A marketing campaign that would avoid these sorts of expectations and reactions would have to prepare viewers for a story of an already existing relationship *surviving* in the face of temptation. A marketing campaign that would leave viewers satisfied that they got what they paid for and ready to tell friends to see the film would have to incorporate some semblance of the notion that this film tells the *truth* about love in today's society, not that the film encourages a viewer to escape into a fantasy romance. Columbia's advertising showed a fantasy cruise ship in the background to Ray and Frannie in a passionate embrace. The advertising suggested that the wrong guy won the girl in the end and probably led potential viewers to expect disco music rather than Tom Waits and Crystal Gayle.

The film industry never had a monopoly on understanding its own product. At the present, *One from the Heart* is a lost film, never having found the right audience or the right critics, which is a tragedy for a film that should have been one of the more respected in recent American film. Lillian Ross closed her piece with Coppola characteristically reflecting on his twin responsibilities as artist and businessman:

You know, some of those Chase bankers told me *they* liked the movie. I told the bank I'll make the first payment with the money we get from the sale of the studio and the money owed us for the foreign distribution of *One from the Heart*. For the second payment, I'll use the money we get from the cable sale of *One from the Heart*, *Hammett*, and *The Escape Artist*. In the meantime, I'll be finishing everything on *The Outsiders* and *Rumble Fish*. So what if my telephone is turned off again at home? Or my electricity is shut off? Or my credit cards cancelled? If you don't bet, you don't have a chance to win. It's so silly in life not to pursue the highest possible thing you can imagine even if you run the risk of losing it all, because if you don't pursue it you've lost it anyway. You can't be an artist and be safe.[13]

The drama in Coppola's life is sometimes difficult to resist: with Coppola we have the conflicting forces of commerce and art locked in a career-long struggle. One almost feels obligated to cheer as a partisan. Still, *One from the Heart* has enough thematic and formal brilliance to stand on its own and may well be a film to be rediscovered in years to come.

## The Outsiders

In 1974, Coppola commented on the screenwriter's task in adapting a well-known novel to the screen:

> I also did a lot of things in *The Godfather* that people *thought* were in the book that weren't. The art of adaptation is when you can lie or when you can do something that wasn't in the original but is so much like the original that it should have been.[14]

Given Coppola's imaginative translations of the literary into the cinematic for the *Godfather* films, and to a lesser extent for *The Great Gatsby*, and given the above musings about what constitutes a good filmic adaptation of a novel, *The Outsiders*, Coppola's ninth directorial effort, seems either rushed or lackadaisical. The 1983 film slavishly follows S. E. Hinton's 1967 youth novel to the point that one wonders why Coppola bothered with a screenplay, why he did not simply film straight from the prose (as he claimed to have done with *Heart of Darkness* for portions of *Apocalypse Now*). Some novels are more cinematic than others, and the abundant violence, drama, and conflict in *The Outsiders* may have justified the decision to remain "faithful" to the structure of a novel that had sold seven million copies.[15] However, S. E. Hinton's dialogue, which is mostly taken straight off the page and uttered on the screen, is so maudlin, so strained, so unreal, that it is difficult to believe that Coppola was vitally involved with this project.

Before going into the film further, however, one important reservation should be expressed. At four or five public screenings of the film attended, I invariably witnessed groups of young teenagers sitting toward the front of the theater, sobbing their eyes out as the film's end credits rolled. Apparently they accepted wholeheartedly what I found overly sentimental and contrived. Coppola all along claimed that *The Outsiders*, as well as *Rumble Fish*, were films for teenagers, and financially *The Outsiders* was a moderate success with that audience. However, if *The Outsiders* was successful in moving teenagers, it seems more the result of Coppola's decision in the adaptation stage to defer completely to novelist S. E. Hinton, who was on the set as a "den mother" to the teenage actors, than of an innate understanding of young people on Coppola's part. In comparison, Coppola was far less reverential with Mario Puzo in their collaboration on the *Godfather* films. It may be that Coppola felt out of his element with Hinton's Tulsa teenagers in a way he did not with Puzo's New York Italians, but the decision to defer to Hinton made the film very popular with basically one subsection of the total audience.

Still, a nagging question remains, which David Ansen of *Newsweek* put bluntly: "Who would have expected a teary teen soap opera from the maker of *The Godfather* and *Apocalypse Now*?"[16] Probably no one, but Aljean Harmetz's production account in the *New York Times* offers an interesting explanation of how Coppola came to the project:

Trying to stave off bankruptcy, Mr. Coppola said he was spending his days in "meetings, issues, compromises, a seven-day-a-week imbroglio." In *The Outsiders*, he saw not only a movie he wanted to direct but a way of fleeing his problems. "It was chaos incorporated at Zoetrope," he said, "like fighting a war. I used to be a great camp counselor, and the idea of being with half a dozen kids in the country and making a movie seemed like being a camp counselor again. It would be a breath of fresh air. I'd forget my troubles and have some laughs again."[17]

That the novel had cult status and was required reading at many junior high schools, and that Zoetrope had recently made a large profit on another children's novel, *The Black Stallion*, made the decision to film *The Outsiders* a bit less whimsical and impetuous. But regardless of the financial motivations, the story of how the novel came to Coppola's attention sounds Capraesque and reveals much about Coppola's idealistic side.

Jo Ellen Misakian, a librarian aide at the Lone Star Junior High School in Fresno, California, was impressed with the novel's ability to stimulate young teenagers who normally did not read. Teenagers love Hinton's books because of her plain-spoken insight into teenage alienation; educators love the books because they depict bad boys who long to be good and thus are a tool to use against discipline problems. Over a number of years, Misakian wrote letters to various people—including Hinton, Lloyd Shearer, and a local newspaper columnist—about why such a popular novel had never been filmed. Eventually, because Coppola's name was associated with *The Black Stallion* (a Zoetrope production with Caroll Ballard directing), Misakian sent a petition signed by 108 children and teachers to Coppola asking him to film *The Outsiders*. Coppola's response was: "Look at the cute letter. I bet kids have a good idea of what should be a movie," and he assigned Fred Roos to look into the matter. Coppola's faith in children's taste went along with a laudable commitment on Zoetrope's part to internship programs for young children designed to make them more knowledgeable about the filmmaking process. It is perhaps ironic that Coppola's faith in children's wisdom was misplaced; the children's petition was organized by an adult.

Roos assigned Kathleen Knutson Rowell to do a screenplay. Eventually, Coppola read the novel, and as *Variety* reported, he immediately decided it had possibilities as a combination of *The Godfather* and *Gone With the Wind* for kids, and decided to direct it himself. Later the screenplay credit went to a bitter arbitration with the Writer's Guild.[18] Coppola claimed to have done 14 drafts of his own screenplay, but lost credit on a rule that a director must write more than fifty percent of a script to receive credit. Probably because Coppola decided to stay so close to the text of the novel, the judges saw little evidence of writing on his part, and the eventual credit went solely to Rowell.

The premise of both the film and novel is that a young, Oklahoma "greaser" is writing an essay about some recent traumatic events as a form of self-therapy. Basically, the story is about the lower class greasers and the upper class "socs" (short for socialites), and the loose, class warfare going on between them. One tends to empathize with the greasers, but a few of the soc characters have problems as well.

The only real plot departure from the novel to the film is the opening. Hinton begins with Ponyboy leaving a movie theater alone, being jumped by socs, and then rescued by the gang. Only later does he go to a drive-in, which we see early in the film. Coppola, instead, opens with Dallas (Matt Dillon) in front of an old-time drugstore in a shot reminiscent of *The Last Picture Show*. The only music in the soundtrack identifiably from the 1960s, "Gloria," comes on as Dillon meets Ponyboy and Johnny. They strut to a vacant lot and see some younger children playing cards. Dallas reflects for a moment on how he hates kids, and they chase the children away. This section of the film feels very authentic, exciting, and easily establishes interest in these hoods, which carries through their antics at the drive-in. However, the tone of this section, well established by the driving, rock rhythms of "Gloria" and the realistically photographed Oklahoma skyline, is never really returned to in the remainder of the film. Instead, the imitation *West Side Story* score of Carmine Coppola predominates, and its over-emotional, exaggerated, melodramatic sound complements the plot and dialogue, which progressively becomes more maudlin and artificial. Correspondingly, the photography becomes lushly romantic, with vivid red skies reminding us of the more lyrical moments of *Gone With the Wind*. As Coppola himself observed:

The key to *The Outsiders* is the score; the fact that it's this schmaltzy classical movie score indicates that I wanted a movie told in sumptuous terms, very honestly or carefully taken from the book without changing it a lot, with young actors—putting the emphasis more on that kind of *Gone With the Wind* lyricism, which was so important to the young girl (Susie Hinton) when she wrote it.[19]

Coppola also remarked about the film: "It's not that I couldn't make that sixteen other ways." The brief opening section with Van Morrison singing "Gloria" must have been one of the other sixteen ways, and had Coppola sustained that mood, the film might have appealed to a wider audience. As it is, much of the dialogue makes an adult squirm, as when Ponyboy and Cherry get a coke at the concession stand and Cherry remarks "You think the socs have it made, the rich kids, the South side socs, well, I'll tell you something, Ponyboy, and it might come as a surprise, but things are rough all over." Later, after Johnny has killed someone and he and Ponyboy are hiding in the country and admiring a sunset, Ponyboy recites a poem by Robert Frost. Johnny remarks: "I never noticed colors and clouds and stuff until you kept reminding me about it. Kind of like they were never there before."

The key to the appeal of *The Outsiders* is that everyone has feelings, even an older brother who seems to hate you, even the hoodlums and juvenile delinquents, even the superficial rich kids who have everything handed to them on a silver platter. This is manifested throughout the story by adolescent males repeatedly crying and expressing affection for each other. It is interesting that the pen name S. E. Hinton was used because editors thought the novel would lose credibility if young readers knew the author was a female. In fact, these fourteen-year-old males act emotionally very much like stereotypical fourteen-year-old females, although the outward trappings of fist fights, interest in cars, and athletics seems very masculine. The fantasy element of the story is that teenage boys can lose the culturally imposed stoicism of the macho persona and that females can finally understand them when this persona disappears. That this fantasy bears absolutely no relation to the realities of urban street gangs or in general to the youth of America bothers only the realistic minded, and perhaps a few adult film critics.

Be that as it may, the film disturbs the auteurist notion that there should be consistency in the auteur's canon. The adolescents who enjoyed *The Outsiders* would be bored with the profundities of *The Conversation*, and most of the adults who enjoyed *The Conversation* were probably bored with *The Outsiders*.[20] In the interview with Thomson, Coppola seemed clearly sensitive about the problem of violated expectations and rationalized:

I believe directors should direct—they *are* directors. If I get a job to direct *Streetcar Named Desire* in a play, the theatre, I'm going to do my best to do *Streetcar Named Desire*, I'm not going to try to imprint it with my own bizarre imagination, although I could. That was the attitude. I took it (*The Outsiders*) to do that, and I was very proud of the fact that I was able to do that. Go take something, assess what it is and make it like it is.[21]

However, the problem with Coppola's rationalization is that in his career he has proven himself to be something more than a director. At times a visionary, an entrepreneur, a revolutionary, an artist, a creator, he has always been more than simply a transcriber of someone else's work. There is no law that prohibits auteurs from temporarily stepping outside their usual role and doing something simply as an interesting exercise, which seems to be the case with *The Outsiders*; but the result will be some disgruntlement from admirers who expect more, and venom from detractors, as evidenced by the following. From Vincent Canby: "Francis Coppola's *The Outsiders* coming on the heels, so to speak, of *One from the Heart*, leads one to suspect that Mr. Coppola is no longer with us, but up with his entourage observing the world from a space platform."[22] From Gary Arnold: "This is another squishy one from the heart, I suppose, but the heart-of-darkness exertions of *Apocalypse Now* may have left Coppola in a suspended state of artistic convalescence."[23] From David Denby: "The movie is a frightening failure; one searches in vain for signs of Coppola's greatness ... Coppola has tried for kinetic excitement and passion, and what he's come up with is a kind of cinematic equivalent of fast-moving purple prose. It's an overblown, inauthentic movie, and a dull one too."[24] A good many of the most respected film critics simply ignored the film, which may be the most appropriate response if the film was simply aimed at people who do not read film reviews.

The one aspect of the production of *The Outsiders* that seems most typical of the real strength of Coppola as a director is his work with the teenage actors. Coppola went to elaborate lengths, reminiscent of *The Godfather* production, to ensure that the actors identified with their parts both on the screen and off. Actors playing socs were given plush quarters while the greaser actors were given second-class accommodations. Fraternization with only one's respective group was encouraged. The actors had interviews arranged with local youths and older Oklahomans who had been young during the 1960s. Many of the principals in recent interviews have spoken of the production as the best experience in their careers. In retrospect, the casting seems very inspired, and many of the supporting characters have gone on to major roles in subsequent films, reminiscent of the way *American Graffiti* launched a generation of young actors.[25] Still, the pleasure in watching the ensemble acting does not totally compensate for the disappointment in the content areas.

### Rumble Fish

In earlier chapters of this study, Coppola's struggles with becoming sophisticated politically have been discussed: his own admission that "making it" in Hollywood was an all-consuming task, the problems with glorifying the Mafia in the *Godfather* saga, the signs of an emerging consciousness toward multinational corporations in the Third World, and an evolving consciousness toward American involvement in Vietnam evidenced in the production process of *Apocalypse Now*. *One from the Heart* allusively comments on the tarnished American dream of the 1980s. *The Outsiders* is an unpretentious stylistic exercise, not an example of auteur cinema. But with *Rumble Fish* we are in the territory of a self-conscious art film, and any kind of political perspective seems strangely lacking.

*Rumble Fish* appeared in October 1983, midway into the Reagan era, when cuts in social welfare programs and a revised tax structure made the disparity between the rich and poor in American society once more a salient issue. Yet *Rumble Fish*, with its tale of an alcoholic ex-lawyer living on welfare with his two high school dropout sons in a bleak urban environment, seems curiously removed from any sort of social observation. My college students commented that it seemed like science fiction to them. Closer inspection of the creative process suggests a weird amalgamation of historical time: Coppola's remembrance of growing up in the beat-generation 1950s with his older brother August, S. E. Hinton's late 1960s experience in Tulsa, Oklahoma, and the more contemporary mannerisms of the young actors, particularly Matt Dillon, Diane Lane, and Vincent Spano. Perhaps with such disparate historical phenomena Coppola was quite right in trying to universalize the film's perspective toward mythic abstraction.

Still this is an art film in the 1980s, and this chapter is focusing on the reception of Coppola's films. Cuts in NEH funding, the drying up of corporate sponsorship for PBS, and related developments have made this a difficult era for the independent filmmaker, with perhaps the on-going appetite of the new video outlets the only savior. This may be the backdrop to *Rumble Fish* being booed at the New York Film Festival. People sensitive to non-mainstream feature filmmaking know too well the difficulty in getting anything "personal" looked at in the current film distribution system and resent what may have seemed to them a $10-million self-indulgence. Later Jim Jarmusch's shoestring-budgeted, hip and cynical *Stranger Than Paradise* would be their darling, coincidentally another black and white film about social dropouts, with even less narrative than *Rumble Fish*.

The American critical establishment's reaction was just as unadmiring. *Variety*'s weekly poll of the first-line New York critics listed nine unfavorable reviews, mostly from the broadcast media and newspapers, one inconclusive review (Corliss in *Time*), and no favorable reviews. This did not include outright pans from David Denby in *New York*, Andrew Sarris in the *Village Voice*, and Stanley Kauffman in *The New Republic*; and "interesting failure" reviews from Janet Maslin and Vincent Canby in the *New York Times*, and Sheila Benson in the *Los Angeles Times*. Roger Ebert of the *Chicago Sun Times* and Jack Kroll of *Newsweek* gave the film favorable reviews, but Ebert hedged: "If you care how the story turns out, you're in the wrong movie."[26] And Kroll demonstrated little understanding of the film, concentrating on Coppola as "an artist who won't surrender."[27] Perhaps the only unequivocally favorable review by a major writer on the North American continent was Lawrence O'Toole in *MacCleans*. O'Toole noted the film's booing at the New York Film Festival and hypothesized: "The real reason may be that in 1983 extreme style is a form of abrasiveness. Truly unique, dark-minded moviemaking, such as *Rumble Fish*, *The Moon in the Gutter*, or even *Daniel*, in an era that cleaves to what is safe and innocuous, is an increasingly risky business."[28]

O'Toole's evocation of the film *Risky Business* was probably intentional and sly. *Risky Business* was also an extremely stylized film about teenagers with its own abstract symbols for the passing of youth to experience (think of the crystal egg, the father's Porsche, the train set/subway montage, etc.). However, while writer/director Paul Brickman quite obviously buttressed the film with gags, sex appeal, and a happy ending that he later disowned, the film also played off a shrewd political analysis of the materialistic, suburban, would-be Yuppies of the 1980s. The social parody paid off— *Risky Business* did *very good* business. Coppola showed far less commercial caution with *Rumble Fish*, and perhaps a bit of self-indulgence, as evidenced by his remark to David Thomson: "I really started to use *Rumble Fish* as my carrot for what I promised myself when I finished *The Outsiders*."

Some might think it megalomaniacal to conceive of a $10 million film involving hundreds of production and post-production workers—as well as the attention of millions of viewers to pay for the film—as a "carrot" for oneself. Another sort of resentment was reflected in a disgruntled Zoetrope employee's remark: "Just remember: this isn't the story of a little guy against the system, Francis *is* the system."[29] However, despite his financial standing, despite the multitudes working for him, in fact just because Coppola makes multimillion dollar personal explorations, Coppola is not "the system." *Rumble Fish* is the strongest evidence yet that Coppola is a challenge to "the system." This was perhaps no better demonstrated than by the reaction of Robert Evans, the former head of production at Paramount, as quoted by Michael Daly: "Evans went to see *Rumble Fish*, and he remembers being shaken by how far Coppola had strayed from Hollywood. Evans says, 'I was scared. I couldn't understand any of it.' "[30] The system produces films that do not require abstract or symbolic thinking. *Rumble Fish* is a demanding film for people with expectations conditioned by standard Hollywood product.

Critics generally have more tolerance for non-mainstream films, but they must face a real dilemma in trying to make connections between the work of a man who in one breath makes *The Outsiders* and in the next makes *Rumble Fish*. Coppola's intentions, his role as an author, and the results differ greatly with this pair; the incongruity follows the pattern of the rest of his career. The earlier equation stating that Coppola made one commercial film to finance another personal film (e.g., *The Godfather* for *The Conversation*) was always somewhat flimsy. Business considerations affect the "personal films," and personal vision is injected into the films made for commercial considerations. With *The Outsiders* and *Rumble Fish*, however, the distinctions between "commercial" and "personal" do seem more polarized. *Rumble Fish* is Coppola's most uncompromising film, audacious, original, and well-realized. The film is perhaps short-sightedly apolitical, but it also has a stubborn, single-minded air about it. Coppola seemed to realize he can afford an occasional self-indulgence and still have a filmmaking career. *Rumble Fish* and *One From the Heart*'s commercial failures had little impact on Coppola's bankability for *The Cotton Club*; in fact the producers thought Coppola might be easier to work with after he had received a "come-uppance" from the previous films. The legal battles over creative control that Coppola eventually won on *The Cotton Club* seemed to indicate otherwise.

Despite the above observations on *Rumble Fish*'s apolitical quality, Hinton's original novels, *The Outsiders* and *Rumble Fish*, were heartfelt cries against societal determinism. They proceeded from the liberal view that juvenile delinquents' problems stem from class barriers and urban environments rather than from inherent personality. In *The Outsiders*, this "message" was expressed bluntly; a greaser would lament: "If only there were a world where there were no greasers and socs . . . " With teenagers, subtlety is usually not a great virtue, and some of Hinton's success with *The Outsiders* should be attributed to her simplicity and directness. With *Rumble Fish*, however, an older, more mature Hinton returned to the same basic theme but fashioned the "message" in a far more complex, symbolic parable. Although the subject remained the same (teenage hoodlums and their struggles with existence), the characterization in *Rumble Fish* was much more psychologically complicated than it had been in *The Outsiders*. Relationships between characters emerge on a metaphoric level not easily unraveled. The oppressive society is now more amorphous, its impact more veiled.

Coppola decided, halfway into the production of *The Outsiders*, that he wanted to retain the same production team, stay in Tulsa, and shoot *Rumble Fish* immediately following *The Outsiders*. He and Hinton worked together on Sundays, their day off from *The Outsiders*, and put together a screenplay. Hinton told Coppola he was "the only person who had ever understood it, fully."[31] *Rumble Fish*, as a novel, had the craft and artistry that *The Outsiders*, despite its gut appeal, did not, and cynics might observe that Coppola was salving his conscience like studio era producers who occasionally produced arty, literary adaptations to counterbalance their more typical commercial fare. However Coppola, in a convincing interview with David Thomson,[32] claimed that his real attraction to *Rumble Fish* lay in a strong personal identification he had with the subject matter, which was about a younger brother who hero-worships an older, intellectually superior brother. Coppola explained at length how during his youth his older brother, August, although five years older, included Francis in his activities, introduced him to an exciting world of intellectual ideas, and provided a very strong role model. Later August became a novelist and professor of comparative literature, and Coppola credits him for the beginning of Coppola's own creative writing and his teenage introduction to such writers as Camus, Joyce, Gide, and Sartre. A dedication to August appears as *Rumble Fish*'s final end credit.

Because of his strong personal identification with the material of the novel, and also because there was no imperative to produce a "faithful" adaptation to please millions of nonexistent fans, Coppola emerged far more as an "author" of the film *Rumble Fish* than he had with *The Outsiders*. The film follows Hinton's story and characters, but Coppola's cinematic presence is felt, and there are subtle but revealing differences between the novel and the film. Coppola later said he wanted to make *Rumble Fish* more in the direction of *Apocalypse Now*, whereas he felt *The Outsiders* had been in the direction of *The Godfather*, and although *Rumble Fish* lacks both the visual spectacle of the Vietnam War and an epic narrative, it certainly has *Apocalypse Now*'s expressionistic mood and singularity.

Coppola established this mood with visuals strikingly unusual for a contemporary feature film. One of the dominant techniques, time-lapse photography either of clouds scudding across the sky or shadows racing along a wall, is more typical of shorter, abstract/experimental films or the Coppola-distributed *Koyaanisqatsi*, but nicely establishes the theme of time passing faster than the characters realize. Thematically related, shots of clocks abound, including a man-sized, handless one reminiscent of the clock in *Metropolis*. The black and white photography, corresponding to the Motorcycle Boy's color blindness, has a film noir quality, expressed in frequent oblique angles, exaggerated compositions, dark alleys, and foggy streets. (Shadows were *painted* on the alley walls to get the proper effect.) In short, the film stylistically resembles nothing in contemporary feature filmmaking, American or European.

David Thomson located the film within past cinematic and literary traditions: "*Rumble Fish* is Coppola's best film, the most emotional, the most revolutionary and the most clearly in love with the 1940's movies. It has a mood from Camus and the French Existentialists, but it looks and feels like Welles and Cocteau. . . . It is deliberately an American art film—as full of the heart's creaking sound as *Kane*."[33]

However, that the film looks and feels like an art film is not enough to dismiss the charge made by many of the film's detractors that the film's style was the empty shell of a meaningless narrative with superficial characterizations. In the remainder of this discussion, I will suggest that there is more depth in the film than its detractors have acknowledged. In particular, the family relationships between the main characters have nuances and complexities that go beyond that of most contemporary film characterization. To get at Coppola's part in providing that depth, we need to consider in some detail the transference of Hinton's novel to film, always being careful not to allow the written text to become a necessary explication for the visual text. So first, I will trace the novel and film's narratives concurrently.

## Novel Versus Film

The basic premise of the story is that a young disadvantaged hoodlum from a broken home, Rusty-James (Matt Dillon), idolizes his older brother, the Motorcycle Boy (Mickey Rourke), to the point where he wants to *become* him. He frequently asks anyone listening whether he looks like the older brother, which is usually greeted in the negative. Rusty-James does not have his brother's intelligence or larger-than-life qualities. His strengths are more intuitive than intellectual; he is not aware of a world other than that immediately around him. His brother, on the other hand, is aware of the world around him, but profoundly disaffected by it, expressed metaphorically by his color blindness and intermittent hearing problems.

Hinton starts her novel in the present, but tells the rest of the story in flashback. In the beginning of the novel, Rusty-James is on a beach in California and unexpectedly meets Steve (Vincent Spano), a long lost friend from junior high days. Steve starts Rusty-James, the novel's first-person narrator, thinking about the painful memories that led to his coming to California, and the rest of the novel is a flashback to those events. With the foreknowledge that Rusty-James has escaped his former circumstances, the novel's narrative becomes an exposition of why Rusty-James is able to leave, while the Motorcycle Boy is trapped in a metaphysical quicksand.

Although Coppola eschewed this flashback structure, the remaining narrative events up until the conclusion of the film are fairly close to those of the novel. A few scenes further establishing Steve and Rusty-James's relationship in the novel are missing in the film; this seems in line with Coppola's narrowing the focus to the brothers' relationship. The exact dynamics of the brothers' relationship differ from novel to film, and suggest to some extent Coppola's infusing his own fraternal feelings into the narrative and changing some of its direction. Lawrence O'Toole commented: "Hinton's novel built to a moving conclusion, but Coppola's movie is more nihilistic: when Rusty-James reaches the ocean on his brother's bike, Coppola does not give the audience a happy ending, but rather suggests that it may be too late for Rusty-James as well."[34] O'Toole is right that the novel builds to the conclusion better than does the film, but wrong about the nihilism of Coppola's ending; he misreads the film's final image, as will be discussed shortly.

The film's conclusion, wherein Motorcycle Boy suicidally breaks into a pet store and removes the fish of the film's title, seems less motivated in the film than in the novel, where, as O'Toole noted, there was a sense of progression. The film emphasizes the texture of the brothers' relationship more than the narrative momentum. This seems a result of Coppola's own personal identification with the characters, specifically as a younger brother looking up to his older brother, August, which he reflected on at length in an interview with David Thomson: "I did most of what I did to imitate him. Tried to look like him, tried to be like him. I even took his short stories and handed them in under my name when I went to the writing class in high school myself. My whole beginning in writing started in copying him, thinking that if I did those things, then I could be like he was."[35] This does sound like Rusty-James's reaction to his older brother, but the Motorcycle Boy of the film is more attendant, more paternalistic toward Rusty-James than the Motorcycle Boy of the novel; he is more like Coppola's description of *his* older brother. Hinton's Motorcycle Boy is more withdrawn, more volatile, as Rusty-James describes: "I was a little surprised he'd worry about me. See, I always thought he was the coolest guy in the world, and he was, but he never paid much attention to me. But that didn't mean anything. As far as I could tell, he never paid any attention to anything except to laugh at it."[36] To some extent this is reminiscent of Ponyboy's inability in *The Outsiders* to perceive his older brother's love for him, a theme found in other Hinton novels, particularly *Tex*. Nonetheless, the novel's Motorcycle Boy is so estranged from everyone that the climactic break-in at the pet store is well prepared for and dramatically logical. The insanity of the action matches the insanity of the character. In the film, because Mickey Rourke gives the character a charisma that connotes warmth, the break-in seems more unexpected and enigmatic. The surprise forces us to re-evaluate what we know about the Motorcycle Boy, and the pain behind his cool exterior becomes apparent.

The film's Motorcycle Boy, in a moment of clairvoyance, seems to know and understand his fate: before leaving the pet shop he tells Rusty-James to take the motorcycle and follow the river to the ocean. Shortly thereafter, the police gun down Motorcycle Boy as he attempts to take the fish to the river. Rusty-James symbolically completes his brother's task by throwing the fish in the river and then departs on the motorbike. The last image of the film is Rusty-James arriving at the ocean. The novel simply ends the death scene with Rusty-James in hysteria, shoved up against a police car, the fish still floundering on the ground, and no explanation of how Rusty-James gets to California. An epilogue-type chapter follows with Rusty-James in California, five years later, saying goodbye to Steve and reflecting on the events just narrated. The epilogue seems to confirm Rusty-James has taken on some of his older brother's properties: Steve remarks on how much he now looks like the Motorcycle Boy, and at one point Rusty-James ceases to hear Steve talking, much like his brother used to do. This reinforces a key detail in the narration of the novel's death scene, which is that in Rusty-James's moment of hysteria his hearing suddenly diminishes and he sees the world in black and white. This appropriation of his brother's sensory perception of the world implies a psychological transference.

The film's rendition is more problematic; Matt Dillon will not suddenly resemble Mickey Rourke without plastic surgery, and consequently a key visual metaphor is lost. Instead, when Rusty-James is shoved up against the police car—the moment in the novel that he sees the world in black and white—the filmic Rusty-James suddenly sees his own reflection in color and a flashing light in red. (The only other color image in the black and white film is the Siamese Fighting fish, which take on such strong connotations for the Motorcycle Boy.) Knowing the novel, this might seem backwards. Rusty-James is the narrator, not the color-blind Motorcycle Boy. A literal translation of the novel would involve shooting the entire film in color, and then shooting the traumatic moment after the Motorcycle Boy's death in black and white. Instead, we must rationalize that since the novel is told by the adult Rusty-James, who has acquired some of the psychological properties of his older brother, as symbolized in their superficial physical resemblance, then it is appropriate in the film to see things in black and white, and that color is used dramatically to demarcate the moment of transference brought about by Motorcycle Boy's death. From the viewpoint that the original novel should have no impact on our understanding of the film, it could simply be said that Motorcycle Boy's view of the world dominates the narrative and makes appropriate the black and white look of the film. The infrequent use of color indicates moments of transcendence.

The film's final re-working of the ending of the novel is the long lens shot of Rusty-James arriving at the glistening ocean beach on the stolen motorcycle. In the novel he spent time in reform school before going to California, but there is more than time compression involved in the adaptation strategy here. Earlier in the film, Motorcycle Boy tells Rusty-James that during his departure he had never gone to the ocean, that California had gotten in the way. Thus, although Rusty-James takes on some of the traits of his brother—in the novel he comes to resemble him, and in the film he completes the action of dumping the Siamese fish in the river and inherits the motorcycle—Rusty-James is ultimately able to escape the environment that kills Motorcycle Boy, the environment symbolized by the fish bowl, the escape symbolized by the arrival at the ocean. (This also recapitulates the actions of their mother, who left Tulsa for California.) From a mythical perspective, oceans suggest a losing of the self and a joining with man's larger destiny; Coppola is certainly aware of Fellini's use of the ocean at the end of *La Strada* and *La Dolce Vita* or, more appropriately, Truffaut's at the end of *The 400 Blows*. From a psychoanalytic perspective, Rusty-James's ability to escape, to arrive at the ocean, seems bound up in his intuitive strengths, his lack of his brother's numbing introspection, which produces an alienation from the world (as well as an inability to escape from it). Although the father remarks how Motorcycle Boy is like his mother, he is in fact an unhappy melding of both his father's and mother's qualities—her acute perception and wild spirit, but his father's intelligence and stasis. The combination prevents Motorcycle Boy from reaching the symbolic ocean, or any other kind of self-fulfillment. Finally, if we want to construct an autobiographical allegory of the Francis/August relationship, Francis is the brother who went to California to achieve fame and fortune.

Understanding the dialectics of Rusty-James's and Motorcycle Boy's personalities within the hereditary scheme of the family is made easier in the novel where more background is given at greater length. The mother had deserted the father and left for California, which prompted the father's alcoholism. Rusty-James asks his father whether his mother is crazy, to which the father explains:

Our marriage was a classic example of a preacher marrying an atheist, thinking to make a convert, and instead ending up doubting his own faith. . . . I married her thinking to set a precedent. She married me for fun, and when it stopped being fun she left. . . .[37]

Characteristically, Rusty-James does not understand what his father is talking about, since anything abstract is lost on him. He responds by telling his father that he thinks he will look like Motorcycle Boy when he gets older. He narrates: "My father looked at me for a long moment, longer than he'd ever looked at me. But still it was like he was seeing somebody else's kid, not seeing anybody that had anything to do with him. 'You better pray to God not.' His voice was full of pity. 'You poor child,' he said, 'You poor baby.' " After Motorcycle Boy's death and after Rusty-James has experienced the momentary loss of color, he tell us: "I was in a glass bubble and everyone else was outside it and I'd be alone like that for the rest of my life. Then a pain sliced through my head and the colors were back. The noise was deafening and I was shaking because I was still alone."[38] Rusty-James's appropriation of his brother's outlook on the world is only temporary. Then in the epilogue, Steve tells Rusty-James that although he looks like his older brother he does not sound like him. This seems symbolically to clarify that although Rusty-James has taken on many of his brother's qualities, he has not taken on *all* of them and will finally survive. The following passage suggests that Rusty-James has achieved some harmony in his life, which the visuals of the film's final image seem to approximate:

I looked out at the ocean. I liked that ocean. You always knew there was going to be another wave. It has always been there, and more than likely it always would. I got to listening to the sound of the waves and didn't hear Steve for a second.[39]

As should be established by now, *Rumble Fish*'s narrative and characterization are complex, and the above analysis in no way exhausts its nuances or the levels of interpretation that could be brought to bear upon it. Perhaps out of pride in the level of abstraction that the story works on, the first screen credit that appears following the last image is Coppola's screenwriting credit.

Hollywood films are almost always easily intelligible; for the moment I would like to avoid the argument about whether that is a positive or negative attribute. *Rumble Fish* almost avoids intelligibility in its concentration on mood and ambiance. The above explication is very dependent on knowing the novel. It is a film that bright undergraduates continue to question, even pester me about. They are haunted by it; it has an eerie beauty. It seems to say something about inner aspects of their personalities with which they are not normally in touch. It is possible that this film in its originality and departure from standard genres verges on being a cinematic Rohrschach test. Of all Coppola's canon, it is probably the film that would be most interesting for Reader Response criticism with that approach's focus on individualistic reactions to artistic texts. Conventional Hollywood cinema demands a commonality of response to its texts because that commonality is the best insurance of financial investment. *Rumble Fish* and *One from the Heart* in their financial failure illustrate too well the peril in straying too far from the beaten path of conventionality.

But finally, this is a chapter concerned with the reception of films bearing the appellation "a film by Francis Coppola." Director cinema as an apparatus conditions our response. The name Francis Ford Coppola connotes spectacles, Hollywood entertainment combined with artistic sensibility, Italian weddings, and napalm in the morning. Coppola the individual seems stifled by those expectations: he at times would rather momentarily be Nicholas Ray, or Vincente Minneli, or even Kenneth Anger. And at least with the three films considered in this chapter, he had developed the financial autonomy to experiment with those desires. However, this same experimentation challenges the worth of director cinema if as an apparatus it threatens our capacity to appreciate and enjoy films as distinct and original as *One from the Heart* and *Rumble Fish* because they undermine the consistency upon which director cinema relies.

## NOTES

1. Christopher Potter, "Where, oh where has once-great Coppola gone?" *Ann Arbor News*, November 12, 1983, p. B1.

2. Aaron Latham, "The Movie Man Who Plays God," *Life*, August 1981, pp. 61–74.

3. Jeffrey Wells, "Francis Ford Coppola/Part 2," *Film Journal*, 85, no. 1 (September 21, 1981), 10.

4. Vincent Canby, "Obsession with Technique," *New York Times*, February 21, 1982, p. D13.

5. Sheila Benson, *Los Angeles Times*, January 22, 1982, Calendar, p. 1.

6. Carrie Rickey, "Let Yourself Go!" *Film Comment* (March–April 1982), 43–44.

7. Jonathan Cott, "The Rolling Stone Interview: Francis Coppola," *Rolling Stone*, March 18, 1982, p. 25.

8. *Variety*'s paraphrase was "Dazzling body, empty heart," (January 20, 1982), p. 20. David Denby titled his review "Empty Calories," in *New York*, February 1, 1982, p. 54. Denby's blurb was: "*One from the Heart* is all visual candy. Without characters or plot, it's a bizarre and pointless movie...." Pauline Kael's review

was titled "Melted Ice Cream," in *The New Yorker*, February 1, 1982, pp. 118–120. She commented: "It's easier to get by with an empty hat in the context of Vietnam than it is in a metaphorical Las Vegas... This story being negligible, what we're asked to respond to is Coppola's confectionary artistry."

9. Cott, p. 25.

10. Lillian Ross, "Some Figures on a Fantasy," *The New Yorker*, November 8,1982, pp. 48–50+.

11. Ibid., p. 110.

12. Ibid., pp. 108–109.

13. Ibid., p. 115.

14. Marjorie Rosen, "Francis Ford Coppola," *Film Comment*, 10 (July/August 1974), 47.

15. A good account of the novel's background and a not very flattering view of the film's production is contained in the late Arthur Bell's "One from the Crotch," *Village Voice*, April 5, 1983, pp. 53, 93.

16. David Ansen, "Coppola Courts the Kiddies," *Newsweek*, April 4, 1983, p. 74.

17. Aljean Harmetz, "Making *The Outsiders* a Librarian's Dream," *New York Times*, March 23, 1983.

18. See "Coppola Loses Credit," *Variety*, June 29, 1982, p. 7; also "Coppola in Screen-Credit Brouhaha," *New York*, August 30, 1982, p. 10. Neither piece goes into the issue in much depth.

19. David Thomson and Lucy Gray, "Idols of the King," *Film Comment*, 19, no. 5 (Sept./Oct. 1983), 62.

20. A 14-year-old, Garrick Stoner, wrote an article for the *Chicago Sun-Times* explaining why *The Outsiders* was such a good movie. The title explains all: "Critics don't count for Teens who see their lives in *Outsiders*." *Chicago Sun-Times*, April 28, 1983, p. 90.

21. Thomson, p. 65.

22. Vincent Canby, "Film: *Outsiders*, Teen-Age Violence," *New York Times*, March 25, 1983, p. C3.

23. Gary Arnold, "Greasy Kids Stuff," *Washington Post*, March 25, 1983, p. C1.

24. David Denby, "Romance for Boys," *New York*, April 4, 1983, p. 73.

25. For example, Tom Cruise as Steve went on to *Risky Business, All the Right Moves*, and *Top Gun*. Rob Lowe as Soda Pop went on to *Class, Oxford Blues*, and *About Last Night*. Ralph Macchio went on to *The Karate Kid* and *Teachers*. C. Thomas Howell and Patrick Swayze went on to *Red Dawn*. Emilio Estevez to *Stakeout; Repo Man*; and *The Breakfast Club*. Going into the production, Matt Dillon and Diane Lane were the best known of the cast.

26. Roger Ebert, "*Rumble Fish* Takes Eerie Look at Piranhas as Teens," *Chicago Sun-Times*, October 24, 1983, p. 37.

27. Jack Kroll, "Coppola's Teen-age Inferno," *Newsweek*, November 7, 1983, p. 128.

28. Lawrence O'Toole, "Strange Young Men in a Strange Land," *MacLeans*, 90 (October 24, 1983), 60.

29. The remark was made amid the speculation about *One from the Heart*'s imminent collapse. Richard Corliss, "Presenting Fearless Francis!" *Time*, January 18, 1982, 76.

30. Michael Daly, "A True Tale of Hollywood," *New York*, 17, no. 19 (May 7,

1984), pp. 50, 51. Later in the article Daly describes a rough cut of *Cotton Club*: "Some moments had the commercial promise of *The Godfather*. Others had overtones of *Rumble Fish*. 'I didn't know which way Francis was going to go,' Evans says. 'I was only hoping he wouldn't esoteric it up.' " Daly, p. 57.

31. Jay Scott, "The Wild Ones," *American Film*, no. 6 (April 1983).

32. Coppola told Thomson: "It's very personal. *Rumble Fish* does come out of a certain period of my life when I was about seven, eight, nine, in an area not too far from here . . . I had a brother five years older—I *have* a brother five years older than me who was my idol, who was very, very good to me. Just took me everywhere and taught me everything." Thomson, pp. 65–66.

33. Thomson, p. 61.

34. O'Toole, p. 60.

35. Thomson, p. 66.

36. S. E. Hinton, *Rumble Fish* (New York: Dell, 1975), p. 49.

37. Hinton, pp. 104–105.

38. Ibid., p. 108.

39. Ibid., p. 111.

# 9

## *Coppola Comes to Harlem*

### *The Cotton Club*

In the critical method of this *auteur* study of Francis Coppola, I have self-consciously reined in urges to psychoanalyze the subject, reasoning that such critical practice usually reveals more about the analyst than the subject. The subject's thought processes are at issue in the question of artistic intentions, but all discussion in that area has been carefully buttressed with Coppola's published remarks on the matter. Artistic intentions, in this study, are not important in the literary sense of establishing privileged meaning that must be ferreted out of a film text, but rather for understanding the structuring process imposed on creativity in Hollywood films. We are examining how one man functions in this system, what Hollywood has allowed him to produce and what he has forced Hollywood to allow him to produce. Personal psychology is a factor in how Coppola functions in Hollywood—the journey of his career is at times quite idiosyncratic—but fully diagnosing the driving psychology of this individual is not the aim of this study. Coppola's personal pathology remains simply a difficult factor to be considered with some trepidation.

But as a way of leading into a discussion of *The Cotton Club*, a film with a production background that was a demolition derby of conflicting personal psychologies, for speculative purposes let me momentarily drop the scruples about armchair psychoanalysis and consider Coppola responding to Gene Siskel's question as to whether there was a "master image" in the film:

A single shot can "contain" an entire movie. Henri Langlois believed that. But the trouble with that theory when applied to *The Cotton Club* is that it's such a sprawling movie with such a large cast. We have 287 characters and dozens of show numbers. So it's hard to come up with an image that contains all that. But the one image that came to my mind when you first asked the question didn't involve the shows in the Cotton Club. It was the image of Diane Lane singing with her blond wig and Richard Gere accompanying her with his cornet. That he really played the cornet in the film meant a lot to me and to him. And I really loved it when she sang "Am I Blue?" and he played the cornet obligatto. Personally, I always like the image of a girl singing and a guy playing a trumpet alongside her. But that image doesn't include the black story or the Cotton Club show; so it really doesn't contain all of the film. And that's because I always wanted the movie to be segregated. I always hate in the movies when white characters have black sidekicks. For one thing, they never did. And that especially wasn't true in the world of the Cotton Club, where everything was segregated.[1] (Gene Siskel, "Coppola: America's Tilt-a-Whirl Director," *Chicago Tribune* (December 16, 1984). Copyrighted, *Chicago Tribune Company*, all rights reserved, used with permission.)

The image that jumps into Coppola's head in this passage constitutes a free association with the initial concept of "the master image." Coppola is intrigued with his association, but he seems to sense immediately its implications, and the admonition that the image does not sum up the black portion of the narrative follows quickly in an attempt to deny the momentary truth of the association.

Why from a movie rich in the lore of the Harlem jazz era, an era when black musicians altered the course of American popular music, does Coppola extract an image of two white amateur musicians who were simply doing their best to cover a basic lack of virtuosity? Why not extract an image of the Hines brothers tap dancing, arguably approximating some of the excitement of the original Nicolas Brothers. Or Lonette McKee in her Lena Horne inspired singing of "Ill Wind"? Or Larry Marshall doing an excellent Cab Calloway imitation? In my initial viewing of *The Cotton Club* my impression was that the image of Diane Lane singing "Am I Blue?" in her brightly lit, sterile looking Art Deco nightclub was meant to suggest the shallowness of white music of the era in comparison to the richness of the black music represented at the Cotton Club. (Perhaps a good example of the dangers in attempting to guess artistic intention.)

Coppola's explanation that it meant something to him that Gere and Lane improved their musical abilities in preparing for their roles suggests a perspective on Coppola's personal involvement with the film and a possible meaning for the free association in question. Coppola's stated rationale for coming on Robert Evans' project as a hired hand was that he fell in love with the Jazz Age subject matter.[2] Who wouldn't? The considerable pleasure that can be derived from the film resides in Coppola's commendable recovering of much of that material—the Duke Ellington music, the dancing style, Cab Calloway and "Minnie the Moocher," and the other non-narrative elements. But ultimately, the film's narrative never totally embraces the subject matter of the film's title. The jar between the narrative and the non-narrative elements suggests finally that Coppola's involvement with the subject matter was much like Gere and Lane's attempting to master the musical aspects of their roles; though well-intentioned, it remains dilettant-ish, never fully taking the material to the heart. Just as Coppola's scruples about showing blacks as sidekicks led to his segregation of the fictional black and white characters in the film's narrative, in a sense Coppola essentially segregated himself from the black experience. Even though this is a film with abundant black talent, it is not a film *about* blacks, and the lethargic black response at the box office is not surprising. There is evidence that Coppola showed a liberal's concern with not exploiting the black entertainers of the Cotton Club for a second time. However, besides bringing in 1920s gangster expert William Kennedy to help in writing the screenplay, Coppola should have brought in an equally talented black writer. An enormous amount of money was spent on research and technical advisors to give the film nuance and verisimilitude in re-creating the Cotton Club; but the film lacks a fundamental black sensibility in its creative heart.

That lack led J. Hoberman to comment that on the one hand: "Coppola has taken pains to be authentic and it shows; one needn't apologize for the film's integrity." But on the other: "The black characters are so politely drawn they barely exist."[3] Perhaps bringing in a black writer is too facile a solution to the problem of providing the "center" that the film lacked from its very inception. Coppola's task was not just to take the sow's ear and make it into a silk purse, but to take its fat midsection as well.

However, it was not just the extravagance, waste, and exorbitant expenses of a $47 million production that compromised *The Cotton Club*—the same conditions existed with the more compelling *Apocalypse Now*. Besides Coppola's inability to provide anything more than a polite liberal's political perspective to the racial issues, fundamental problems with the production lay with the givens and methods established by Robert Evans, the producer and originator of the project. This was Coppola's first directorial effort since 1974 that had been originated by someone other than himself, and the results tell much about why Coppola places so much importance in creative control and the power to originate his own projects. The final film is often a showcase for what Coppola does best, his editing, his passion for research, his ability to bring out the best in collaborators—but it still lacks that center that organizes all these attributes into an organic whole. If finger-pointing is in order, Coppola should not be absolved of blame for *The Cotton Club*'s inadequacies. But if the film's production story is viewed as one more parable of how vision and art is stultified in the Hollywood milieu, then Robert Evans is potentially the tale's heavy.

We should recall that this was not the first interaction between our protagonists, Coppola and Evans. Evans had been chief of production at Paramount during the making of *The Godfather* and had overridden Coppola and Puzo by deleting the final scene of Kay lighting candles at a Catholic church to atone for Michael's sins. The result was more emphasis on the preceding shot of Michael shutting the door in Kay's face, which, in light of Kay's later rebellion in *Godfather II*, was a more sensible choice. During the strife of *The Cotton Club*, Evans' claims concerning his role on *The Godfather* became more grandiose: "When Francis turned in *The Godfather*, it looked like a section out of *The Untouchables*. . . . We changed the picture around entirely."[4] Coppola later claimed that what Evans contributed to *The Godfather* "was like what five other executives did."[5]

During the 1970s, Evans developed a reputation as "a painstaking, creative producer of the old school,"[6] based primarily on his success as chief of production at Paramount. During the longest tenure of any modern studio executive, he oversaw production of 300 feature films and developed a reputation as a workaholic. Leaving Paramount to do independent productions, he achieved his pinnacle of fame as a producer with the stylish *Chinatown* in 1975. Considerable celebrity also accrued with his much publicized marriage to Ali MacGraw, which earned him the nickname "the Hollywood prince." Following *Chinatown* Evans' career took a downturn with a series of financial failures culminating with the abysmal *Players* (1979). The same agent who called Evans' attention to *The Godfather* brought him the oversized picture book *The Cotton Club* by James Haskins.

Haskins is a prolific writer with about thirty books to his credit, mostly about black celebrities, and he published *The Cotton Club* to minor fanfare in 1977.[7] Although the book seems quickly written and not meticulously researched,[8] it is interesting reading, never tedious, and one gets a vivid picture of the club, its policies, its attraction, and its historical context. Important to note is that in no way, shape, or form is there any kind of narrative in the original book, other than the exposition of the rise and fall of the club; Haskins does straightforward historical writing. Turning such material into a film has a precedent in Evans' career with *Urban Cowboy*, which started as a magazine piece about Gilley's, a popular Texas Country Western music bar. As with *The Cotton Club*, a story was contrived to fit the locale; and likewise a top male sex star, John Travolta, was brought in for box office pull. One could argue that the Italian disco king was as inappropriate at the country-western Gilley's as Richard Gere was playing the cornet at *The Cotton Club*.

Before Evans received *The Cotton Club*, however, two black producers, Charles Childs and Jim Hinton, optioned the rights to the book with the intention of developing a television mini-series, á la *Roots*, or a Broadway musical. Without a story-line, however, or much interest from the conservative networks, they floundered and were probably delighted to sell the property to Evans for the price of $350,000. As Haskins' research could easily be duplicated with that amount of money available, the exorbitant amount must have been designed mostly for publicity value. The same philosophy applied to the million dollar fee paid to Mario Puzo to develop a narrative from the material, a narrative which was eventually discarded. Evans from the outset was determined to go first class; Haskins probably in his wildest imagination could not have envisioned that his picture book would eventually result in a $47 million movie.

Evans' initial attraction to the subject was the commercial prospect he saw in a milieu that would combine jazz entertainers with underworld figures: "Gangsters, music, and pussy, how could I lose?" he was later to remark.[9] He also reckoned that blacks still wanted to be reminded about the oppression of the past and would support at the box office a film with a number of black performers. On Ted Koppel's "Nightline" Evans made the ludicrous proclamation that *The Cotton Club* would be the first fully integrated film since *Gone with the Wind*—the ignorance and insensitivity of such a remark is monumental. Prior to the production he commented that the prospective film would not star Diana Ross[10]—presumably because of the failure of *The Wiz* and not because of the biography of Billie Holliday, *Lady Sings the Blues*, which unlike *The Cotton Club* gave a black musician star billing. Evans did pursue Richard Pryor to star in the film because of his crossover potential for white audiences. Pryor eventually balked at the idea of Evans directing, which was the original plan, and asked for four million dollars, to which Evans would never agree, thus the less-expensive Gregory Hines was signed to take the black lead. Throughout the pre-production, Evans was convinced the film needed a white star to ensure box office draw. He initially approached Al Pacino, at one point had Sylvester Stallone in tow, and finally settled on Richard Gere. Gere had two crucial stipulations in taking the part: that he play a "nice guy" and that he play the cornet, which Gere had studied in high school. Those two stipulations were to curtail severely the directions Coppola and Kennedy could later go with the screenplay.

The upshot is that Evans was seeking a formula, a way to package success after a series of personal financial failures. He had no passion for the material, no desire to make an artistic statement about the historical oppression of black Americans as represented by Harlem in the Prohibition era, no curiosity in the development of American music.[11] The incentive to make this a commercial success was heightened by Evans' desire to own the film and control the future ancillary rights—similar to Coppola's control and ownership of *Apocalypse Now*.[12] To accomplish this, Evans pursued non-studio funding: Texas oilmen, Arab arms dealers, and finally the principal investor, the Doumani brothers of Las Vegas, who allegedly had Mafia ties. In the scramble to attract private financing for an originally budgeted $24 million film, Evans lost sight of the fact that he did not have a solid script from Puzo, who had been signed on because *The Godfather* aura would attract financing, not because Puzo had any special affinity for the Ellington era. With much of the creative personnel already hired, Dick Sylvert, the production designer, warned Evans that all he had was a "coffee table idea"[13];

Evans asked Sylvert to keep quiet because he was going after new money; Gere and the Doumanis, however, had script approval and were balking at the Puzo script. As a crisis loomed, Evans went to Coppola to be a doctor to his "sick child." As Coppola describes the results:

I looked at it and I saw that there was nothing there, it was a shallow gangster story without any attempt at anything, you know? But in reading some of the research, I started to become more... there's a lot going on in that period and it's very stimulating. It has music, great music and it has theatre—because it *was* a theatre—and it has beautiful dancers. So ultimately I took a shot at the script, then I reworked it... I sort of fell in love with *The Cotton Club*, if I could get to do it the way I see it. It's like an epic in its own way. It *is* an epic. It's a story of the times: it tells the story of the blacks, of the white gangster, about entertainers, everything of those times, like Dos Passos, and the lives all thread through with "Minnie the Moocher" and "Mood Indigo." You can't lose if you handle that right.[14]

Coppola had financial incentives as well for taking the project. Zoetrope's studio was being sold due to the financial failures of *One from the Heart*, *Rumble Fish*, *Hammett*, and *The Escape Artist*. According to different sources, Coppola was personally in debt to Chase Manhattan Bank and other lenders to the tune of $10–20 million, which he was obligated to pay back in $1–2 million installments for ten years.[15] Coppola had already committed to a quick fix of $2.5 million to direct *The Pope of Greenwich Village* with Al Pacino starring. As production delays slowed the starting date of that film, *The Cotton Club*'s similar directing fee, as well as a $500,000 writer's fee, combined with an opportunity to immerse himself in Harlem jazz, became irresistible.

Evans had sobered on the idea of directing *The Cotton Club* himself and was ecstatic when Coppola announced his willingness to assume the responsibility. Coppola, however, had not forgotten *The Godfather* experience with Evans and had an ironclad clause put in his contract specifying his creative control and final cut on the prospective film. This would be later tested in court, with Coppola victorious. When Coppola and Evans had signed their agreement, the felicitous relationship that had existed in the initial script conferences soon ended. Evans still regarded *The Cotton Club* as a Robert Evans film and had a jealous, overprotective relationship with it. A film directed by Francis Coppola by this point in Coppola's career, however, was not easily someone else's film.

The first flare-up occurred over Coppola's casting of Fred Gwynne as Frenchy DeMange. Evans objected that someone known mostly as Herman Munster of TV fame would present difficulties. Coppola, remembering his difficulties casting Al Pacino and Marlon Brando for *The Godfather*, immediately put the issue to a test, threatening to walk out if his authority was not respected. Evans backed down, but acrimony characterized their relationship thenceforth.

The intrigue, in-fighting, and power plays of *The Cotton Club*'s production are well documented in Michael Daly's *New York* exposé, "The Making of *The Cotton Club*: A True Tale of Hollywood." The article, though well-researched, sensitive, and thought-provoking, also has its sensational moments and had Hollywood gossip columns buzzing for months prior to the film's premiere. A producer reportedly offered $500,000 for the screen rights to courtroom documents connected with the film.[16] A common punchline was that there would be no way the film could top the drama of the production. Frontline reviewers, after having heard so much about the strife on the set, often voiced surprise that the film was actually good. What Daly's article did suggest, however, was that though there was incredible stress and anxiety connected both with Coppola's wranglings with Evans and the Doumanis as well as with his Zoetrope-related agonies, Coppola maintained an incredible clarity and concentration when it came to creative matters of how the film was staged. A veteran Coppola watcher would not be surprised; it was simply a recapitulation of his working method on *The Godfather* and *Apocalypse Now*. Unlike *The Godfather*, however, Coppola did not start with a strong narrative with mythic resonance, and unlike *Apocalypse Now* he did not have four years to wrestle with the thematic consequences of the material. *The Cotton Club* was rushed due to commitments that Evans had made to creative personnel signed on before Coppola. In fact $13 million had been spent before Coppola came on the project.

Even so, and despite the rushed nature of the production, Coppola's conception of the film went through an evolution. Daly describes his first impulse with the material:

On April 5, Coppola completed his first draft. He had pieced together a historical montage of the Harlem Renaissance that included civil-rights marches and readings by black poets. Evans says, "Suddenly we had a history lesson that read like a PBS documentary. I hated it. Richard Gere hated it. Francis loved it. And the more everybody hated it, the more Francis loved it."

The day of the Academy Awards, Evans flew to Las Vegas to present the script to the Doumanis and Sayyah. He enclosed a note that he said Coppola had written to him. Signed "F.," this "author's note to the producer" had actually been written by Evans himself. It read, "Well after 22 days, here is the blueprint. Now let's get down to writing a script. As we've said before . . . 'background makes foreground'— now let's get to the foreground. You always use the word 'MAGIC' . . . We're going to touch it again!" The investors were apparently not impressed, and they suspended any further financing.

"To me, it wasn't a script," Ed Doumani says.[17]

Of course subsequent, more commercial drafts brought the investors back on the project. However, Coppola's initial draft should be put in the drift of his career at this point in time. With *One from the Heart*, *Rumble Fish*, and *Apocalypse Now*, as well as interviews of the period and a signed article in the *Washington Post*, Coppola had shown marked boredom and aversion to films with strong narrative elements, instead showing more interest in mood, texture, visual design, and ambiance.[18] Also worth noting was Coppola's respect for historical research and reconstruction as well as a liberal's sensitivity to black problems shown in interviews, where he lauded the current generation of black actors and decried their difficulty finding work. Finally, there was his interest in the development of American music fostered by the musical tradition of his own family. All indications suggest Coppola's first draft of *The Cotton Club* was his purest impulse in connection with this material and that perhaps Coppola's sensibilities would indeed have been better served with a PBS documentary than the film that eventually evolved. From this point forward, Coppola would be subjected to tremendous pressure from producers and actors to make the film more commercial. Not to be slighted was Coppola's own personal compulsion to revive a career that journalists were proclaiming on the skids.

Another perspective on Coppola's task in moving away from that first documentary-style screenplay could be provided by a 1948 remark by documentary director Robert Flaherty: "You cannot superimpose studio-fabricated plots on an actual setting without finding that the reality of the background will show up the artificiality of your story."[19] As an historical film, *The Cotton Club* did not use an actual setting. They instead recreated at a cost of $5 million an exact replica of the original. Former workers from the original club were dazzled by the set's authenticity, and the Smithsonian belatedly tried to purchase it to create an exhibit. Still, Flaherty's point is that one must find the story within the material one is dealing with: in *Nanook* he contrived a narrative about an Eskimo hunting in the arctic. In a similar manner Coppola found that being on location in a jungle altered the way he made *Apocalypse Now*. From that vantage point, what was the material of the Cotton Club as an historical entity, and what would one expect to emanate from it dramatically?

In 1923, Owney Madden, one of the leading mob figures of that time, bought Harlem's Cotton Club from Jack Johnson, the famous black heavyweight fighter, with the purpose of turning it into a front for his gangland activities. Thus from the outset we find the confluence of two strains of American culture, entertainment and crime, strains still inextricably linked in the present. Harlem of the 1920s was undergoing a renaissance; it was the meeting ground of a vast array of black culture: poets, artists, writers, and musicians. It was also the object of white Americans' awakening curiosity about black culture, particularly toward black styles of dance and music, which seemed to have a spirituality and a sexuality that whites could copy but not capture. One fad of the era became "slumming," going up from Manhattan into Harlem to hear jazz, the new black music, at its source. Duke Ellington, Cab Calloway, Bill "Bojangles" Robinson, Lena Horne, the Nicholas Brothers, Ethel Waters, and many others used the Cotton

Club as a launching pad to wider fame. That they were also "used" in the process is part of the club's function as a metaphor for recent black history. Adam Clayton Powell called it "entertainment sharecropping," but the Cotton Club also provided a window to black culture where talented black artists and musicians could advance themselves and slowly change the attitudes toward, and the economic status of, their race.

The club embodied the morality of the period, the cynicism about authority, the new sexual permissiveness, and the affluence—the $5 admission price was stiff. Gangsters at this time from a certain perspective were doing the public a favor in providing them with the liquor that the government had prohibited with the 18th Amendment. Thus there was the additional attraction of being able to rub elbows with notorious gangsters at the establishment, and Frenchy DeMange was installed as the manager of the club to capitalize on this fascination. Celebrities flocked to the location. The Duchess of Windsor dubbed it "the aristocrat of Harlem."

From this material, one would not think that a nice-guy, white cornet player would emerge as the main character. But such was the production's prerequisite under which Coppola had to labor in developing the script. Perhaps understandably, he sought help. Mickey Rourke had sent Coppola a copy of *Legs*, a novel about Jack "Legs" Diamond, a notorious 1920s gangster, by Pulitzer Prize-winning author William Kennedy. As Kennedy seemed expert in the culture of the 1920s, particularly in relation to gangsters, Coppola enlisted him to work on the screenplay. The collaboration became a close one, and as principal photography loomed, they worked in a manic, feverish style that Kennedy was to characterize as similar to working in the city room of a newspaper. Reportedly, the pair went through forty re-writes of the script, much to the consternation of other production personnel who wondered in what direction the film would go next.

Richard Jameson suggested: "Kennedy's 'Albany Novels' about the murderous glamour of oldtime gangsterism move to a rhythm of pungent detail and suggestive elision that is echoed in the movement of this film—tense and jazzy rather than slow and operatic in the manner of *The Godfather*."[20] Based on Kennedy's tone in *Legs*, it can also be surmised that Kennedy brought a strong sense of cynicism to *The Cotton Club*'s narrative; his approach is iconoclastic and anti-romantic. Thus it is not surprising that Kennedy found the "perpetual task of enhancing Richard Gere" an onerous one. The character in the narrative who probably bears the heaviest Kennedy stamp is Dutch Schultz, who very much resembles the portrait of Legs Diamond in Kennedy's novel. Both have hair-trigger, violent, sadistic tempers in the world of men, but both have nagging shrewish wives who seem to cow them, and from whom they seek escape in a younger mistress. However, in the novel *Legs*, we look at the gangster through the eyes of the crooked lawyer Marcus, who is educated and understands the anti-social evil of the gangster, but is nonetheless attracted and fascinated with him, something like a moth to flame. The perspective forces us to consider our own interest in the legendary gangster. In *The Cotton Club*, however, we view Dutch Schultz through the eyes of Gere's Dixie Dwyer, who takes a moralistic, scolding tone toward Schultz. In perhaps the lamest speech of the film, Dwyer admonishes Schultz: "Do you want to get into everybody's life and run it forever? Do you want to be Genghis Khan for Christ's sake?" Because of historical necessity, Dixie Dwyer cannot be the one to end Schultz's existence; other gangsters do that, and thus Dixie pales as a cathartic figure in comparison to the virile and violent gangsters, much the way Douglas Fairbanks, Jr. did as a musician/good guy foil to Edward G. Robinson's *Little Caesar*. However, in that film, unlike *The Cotton Club*'s Dutch Schultz, Robinson's Rico was the protagonist of the drama. The gangster, despite his anti-social behavior, embodied a mythic dissatisfaction with elements of modern urban life. The powerful, unconscious identification with the gangster was something that Coppola should have known from his experiences with *The Godfather*. His basic impulse in both *The Cotton Club* and *Godfather II* seems directed at de-fusing this identification.

That Coppola and Kennedy felt straitjacketed by Gere's stipulations perhaps led to a scene added late in the writing process in which Dixie, like George Raft, is dispatched to Hollywood for screen tests and to front for an East Coast gangster. A producer watches the rushes of Dixie and comments to an underling: "This kid can't act. The kid stinks as an actor. He has a good face. He has a good voice. Does not look like a fruit. He looks like a gangster. He could be a great gangster." How much more credibility the film would have had if Gere had truly played a gangster and not an historical impossibility, a white musician playing at the Cotton Club.

Kennedy's presence on the film generated much good publicity for the production. He had won a Pulitzer Prize and a MacArthur Foundation "genius" grant. His Albany trilogy of novels was being discovered by literary critics and optioned by movie producers. However, the possibility exists that Kennedy's presence had something to do with swinging the weight of the film toward the gangsters and white characters. Although the film's structure suggests a parallel between two pairs of brothers whose lives are affected by the Cotton Club, one pair the black Williams brothers, the other the white Dwyer brothers, the predominant screen time is devoted to the white characters. Although some of the most memorable scenes occur with the black characters—the brothers' reunion, the visit to the Hoofer's club, a view of their home life—these scenes seem improvised and not essential to the narrative.

The frantic germination stage when Coppola and Kennedy went through supposedly forty drafts was characterized by reduction. Kennedy later commented that he had approached the material as he would a novel but had finished with a short story. Kennedy described writing with Coppola: "Concision is the operative word with Coppola, who will intercut even a short scene with another one to accelerate the pace. I thought I was already a concise writer, but after Astoria I created a screenwriting axiom: What you wrote yesterday, cut in half today."[21] Perhaps this acceleration and distillation contributed to Pauline Kael's observation that the film felt like a music video. Apparently much was shot and left out—one source says 35 musical numbers were shot for the film—and it was announced in 1986 that some of the unused footage will be restored for a four-hour television version. The scripting process also reflects Coppola's increasing facility with word processing and computer information storage systems. Coppola deleted, recalled, and transposed scenes at will, according to Kennedy. The malleability of the script is reflected in an inspection of the August 22, 1983 shooting script, which has major departures from the final film. The entire kidnapping-of-Frenchy section is missing, a subplot of Sandman as a runner for the numbers game is woven throughout, Dixie's servitude to Dutch is more drawn out, the Grand Central Station production finale is missing, and so on. Critic Gene Siskel found the film too short and worried that exhibitors were curtailing the length of films for financial considerations, at the expense of artistic considerations.[22] Perhaps the mini-series approach will rectify that.

In the critical reception to *The Cotton Club*, reviewers were quick to laud the scene wherein Coppola crosscuts between the Hines' dance solo and the machine-gun murder of Dutch Schultz and his mob. Sheila Benson called it "the sequence that makes *The Cotton Club* soar."[23] The scene provided an easy way of talking about the Coppola touch because on the surface it has so many similarities to the baptism/execution montage of *The Godfather* (reviewers had forgotten about the ox slaughter/Kurtz murder of *Apocalypse Now*). However, on closer inspection the scene may be overrated, and instead the best example of Coppola's genius for Eisensteinian montage is the finale. To explain the weakness of the former, we should begin with Coppola's explanation of the tap dancing montage:

> While making the movie I operated on a simple theme that I thought the film was about—the concept of servitude and how you can get out of a position of servitude only through your talent. And so the metaphor came to me when Gregory Hines says, "I'll kill 'em with my tap shoes," meaning that he's too weak to kill 'em any way else.
>
> But that situation doesn't apply to just the blacks in this movie. I find myself in the same situation all the time. When I'm in a tight spot all I have that can help get me out of trouble is a demonstration of my talent.
>
> So when I tried to come up with a way to restate that theme at the end of the picture, I started with the notion that tap-dancing sounds like machine guns. And so what you see is, in effect, the black guy murdering the white establishment with his tap shoes.[24]

Unfortunately, this explanation does not mesh with the text of the film in the way that the baptism/execution montage of *The Godfather* did. In terms of the servitude of the Dixie Dwyer character, he simply exchanges an oppressive boss (Schultz) for a patriarchal one (Madden). In terms of talent being the vehicle for his freedom, he simply gets a lucky break based on his good looks; as the Hollywood producer says: "The kid can't act." Again, the Dwyer plot compromises thematic intent in the film. As far as the black plot, from one view it could be said that the metaphor is true, that historically blacks have broken their servitude through talent, that the athletes and entertainers have paved the way for the rest. Another view says that for every Sandman Williams who attains economic independence based on his talent there are 10,000 ordinary blacks who are oppressed because of the color of their skin, and that the elevation of a few contributes to the oppression of the many. In terms of the film, it is not Dutch Schultz who is exploiting Williams, but the genial Madden; thus Coppola's metaphor that Sandman is "murdering the white establishment" does not really stand up. (Had the subplot that Sandman was running numbers to survive while building his dancing career been left in, the montage would have made a bit more sense.)

Far more satisfying and ingenious is the final production number montage wherein the conclusion of the narrative is blended together with a Cotton Club production spectacular such that it becomes difficult to distinguish between the two locations. On stage, Gregory Hines seems to be leading the troupe through a Grand Central Station number, dancing porters and ticket takers, etc. But on the same set we also see Schultz's widow escorting his coffin to a train, Sandman and Lila going off on a honeymoon, Tish Dwyer escorting Dixie to the train, and then Dixie meeting Vera at the train. Breaking down the proscenium arch so that production numbers soared in a way not possible for a theater audience to observe was a Busby Berkeley trademark, but the Berkeley spectaculars were always discrete from the flimsy narrative that framed them; no attempt at integration was made. With *The Cotton Club* we are in the territory of meta-movie; the distortion between the staged and the real becomes a commentary on the entire fictional enterprise, not a lyrical ode to fantasy in the sense that Michael Powell and Emeric Pressburger used this device in *The Red Shoes* (1948). On one level we see a reversal of the obvious narrative direction; the film has suggested the impossibility of romantic union between Sandman and Lila, as well as Dixie and Vera. Suddenly with no explanation this is reversed. As such it resembles the deus ex machina of the messenger that rescues Mack the Knife at the end of Brecht's *Three-Penny Opera* or the fantasy reversal ending of Murnau's *The Last Laugh* (1924). The impossibility of the ending invites a reconsideration of our experience of the fiction. Furthermore, the contrivance of the ending extends the contrivance of the entire film, of a film about the black Cotton Club and its music, dependent on concocted white violence and romance for its viability. The drive and energy of the Ellington music in the production number overwhelm concern for the narrative, just as in the larger sense the memorable and exceptional aspects of *The Cotton Club* as a film are the musical production numbers and not the worn out rehash of the gangster saga. Coppola gives us the romantic union that the musical genre seems to demand, but it is not given to us straight; there is a knowing wink. In conception, this is the best realized ending of the entire Coppola canon, and had the same daring and ingenuity been displayed throughout it would have been a much more inspiring film.

In some ways, *The Cotton Club* compromises the vision of Coppola's *Godfather II*. Coppola had been disturbed with the crowds cheering Michael as he slammed the door in the face of Kay at the end of *The Godfather*. He had made people identify with a monster, and so he sought to destroy the gangster myth with *Godfather II*, to show Michael for what he really was. That vision was tarnished somewhat by the insistence that there were "good" gangsters who were turn-of-the-century Robin Hoods, represented in the section dealing with young Vito. We see the good gangster myth continued in *The Cotton Club* with Owney Madden, who seems a level, fair, intelligent gangster, much preferable to the psychopathic Schultz. The historical reality that Madden was a murderer and was always willing to use ruthless violence against legitimate competition is, of course, obscured; what will remain in our minds is that he got his watch smashed by Big Frenchy.

The charisma of Bob Hoskin's Madden overshadows some of the more interesting characteristics of James Remar's Dutch Schultz, possibly the most complex character in the film. Schultz is the one character, aside from the musicians, who truly seems to like music, and in the opening scene he demonstrates a connoisseur's knowledge of lesser known jazz musicians. This man, capable of murdering Joe Flynn for a racist insult, in turn exploits blacks, although he expresses an integrationist's interest in getting "Micks" into his gang. Impulses of gratitude and friendship are twisted into cruelty in a murderer who can be reduced to a whining boy by his wife. Visually, Coppola in several shots evokes Herzog's *Nosferatu* by Schultz's posturing and the lighting style; the pathetic vampire image is apt.[25] However, in the end Schultz is reduced to a movie convention, as he dies in the manner of the gangsters of *Scarface*, *Little Caesar*, and *The Public Enemy*, and we watch Madden go off to his horse farm in Arkansas. (The real Madden married a postmaster's daughter and died of emphysema at the age of 73 in 1965.)

With *The Godfather* there was the sense that gangsters were mythic characters somehow removed from interacting with everyday people; exactly how they made their money was never clear and they did not seem to harm the innocent bystander. *The Cotton Club* presents a somewhat grittier view. At one point gang warfare leads to innocent children being shot. The black businessmen who are being squeezed by the Schultz mob are given a scene where they pass up the chance to respond violently. When Tish Dwyer hears that her son saved a gangster's life, she responds: "Why did you help that awful man?" But again the violence against blacks seems to emanate specifically from Schultz, not from Madden. The same Tish Dwyer who had turned her nose up at Schultz later calls Madden "Mr. Broadway" and introduces him to her son. In this fictional universe there are good gangsters and bad gangsters; they move on a mythic plane only marginally connected to reality, but without the self-reflective perspective of a film such as *Bonnie and Clyde.*

The classic gangster films, detective films, or other urban action films of the 1930s and 1940s often momentarily broke their narrative progression for a brief stint by some famous jazz musician—for instance, in *Song of the Thin Man* Nick Charles' pursuit of the killer is interrupted by a Gene Crupa drum solo. The music interlude would have no connection with the narrative, but before television the audience had not been saturated with images of musicians entertaining and enjoyed these little excursions. Although *The Cotton Club* was conceived forty years later with the notion that it would combine the best of the Warner Brothers gangster and musical genre films of the classical period, there is not the same leisure about presenting musical interludes. The dictate of pace for a modern audience generally allows only musical numbers that support the narrative rather than interrupt it. Typically, other action is cut into a song, as with Lonette McKee's singing of "Ill Wind" juxtaposed with a montage of Harlem gang warfare. (A much more effective montage than the tap dance/ machine gun juxtaposition, I might add.) A few scattered numbers appear in complete form rather gratuitously, for instance the "Minnie the Moocher" number performed by Larry Marshall, which only seems to be in the film because it is such a good impersonation of Cab Calloway. The fact that we have moved from the club's Ellington period to the Calloway period really has no bearing on the narrative. One of the best examples of a number supporting the narrative progression is the "Crazy Rhythm" dance duet between the Williams brothers. The song's words "You go your way, I'll go mine" take on irony because the brothers are enacting a public reconciliation after an earlier falling apart. Demonstrating the fortuitous nature of some of any film's best moments, the song was only picked at the last minute because another song's rights proved too expensive. This particular scene had added resonance because the Hines brothers in real life had broken up their brother act, and at Coppola's urging were re-creating for film some of the feelings that had transpired. It is interesting that despite Coppola's recent disaffection with the narrative portion of filmmaking, he apparently felt a strong compulsion to maintain narrative drive with the production numbers.

Many reviewers complained that stylistically Coppola and cinematographer Stephen Goldblatt did not know how to film the dance numbers, as cutting, close-ups, and use of the moving camera appear throughout. Fred Astaire during his classic period was an advocate of the single-take, fairly static full-body-shots as the only way to preserve the integrity of the dancer's art. (Similar to Chaplin's aesthetic of camera placement.) Going against this notion, Coppola had fired Hermes Pan, Astaire's choreographer during *Finian's Rainbow*, and adopted a disjunctive method of filming musical production numbers that seemed to jazz up the 1947 musical for the 1968 audience. Film technique compensated for the inadequacies of the performance element. *The Cotton Club*'s tradition is more that of a backstage musical focusing on the lives of entertainers than the tradition of the operetta, where ordinary characters burst into song or dance in the middle of ordinary life, as was seen in *Finian's Rainbow*. Thus, borrowing from the more "realistic" tradition, as well as a tradition placing more emphasis on performance virtuosity, would seem to demand the Astaire approach to camera placement. However, while this film borrows, it is never a full-scale recapitulation of the studio era musical. Many felt that it was a self-conscious "art film," and the dutch angles, the expressionist lighting styles, and the mediated performance numbers would support this view. The only scene that leaves the reality of the performance untampered with is Big Frenchy's smashing of Madden's watch, which is a study in comic timing.[26] From the musical purist's point of view, the dance numbers should have been presented uninterrupted in the manner of the watch scene. However, this film is characteristic of Coppola in presenting a hybrid of styles, never letting us escape totally into the conventions and expectations of a particular genre of filmmaking.

That the film did not give itself more wholeheartedly to the musical elements was the origin of a rather heated debate in the *Village Voice* about whether the film was racist. The controversy began when Stanley Crouch interviewed black workers on the film for a piece titled "The Rotton Club" and suggested the film was no better in its production racial policy than the original club. He interviewed Howard "Stretch" Johnson, who had been a chorus boy at the Club in the 1930s and later became a professor of sociology and served as the film's technical advisor. Johnson commented:

They had the opportunity to present great black entertainment on a scale never before shown on film. But they lacked the courage and the faith in the public. What they chose to do was present falsehood by focusing on the gangsters. Had they gone whole hog and really shown how the black talent gave poetic expression of life and love in their art, all the while surrounded by these other elements, the viewer would have seen *why* people went to The Cotton Club. They didn't go up there to see gangsters. . . .

There is some of the greatest entertainment on film you ever saw in your life, but they only show snippets of it. It was too powerful. When Gere saw those black performers performing the way they did, he ran scared and threatened to raise holy hell, threatened to leave the film after they had half the footage.[27]

Crouch went on to question why Bob Wilbur, a white jazz historian, had been hired to re-create the Ellington sound with a mostly white band. Angry letters responding to Crouch suggested that Crouch was a black racist and that Wilbur was a pre-eminent historian of that period, and that for the most part the only musicians interested today in re-creating that period's sound are white. Coppola had used black musicians to play as the on-screen Cotton Club orchestra and then dubbed over them later with Wilbur's musicians with the intention of getting the most authentic sound possible. The on-screen musicians were understandably disturbed that their playing was not acceptable for the film, but a white amateur's, Richard Gere's, was. Such paradoxes seem to characterize the production on every level.

Other black writers and the black press seemed to treat the film gingerly, happy that a large body of blacks were being employed, but dissatisfied with the results. A writer in the *Black Film Review* summed it up:

It seems to me that Coppola has given us something not so dissimilar to the real Cotton Club, and instead of exploring the peculiarities of a situation where blacks found themselves conforming to white expectations, placed us, as viewers, in the position of whites who came to the nightclub. We see singers and dancers on stage and in their dressing rooms, but their stories (and the real story of The Cotton Club) remain to be told.[28]

In terms of Coppola's career, it seems ironic that black audiences flocked to *The Godfather* despite its lack of even token black characters and the open racism of some of the central characters. Blacks recognized a cynicism about the way society was run in that film that was close to home. The Corleones' taking care of one's own could be taken as a prescription for how blacks could survive and prosper in an Anglo culture. With *The Cotton Club* blacks felt they were being paid lip service, the Gere/Lane romance was obviously more central to the narrative than the Hines/McKee counterpart, and the black box office reception was weak.

The overall box office reception was by no means disastrous. *Variety* estimated the film grossed a respectable 25 million dollars domestically, which put it in the top three or four holiday films of the 1984 season. Orion gave it the heaviest advertising push of the season, which probably contributed to the record sum paid for video cassette rights for the film. The film did well internationally as well.[29] Still, it's difficult to imagine the film paying back the $47 million reportedly spent on the production. Ironically, the film that ran away with the 1984 box office championship was *Beverly Hills Cop*, which made a mockery of the idea that white audiences would not support a film with a black star at the center (although it remains to be seen whether Eddie Murphy playing a black man in a black man's world would have such appeal).

A representative survey of the critical response to the film shows a very even split.[30] Jack Kroll called it "one of the few original films of the year," and "something of a miracle."[31] Roger Ebert found many echoes of *The Godfather* in the film, called it "one of the year's best," and observed that it was a "somewhat cynical movie about a very cynical time."[32] Paul Attanasio wrote about the meta–movie elements and concluded that the film: "adventurously questions the formulas of Hollywood; its success in doing so without a hint of boredom or pretension augurs a whole new way of making movies. It's the most entertaining art film of the year."[33]

The negative reviews were reminiscent of the reaction to *One from the Heart*, complaining of shallow, cold, visual pyrotechnics without substantive content. The most interesting of the middling reviews were Hoberman's and Andrew Sarris's in the *Village Voice*. Sarris's first filmgoing experience after a six-month severe illness was *The Cotton Club*, and in the review he playfully refers to himself as "Rip":

On the plus side was Francis Coppola's undeniable flair for making *cinema*, in the French phrase, a level of cinema, moreover, that most of his contemporaries seem to have forgotten existed. Rip felt about Coppola's direction the way he felt about Brando's acting. He hadn't liked either entity much lately, both both were always something special even during their most misguided virtuosity. For Rip, Coppola was an authentically modern dissonant auteur who would be studied for years to come.[34]

Sarris's rather chatty, gossipy review never does explain what he feels is "special" about the film, at one point remarking without elaboration: "The brilliance of *The Cotton Club*, Rip concluded, was ice-cold and almost completely lacking in emotional affect." This seems to support the earlier contention that Coppola is a "modern dissonant auteur," in that the modernist approach tends to eschew audience identification with movie star personas, perhaps for Sarris resulting in an emotional coldness. In the world of exorbitantly expensive film production, movie stars are seen as a necessity, but Coppola's basic impulse seems to be to subvert their power. Hence the impression in both positive and negative reviews is that there is a lack of fire in the Gere/Lane relationship. But contrary to the evaluation of Gere and Lane's performance, the supporting players in most reviews are applauded for making strong although brief impressions. Coppola *is* at odds with the notion that a film should be constructed around a star persona, but his ability to exact vivid performances from an ensemble is as strong as ever in *The Cotton Club*. Thus Coppola does not easily fit the modernist cubbyhole.

This can be demonstrated in other elements as well. Coppola places great demands for verisimilitude, a hallmark of the classical Hollywood cinema, in his fastidious research and mania for accurate re-creation of historical periods. But the same mimesis is muddied with expressionist camera techniques and the production finale's modernist violation of spatial/temporal continuity and narrative causal linkage. In some ways *The Cotton Club* is disappointingly conventional: the use of Gere as the star anchor of the action, the programmatic gangster violence, the unremarkable romances; but then these elements jar with the abrasive, modernist elements, which almost demand that we not take seriously the companion classical narrative elements.

Coppola's singularity resides on the ambiguity such filmic schizophrenia produces. In our culture a $47 million "Art film" is oxymoronic and Coppola is a subversive. Coppola states that his ultimate objective is to make more films faster and cheaper so that his brand of experimentation is not so financially dangerous. The strategy of playing off commercial films versus personal films seems to be breaking down: Coppola seems to no longer have the patience for the separation. Whether the resulting hybrids will vault him toward the goals he has established remains to be seen, but these films have a way of unsettling notions of what popular culture should be, and that in itself is valuable.

## NOTES

1. Gene Siskel, "Coppola: America's Tilt-a-Whirl Director," *Chicago Tribune*, December 16, 1984, Sec. 13, p. 8.

2. David Thomson and Lucy Gray, "Idols of the King," *Film Comment*, 19, no. 5 (Sept./Oct. 1983), p. 75. Coppola comments: "I knew that *The Cotton Club* material was so rich that, if I had control, there was no reason why I couldn't make a beautiful film out of it."

3. Hoberman, "Tall, Tan, and Not So Terrific," *Village Voice*, December 18, 1984, p. 77.

4. Julie Salomon, "Budget Busters: *The Cotton Club*'s Battle of the Bulge," *Wall Street Journal*, Dec. 13, 1984, p. 22.

5. William Kennedy, "William Kennedy's Cotton Club Stomp," *Vanity Fair* (November 1984), 48.

6. David Pirie, *Anatomy of the Movies*, (New York,: Macmillan, 1981), p. 80. The book includes a seven page article by Evans on his career. Besides Pirie's book, another good account of Evans's career is: Paul Rosenfield, "Bob Evans: The Other Gatsby," *Los Angeles Times Calendar*, December 4, 1983, pp. 30+.

7. Jim Haskins, *The Cotton Club* (New York: Random House, 1977).

8. Joel E. Siegel commented: "It's an interesting but shockingly slipshod study of the Jazz Age Harlem night spot where great black artists performed for "whites only" audiences. In the final chapter, Haskins informs us that 'Harold Arlen is dead as well, but his life and career were long and successful,' an observation that should come as a big surprise to composer Arlen, who remains among the living in his Central Park West apartment. A new edition of the book, keyed to the film's release, repeats the unfortunate error." "One from the Godfather," *City Paper (Washington)*, 4, no. 52 (December 28, 1984), p. 12.

9. Michael Daly, "A True Tale of Hollywood," *New York*, May 7, 1984, p. 43.

10. Aljean Harmetz, "Producer of *Popeye* to try *Cotton Club*," *New York Times*, December 12, 1980, p. C14. The exact quotation was: "We won't have Diana Ross playing Lena Horne." At the time of this article, Robert Altman was to be the director.

11. Evans told a group of USC film students that his tie to the era was that his father had been a dentist in Harlem.

12. Daly, p. 45.

13. Dale Pollock, "Trouble at the Cotton Club," *Los Angeles Times Calendar*, December 4, 1983, p. 31.

14. Thomson, p. 74.

15. Although the reports vary, Dale Pollock's interview/personality piece seems authoritative: "He's temporarily saddled with annual payments of $2.5 million to assorted banks and lenders..." "Coppola the Artist," p. 1A. See also Lillian Ross' "Some Figures on a Fantasy," *The New Yorker*, November 8, 1982, pp. 48–50+.

16. Barbara Gravstark, "Tapped for Stardom," *American Film*, 10, no. 3 (December 1984), p. 31.

17. Daly, p. 46.

18. Pollock, "Coppola the Artist," p. 26. Coppola commented: "I'm interested in more of a spatial story, where you dump whole buckets of story on the audience and it *absorbs* the film. That's *Apocalypse Now* and *Cotton Club* certainly. I have a kind of spatial brain—I don't think in a linear way."

19. Siegfried Kracauer, *Theory of Film* (New York: Oxford Press, 1971), 260.

20. Richard T. Jameson, "It Is, Too, Good," *Film Comment*, 21, no. 2 (March/April 1985), 52.

21. Kennedy, p. 47.

22. Gene Siskel, "Flaws Don't Spoil Show in *Cotton Club*," *Chicago Tribune*, December 14, 1984, p. 1D.

23. Sheila Benson, "The Sequence That Makes *The Cotton Club* Soar," *Los Angeles Times Calendar* (December 23, 1984), p. 3A.

24. Siskel, "Coppola," p. 8.

25. Albert Johnson claimed that the image was "an homage to Mervyn LeRoy's *I am a Fugitive from a Chain Gang*," thinking of that film's last scene. "*The Cotton Club*," *Film Quarterly*, 38, no. 4 (Summer 1985), p. 19.

26. When asked about the watch scene, William Kennedy responded: "My chief contribution to that was keeping it in the film. That scene came from Fred Gwynne and Hoskins—actually written by Gwynne. People around Francis kept wanting to cut it on grounds that it was too wacko. I loved it and lobbied for months to keep it." David Thomson, "The Man Has Legs," *Film Comment*, 21, no. 2 (March/April 1985), 54.

27. Stanley Crouch, "The Rotten Club," *Village Voice*, February 5, 1985, p. 57.

28. Jerome Bailey (?), "The Cotton Club," *The Black Film Review*, no. 2 (February 1985), 5.

29. The film was number one for two weeks in Paris. French distributor Pierre Kalfon attributed this to his decision to downplay the gangster violence and emphasize the music in his marketing strategy. He commented: "I'm a former musician myself and I immediately realized the importance of Cotton Club to jazz. It is a film full of life, movement, music and joy—and that's what is drawing French filmgoers into the theater, not guns and violence." Kalfon also created a half-hour

documentary for French television about the Cotton Club, which coincided with the release of the film. "Gallic Distrib Produces TV Spec to Shed Light on *Cotton Club*," *Variety*, January 2, 1985, pp. 7, 20.

30. Coming out for the film were: Jack Kroll (*Newsweek*), David Sterritt (*Christian Science Monitor*), Paul Attanasio (*Washington Post*), Andrew Sarris (*Village Voice*), Gene Siskel (*Chicago Tribune*), Roger Ebert (*Chicago Sun Times*), Jack Mathews (*USA Today*), Klad (*Variety*), Catherine Rambeau (*Detroit Free Press*), Sheila Benson (*LA Times*), Tom Milne (*Sight and Sound*), Michael Healy *(Denver Post)*, and Joe Pollack (*St. Louis Post Dispatch*). Coming out against the film were: Ian Pearson (*Newsweek*), Stanley Kauffmann (*The New Republic*), Richard Corliss (*Time*), David Denby (*New York*), Pauline Kael (*The New Yorker*), Vincent Canby (*New York Times*), Joel Siegel (*City Paper-Washington*), Susan Stark (*Detroit News*), J. Hoberman (*Village Voice*), Neil Gabler and Jeffrey Lyons of "Sneak Previews," Gerald Nachman (*San Francisco Examiner*), and Bill Cosford (*Miami Herald*). Further reflecting the ambivalent response, many of the positive reviews had qualms about some of the material, and many of the negative reviews had favorable things to say about certain elements of the film.

31. Jack Kroll, "Harlem on my Mind," *Newsweek*, December 24, 1984, pp. 52–53.

32. Roger Ebert, "*Cotton Club* is Simply Great," *Chicago Sun-Times*, December 14, 1985, pp. 53, 57.

33. Paul Attanasio, "*Cotton Club*: Coppola's Triumph," *Washington Post*, December 14, 1984, pp. C1, C2.

34. Andrew Sarris, "O Hollywood! O Mores!" *Village Voice*, March 5, 1985, p. 51.

# 10

## The Hired Hand

Coppola came on *The Cotton Club* as a "hired gun" with an exorbitant director's fee prominent in his motivation. Still, there is the sense that through the script wranglings, the fights with Robert Evans, and the interaction with the performers and jazz-age material that the film became a Francis Coppola film, an auteur film, inasmuch as any big-budget Hollywood film can be dominated by a single individual. However, with *Peggy Sue Got Married* (1986) and *Gardens of Stone* (1987), Coppola's involvement seems much less passionate, perhaps even perfunctory. In his own words:

*Peggy Sue*, I must say, was not the kind of film that I normally would want to do. The nature of my debts is that I have to make gigantic (annual) payments in March, millions of dollars, And so when the time starts getting closer to the payment and I'm looking around saying what should I do, the project that was ready to go and that wanted me was *Peggy Sue*. And at first, I felt the script—although it was okay— was just like a television show. . . . I was very reluctant to do it and finally did it because Fred Roos, who has great taste, said it would be successful.[1]

Although later Coppola characteristically found more in the film to interest him, the motivations for doing the film were of financial retrenchment. Earlier in his career he was able to bargain off one film for another, e.g., *Finian's Rainbow* for *The Rain People*. At this juncture, due to the extravagant personal debts incurred in Omni-Zoetrope's demise, the ante had been upped and instead of a one-for-one exchange, a series of films were needed to settle the balance. In the same period Coppola was doing short films for large director's fees: *Rip Van Winkle* for Shelley Duvall's Fairy Tale Theater and *Captain EO* for George Lucas and Walt Disney productions, a 17-

minute, 3-D special effects exercise featuring Michael Jackson. Coppola told Gene Siskel that at the worst point the debt had been $50 million and that: "My home was part of the collateral, and I suppose I could have taken the easy way out and declared bankruptcy. But I wasn't brought up that way. So I worked my way back as a professional journeyman director to where I currently owe only $5 million" (October 5, 1986).[2] Citing personal upbringing as a rationale for paying back such an enormous debt to such an enormous bank has a certain grotesqueness about it. Can we reconcile the conscience-stricken, middle-aged Coppola with the young, revolutionary Coppola who had talked of subverting the Hollywood system to make personal films? In recent interviews he seems chastened, ready to do penance, weary of the present, taking no umbrage with journalists' suggestions that an inflated ego had caused his demise. The Machiavellien, ends-versus-means strategy of Coppola's earlier career looms less prominently in the 1980s. Survival and professional respectability seem more paramount.

### Peggy Sue Got Married

Coppola's relatively low level of involvement with *Peggy Sue* was a moot point with the marketing of the film and the media's reception of the film. It was treated as any other Coppola film. Print ads displayed in large boldface a blurb from Siskel and Ebert's television show: "Francis Coppola has made a classic." The ads were heavy with critical quotation, including Rex Reed observing: "It's Francis Coppola's best film since *The Godfather*." A number of reviewers looked for inappropriate thematic links back to films such as *The Godfather* or *The Conversation*. One reviewer even posed the film as an allegory of Coppola the director at a troubled point in his life looking back into his own past for the cinematic magic that would help him understand his current dilemmas.[3]

In the exhibition and the reception of the film we see once again that the director of a Hollywood film is both a commodity in how the film is sold and a signifier in terms of how the film is apprehended and distinguished by the critical apparatus as well as by the general public. Both practices inevitably obscure Coppola's more routine function on this film and perpetuate a myth of personal vision in Hollywood filmmaking that is more relative than is ever acknowledged.

Close inspection of the working draft of the script by Arlene Sarner and Jerry Leichtling, dated December 2, 1984, reveals that if there is personal vision at issue with this film, then it is the largely unheralded fledgling screenwriters' vision. I will explore differences between Sarner and Leichtling's script and the final film that suggest a Coppola touch, but the overall success or failure of the film resides more with the two screenwriters' initial concept or conceit than it does with Coppola's direction or Kathleen Turner's acting. Turner and Coppola's contributions were creative and professional. But the point is we are not in auteur territory with *Peggy Sue Got Married*, however entertaining the film finally is or whatever similarities it may have to other Coppola films. We cannot categorically ascribe whatever is in a film to its director.

The project got its impetus when Sarner and Leichtling, a husband/wife team, contacted producer Paul Gurian in July of 1983 with a 50-page outline. Chronology is important because the eventual film bore some similarities to another time travel film, *Back to the Future*, which had opened in the summer of 1985. Gurian later charged, probably erroneously, that Steven Spielberg had put the Michael J. Fox film on "go" after hearing of Gurian's production.[4] The production of *Peggy Sue* was delayed due to a director shuffle—Jonathan Demme to Penny Marshall to Coppola—and an injury to the originally planned star, Deborah Winger. Robert Zemeckis and Bob Gale had worked on the original script of *Back to the Future* in the late 1970s. Chances are that any coincidences between the two productions owe more to a general cultural nostalgia that lights on the time-travel genre as an appropriate vehicle for its exploration than to any overt idea theft.

As with *Back to the Future*'s story of a teenager going back to meet his parents at a younger age, *Peggy Sue* has a catchy premise: a middle-aged woman going through a divorce mysteriously goes back to her senior year in high school to confront the seeds of her present discontent. Whereas Michael Fox's journey has its outward rewards (he turns his parents into yuppies in the present), Peggy Sue's gain is more inward: she comes to understand both herself and her adulterous spouse better, and the end hints strongly at a reconciliation between the two. Both films rely heavily on gags about the present versus the past. However, whereas Michael Fox is rather dumbfounded with a past that contains no twist-off soda bottles and quaint rock music, *Peggy Sue* trades heavily on a more universal theme of the wisdom of experience versus the arrogant assurance of youth.

The film is a full-scale rendition of the universal fantasy, "If only I knew then what I know now." Ultimately, that fantasy is contradicted, as Peggy Sue does not change much about her past. After a struggle, she still falls for the romantic wooings of young Charlie. However, her understanding of her own past does change. The moralistic theme of wisdom gained through reflection on the past was endearing to baby boomers now facing middle age. Thus, while *Peggy Sue* did not come close to *Back to the Future*'s box office success, it did help put Tri-Star up with the major studios. It was widely viewed as a *Back to the Future* for adults, and Kathleen Turner received an Oscar nomination for her performance.

## Script Changes

Key participants on *Peggy Sue* have observed that the major inflection Coppola put on Sarner and Leichtling's script was that he de-emphasized the gimmicky time travel humor and strengthened the emotional quality of the script. This is evident in the December 2, 1984, script's differences from the film.[5] The original script focuses heavily on Peggy Sue's ability once into 1960 to capitalize on the 1980s knowledge of oncoming technological development. In a lost subplot, the beatnik Michael Fitzsimmons' capitalist father brazenly steals an idea from her for the benefit of his company. The original script establishes Peggy Sue's father as a male chauvinist and a poor money handler. This sets up Peggy Sue's new feminist approach as a potential rescue for the family. She's also effecting some consciousness-raising for her mother. The original script strongly links personal liberation with financial independence.

The film tones down the preoccupation with money. Although it might seem that some of the corresponding feminist analysis is lost, other changes compensate. Nicolas Cage's Charlie is better developed in the final film. A scene is added where Charlie tells Peggy Sue he wants to date other girls and "comparison shop," fully expecting her to burst into tears. The modern Peggy Sue throws it back in his face by promptly agreeing. There is a subtle hint in this addition that Peggy Sue was unknowingly complicit in Charlie's eventual womanizing by her original failure to stand up to him.

In the same vein, the film develops more fully Charlie's failed career aspirations, which lead to his unhappiness and womanizing in the present. This results in more of a sense that Peggy Sue's time journey is not just a discovery of herself but also a discovery of her husband as well. The 18-year old Peggy Sue had no idea of the extent of Charlie's aspirations; the 43-year old Peggy Sue sees this failure as a key to her husband's pathology. The added scene that is key to this perspective is when Peggy Sue sees Charlie singing with a Black R&B group and then being turned down by a recording agent. (Oddly, although this is Peggy Sue's fantasy, she isn't present at the meeting with the agent.)

The Richard Norvik/inventor character (Barry Miller) is toned down in the final film. In the script he is more sexually interested in Peggy Sue with a gag scene where he hypnotizes her and has her take her blouse off. The film confines Peggy Sue's sexual exploration to the Michael Fitzsimmons beatnik character. One deletion in the sequence between Michael and Peggy Sue missed an opportunity to make the film more relevant to the AIDS/safe sex generation. In the script, prior to the sexual encounter with Michael, Peggy Sue goes to a 1960 gas station's men's room and buys a package of condoms. Apparently it was determined that this made Peggy Sue too cold-blooded or anti-romantic and the scene was eliminated, but it would have made an interesting scene, particularly as the character's early marriage was the result of an accidental pregnancy. (One can only imagine the sort of comic inflection an actress such as Turner would have lent to the action.) The film showed less timidity in including a scene in which Peggy Sue and Michael smoke marijuana and a scene in which two contemporary characters use cocaine, this despite recent Hollywood paranoid about the depiction of drug usage.[6]

Coppola conducted his characteristic two weeks of videotaped rehearsals prior to production, which resulted in some dialogue changes and added bits of business as well as strong acting performances. Kathleen Turner does give a fine, intelligent rendition of the character. The star persona Turner brought to the role from films such as *Body Heat, Romancing the Stone,* and *Prizzi's Honor* was unprecedented for a female actress in any previous film directed by Coppola. The success of the acting performance suggests Coppola in dealing with actors has a wider range than the violent, male-bonding films that have made his reputation. Nicolas Cage's performance as Charlie is a striking juxtaposition with Turner's, as he was eleven years younger than she and did not have her celebrity. His acting style is more ostentatious and mannered, a sort of neo-method acting, which makes it both abrasive and at times more interesting. Some reviewers were put off by the high-pitched voice he affected, others felt he captured the awkwardness and hypersensitivity of a 1960 "teenager in love." The overall casting had a typical Coppola flair with Hollywood veterans Maureen O'Sullivan, Leon Ames, John Carradine, as well as his own daughter Sofia as Peggy Sue's younger sister.

In general, despite shifts in tone and emphasis in the performance element, the final film is fairly close to the original script. Scenes with affecting emotional nuance such as the scene where Peggy Sue talks to her dead grandmother on the telephone, are played substantially as written.

Coppola did put a visual signature on the film that was much remarked upon. This was the use of similar mirror shots at both the beginning and end of the film, in effect creating bookends. In the opening shot, we see Peggy Sue in the mirror as she prepares for the high school reunion. The shot pulls back behind her as her daughter enters. Although it is a large mirror and we should be able to see the camera from our angle, the camera seems invisible. Coppola arranged the shot with the choreographed actions of doubles to give the impression of a mirror. In the same manner, at the reconciliation scene at the end, as Peggy Sue invites Charlie over for strudel and the daughter enters again, we view the action through another ersatz mirror. The obvious interpretation of such a marked device would be that Peggy Sue's journey is a sort of Lewis Carroll, through-the-looking-glass experience. However, it seems more than coincidental that mirror shots also dominated *The Rain People.* In that film, we saw Natalie's vampish seduction of Killer almost totally in mirrors. Only when she realizes the impossibility of her fantasy sexual encounter do we see the two characters outside the mirror. By considering the two films together, it would seem that mirror images suggest women's real self out of contact or at odds with a socially constructed self. In the first mirror shot in *Peggy Sue,* we see a television image of Charlie as the 1985 Peggy Sue puts on a 1960 prom dress. She expresses anger at Charlie and the dissolution of their marriage, while the daughter tries to minimize the strife. That Peggy Sue still fits into that 1960 dress and that Charlie is only as real as a television image in this scene take on abstract metaphorical connotation. In the course of the film, Peggy Sue must come to terms with how similar she is to her 1960 self and whether she knows the real Charlie. The daughter's presence in the two scenes suggests both that it is the consideration of family that must effect the reconciliation and that the daughter has achieved wisdom from her mother's experience. The daughter is involved with a musician, just as her mother once was. A connotation of sisterhood is strengthened by the fact that Coppola pretty much dropped the character of Scott, the son, from the original script. Such camera work as these mirror shots was complicated, well-conceived, and not indicated in the original script.

The level of meaning and nuance such devices bring to a film do suggest a type of authorship on Coppola's part with this film. Although Coppola's authorship is, as we have seen, problematic with *Peggy Sue*, there is also a certain responsibility in saying yes or no to a project. The introspection and distinctions made about what is and isn't a Coppola film in this study are of no value to the world in which Coppola makes his career. It is a world where the financial success of the last project is more of a consideration than the degree of authorship the director lent to the final results. Once Coppola says "yes" and does a project, it is forever wedded to his name within the industry. If he loses his power to originate projects of his own choosing, then projects presented to him are dependent on the track record of subjects he has treated in the past. The decision to do *Peggy Sue*, even in a limited authorial role, represents Coppola's careerist determination to break out of the stereotype of male-bonding, action spectacles with which he was becoming associated.

As such, it is interesting that the feminist issues treated in *Peggy Sue* and their resolution bear some striking similarities to those in Coppola's own personally scripted film, *The Rain People*. Both films frame troubled married women searching for an identity apart from husbands. Both films finally come down in favor of family responsibility outweighing personal exploration: in *The Rain People*, as Killer is dying, Natalie promises him that he can come and live with her and her husband. They would be a family, and it seems that Natalie's running from responsibility has led to Killer's death, a loose allegory for the abortion she is considering. Likewise, in *Peggy Sue* just before the moment that Peggy Sue gets pregnant in the greenhouse, Charlie woos her with the locket that will contain pictures of their children. Both films seem to suggest that while relationships with men may be oppressive to personal freedom, children and family are a higher value. Similarly, in the Coppola-scripted section of *Godfather II*, the ultimate threat to Michael Corleone was not Hyman Roth, but Kay's abortion and destruction of his family.

The script of *The Rain People* was generated out of Coppola's imagination and personal experience. *Peggy Sue* seems to represent Coppola more in that he refused to alter it than that he added fresh vision to the project. A ticklish distinction, but the criticisms made of Coppola and *Peggy Sue* seem to apply equally well to *The Rain People* and would seem germane to a consideration of Coppola's career and films.

The leading leftist film journals in the United States, *Jump Cut* and *Cineaste*, ran review/critiques of *Peggy Sue* with Marxist/feminist perspectives. Both reviews depend heavily on analysis of *Peggy Sue*'s ending. If, as it seems, Peggy Sue is taking back her philandering husband, then as Roberta Pearson puts it: "Peggy Sue has learned nothing from her bizarre experience. She still cannot reject the myth of romantic union with which Charlie immediately recapitulates."[7] I argued earlier that Peggy Sue comes through the time journey to understand her husband's need for philandering as an expression of his own career dissatisfaction, which she had ignored. Still, taking him back should be conditional on some sort of new awareness on Charlie's part, which isn't forthcoming in the film. We only see Charlie's remorse and apology. The larger imperative in the end seems to be that the marriage be re-established and that Peggy Sue begin again making strudel, the symbol of her family's historic strength.

Both reviewers note that Peggy Sue's time travel is purely a personal journey. Bob Bartosch observes: "Peggy Sue uses her knowledge of the future to make money and to make her personal life better, not to warn Martin Luther King against being in Memphis on April 4, 1968; or to tell people that Nixon is a crook; or to speak up about the lies being told about Vietnam and what the eventual toll would be."[8] The film does not really take on the question of whether individuals can effect social change, and that may not be appropriate for the fantasy genre in which this film operates. But ultimately there is a certain hedonism in the way Peggy Sue decides to experience the past, an 1980s hedonism. Peggy Sue decides that since she must be dead, she will have a good time about it, and proceeds to hit the liquor cabinet and tell off authority figures. Do the values of the 1950s finally wear down Peggy Sue and prepare her to re-accept Charlie? Bartosch notes that the values of the current political Right are congruent with a return to the 1950s, and explains:

The film's anti-divorce, pro-marriage, "pro-family" stance reflects the current attempt to reassert marriage and "family values" in the face of the historical decline/disintegration of those institutions. Indeed, all elements of the film's ideological project mirror the agenda of the radical Right, the "Moral Majority." This agenda includes the "New Patriotism" (Peggy Sue's impassioned "My Country 'Tis of Thee"), the backlash against the women's movement (Phyllis Schlafly and the defeat of the ERA), and the acceptance of sexual expression and activity only in a marital and procreative context. The reactionary politics of this film reflect the political swing to the right of the Reagan era. Indeed, the 1950s is precisely where Right would like to take the country back to, wiping out twenty-five years of social change.[9]

Bartosch suggests that the film may ultimately have a positive social effect in that audiences may overlook the didacticism and be engaged by how the film "depicts a woman's desire to be free of oppressive social structures." In a less politicized, but still feminist-oriented review in *Ms.*, Susan Dworkin came to roughly the same conclusion. Dworkin felt it was an "almost-wonderful new film," and that it "doesn't pay to dwell on the less-than-wonderful parts," namely the final fifteen minutes.[10]

This brings us straight back to the final problem of *The Rain People* as well. With that film, Coppola admitted his problems with finding an ending appropriate to the questions posed by the narrative. With both *Peggy Sue* and *The Rain People*, we feel strongly women's revolt against cultural roles imposed by our society. Yet the endings seem feeble and overly melo-dramatic. Coppola's intuitive feel for women demonstrated by the bulk of the films is not served by his intellectual understanding of what has tran-spired, which is demonstrated by the poorly conceived endings. He falls too easily back on pat, conservative resolutions that serve the status quo and do a disservice to the depth of the rest of the film.

Coppola, talking about his 1980s production, mused: "The way that I look at my recent career is that I'm constantly storing up bits of knowledge from each film I work on to make better films in the future."[11] The problem with finding an appropriate ending to interesting films has dogged Coppola through earlier successes such as *Godfather II* and *Apocalypse Now*. High on the priorities for those better films of the future should be finding endings that are congruent with the depth of analysis in the preceding material.

### Gardens of Stone

In *Gardens of Stone* (set in 1968), when not referred to in expository dialogue, Vietnam exists visually as a series of washed-out video images of GIs suffering during the war: buddies drag wounded to a helicopter, close-up on pain and anguish. Although the footage was probably shot in 16mm, it is intentionally transferred to video and blown-up to evoke the experience of watching the war on TV. The bulk of the action of the film concerns stateside soldiers, the Old Guard unit, who are responsible for ceremonially burying the dead from Vietnam at Arlington Cemetery at a rate of about fifteen a day. Talk in bars and cocktail parties espouses different theories of what is occurring in Vietnam, but in movies the image usually outweighs the auditory, and the archival footage defines its own perspective on Viet-nam: no sense in trying to understand it beyond the visceral look of Amer-ican death and suffering.

Political scientists and media critics have debated whether with the presence of television America will ever be able to fight another sustained, difficult war. American will to prevail over Third World peasants seems to diminish with nightly television reports of American casualties reminding us of the human price of either being the world's policeman or a colonial aggressor, depending on your point of view. Far better to have a quick, splashy "success" such as the Grenada invasion, which is also forgotten quickly. *Gardens of Stone* assumes the knowledge that Vietnam was a mistake, we saw it on television, and throughout the text of the film the television clips serve as an index to that consensus view.

There is a certain integrity to such a perspective. Truffaut once said something to the effect that anti-war films that showed the war were contradictory because of the cinematic lure of an exploding bomb. Intellectually we may understand that *Apocalypse Now* or *Platoon* are anti-war, but it is still difficult to not be excited by a helicopter attack or a platoon being overrun by Viet Cong. In conception the idea of a film simply about the results of war—young men being buried—sounds like the perfect solution to the dilemma of how to frame an anti-war cinematic statement.

Unfortunately, the level of analysis of *Gardens of Stone* never seems to rise to the possibilities of the concept. The film concerns itself obsessively with military rites and rituals. Besides the omnipresent ritualized funerals, on the lighter side the film gives a long rendition of how a corporal gets his new stripes broken in, what an anal obsessive barracks inspection is like, how to get a proper spitshine on a boot, and so on. Yet none of the ritual is tied analytically to how and why the Vietnam War was fought. More ambitiously and audaciously, Peter Davis' *Hearts and Minds* posited links between such seemingly disparate subjects as how football was played in America and why we got into Vietnam. That film had a macroscopic, cultural view, which *Gardens of Stone* never attempts.

In the more microscopic view of *Gardens of Stone*, small men try to ponder why being in the army at this particular historical juncture is not the honor it was in wars past. Their only final solution to their anxiety and depression is to do their job as best as possible and to look out for their immediate comrades. In the penultimate scene, the protagonist grieves for a young friend killed in Vietnam, asks his anti-war girlfriend to marry him, and decides to go back to Vietnam to save other young Americans, about in that order. The movie eschews much of the political pontification of Nicholas Proffitt's source novel, in which the main character feels Lt. Calley was an innocent victim of circumstances, and that the finger should be pointed vaguely higher up.

A study of average men in an overwhelming national calamity could potentially make for interesting material. It certainly describes the historical situation of a number of individuals involved in the military and the Vietnam War. They had joined with a World War II sense of heroism and purpose and found those values suddenly outmoded. However, the film never seems to relate those new values to the society that changed them. There is an uncomfortable blindness in both the novel and the film in regard to how the rest of society felt about the war. In the pivotal scene, a peacenik, played by Bill Graham, approaches the war hero protagonist, Clell Hazard (James Caan), and obnoxiously challenges the sergeant to a fight by calling him a baby killer. Hazard responds by savagely beating the peacenik to within an inch of his life and then calling for an ambulance as he nervously walks away. Rather than dramatically resolving anything within the narrative, the scene instead trades on wish-fulfillment for the American warrior class: let's beat up these cowards. (In the novel, the scene provides a long-running rupture between Hazard and his girlfriend; in the film, she forgives him almost immediately.) The novel and movie both have the rather curious view that people best qualified to judge a war as a mistake are the military. The peacenik is poaching on Hazard's territory and deserves a thrashing.

With *Apocalypse Now*, we saw how Coppola had the good sense to tone down the militaristic, war-loving elements of Milius' original script and enhance its more visionary glimpses of war's surreal insanity. The overall impact was that many on the left, or anti-war, could agree or find insightful the content of the film, for example, the puppy/sampan scene, which Coppola added late in the narrative, that traded on an awareness of the My Lai massacre. With *Gardens of Stone*, Coppola made little effort to alter or mitigate any views in the novel. As with *Peggy Sue Got Married*, what results is a fairly straightforward transcription of the original writer's ideas.

In public rhetoric, Coppola claimed more affinities with the material than he had with *Peggy Sue*. In the Pressbook for the film he commented: "One of the things that touched me when I read the script was the drill and ritual that gives the Old Guard its splendor. There is a certain beauty and honor in being part of an exercise where hundreds of other people are performing the exact same drill in absolutely perfect harmony." (Shades of Busby Berkeley and Leni Riefenstahl!) In other interviews, he noted that one of the attractions for him was the sense that the script gave male soldiers emotions and feelings not characteristic of movies about the military. One wonders how to regard such an approach in an era of *Top Gun*, *Officer and a Gentleman*, *Stripes*, *Private Benjamin*, *Rambo*, and *Uncommon Valor*, which collectively have made military recruiting better than ever. J. Hoberman observed: "Coppola has jumped back on the militaristic bandwagon, tacking hard to the right and taking an unforgivably simplistic view of the 1968–69 period."[12] Yet in the same interview where Coppola praises the military for all the invaluable assistance they gave him on the movie, he comments that he is optimistic about the future because: "In the future it's not how much steel you make, it's how creative you are . . . once and for all this creative offensive is going to put the military down. The military is more part of the industrial age. We're entering the creative age"—reflecting his oft-stated view that we are moving toward a technological utopia.[13] If

Coppola sees no contradiction in making a film that glorifies military ritual even as he sees the military as a dying, repressive institution, then perhaps he has not progressed far from his 1974 comment that he had never attained a political sophistication because he was "too busy trying to make it." With the debts incurred by Zoetrope's demise, he is still trying to make it.

Still, there is an inflection on *Gardens of Stone* that is decidedly different from the pro-military films quoted above. As noted at the outset, it is an atypical anti-war film in that it never makes war visually exciting. Even as it seems pro-military in the loving depiction of male bonding and camaraderie expressed in elaborate ritual, it never gives serious credence to the gung-ho ideas of young Willow (D. B. Sweeney). This character plays the surrogate son figure to James Caan's Sgt. Hazard and is full of ideas such as "the right soldier in the right place can change the world." He feels it is his destiny to be a soldier/warrior. Ultimately, however, his zeal is naive, immature, and gullible, and despite Hazard's efforts to dissuade him from going to Vietnam, he gets himself unheroically killed and leaves a young widow. This is hardly the sort of material to make an impressionable 18-year-old run to a recruiting office. While most of the current pro-military films trade on macho, nonconformist, rebellious heroes epitomized in Tom Cruise's "Maverick" in *Top Gun*, *Gardens of Stone* casts a benign view toward authority and world-weary experience as embodied in Caan and Sgt. Major Goody Nelson, played by James Earl Jones. Nor are these "lifers" the sort of crusty, tougher-than-thou D.I.s, most recently played by Clint Eastwood in *Heartbreak Ridge*. In one scene Goody rather comfortably sits behind his desk doing paperwork.

No doubt the somber perspective had to do with the film's dismal box office performance. While the film received heavy media coverage due to James Caan's emergence from a five-year retirement to work with Coppola and Angelica Houston's first major film since *Prizzi's Honor*, it faded from sight quickly and got mostly negative notices. Not a few critics speculated that the leaden tone of the film had to do with Coppola's son, Gian-Carlo, a crew member, being killed in a boating accident during the production. The Chapel where the service was held for young Coppola was the same used for the scene in which Hazard visits the body of Jackie Willow, his surrogate son. Coppola continued working on the film the day after the accident as therapy for his grief.

## Proffitt's Novel

The original novel *Gardens of Stone* appeared in 1983.[14] Proffitt, a first-time novelist, had served in the Old Guard for three years and later did a stint in Vietnam as a war correspondent for *Newsweek*. As such, the novel is heavy on authentic detail, even as the prose has a journalistic spareness about it. The film is fairly faithful to the novel with one exception, the deletion of the novel's turgid sex scenes, which prompted a book reviewer to comment that it was a pseudo-James Jones pot-boiler. Perhaps it was screenwriter Ronald Bass's decision, but the move is similar to Coppola's clean-up of Puzo's *The Godfather*, where Coppola excised the material about Sonny's giant penis and other sexual matter. With *Gardens of Stone*, there is a problem in that without the sex scenes, the relationship between the war protestor/journalist Samantha Huff (Angelica Houston) and army sergeant Hazard becomes even less believable and more schematic. Whereas in *The Godfather* the toned-down sex had the impact of enhancing the themes of dynastic power, here the elimination merely makes the characters more one-dimensional. It seems to go along with a general diminishment of sexuality in 1980s, AIDS-aware Hollywood.

As with the film, Proffitt's novel is clearly in love with the military. All the civilian characters are inferior to the moral superiority of the military characters. Typical of this is a scene that got lost in the editing room and that leaves the film somewhat difficult to follow. In the novel, when Jack Willow's father dies, we follow Jack back to Harlan County for the funeral. Jack is so disgusted with the lack of proper respect for the dead and ceremony in the civilian funeral that he decides to take the body back to Arlington for another service and burial military style. In the film we merely learn the father has died and then Jack asks Hazard if he can change his mind and bury him in Arlington; the request seems odd and the father's death unmotivated. The film confines its contempt for civilians to the scene where Hazard punches out Bill Graham's peacenik. The following scene with Graham in the hospital with his jaw wired shut drew big laughs at showings I attended.

Proffitt's novel has a more complex narrative structure than the film with flash forwards to Willow's time in Vietnam, which is covered in some detail, and flashbacks to Willow's romance with his girlfriend in high school. Time and budgetary constraints must have limited this in the adaptation, but the film does start with Willow's funeral and a voice-over from Willow's corpse, a bit like William Holden's corpse talking to us at the beginning of *Sunset Boulevard*. However, in the film, Willow's experiences in Vietnam are only treated in a letter read by Hazard. As such, some of the power of watching the young war lover becoming totally disillusioned is lost in the film.

One of the central conceits of the novel, which appears more briefly in the film, is that the three main male characters, the two sergeants and Willow, share an avid love of military history. They quiz each other on key books going back to the Romans as if it were a doctoral exam. Proffitt's point is that within the military individuals exist apart from the usual anti-intellectual men-of-action we see in movies. These three would seem to be renaissance men; Caan has tastes in Persian rugs and gourmet cooking, Goody talks about Kabuki theater. Still, breaking stereotypes is one thing, stretching credibility by multiplicity is another. As J. Hoberman acidly observed: "Like Donald Duck's nephews, Caan, Jones, and Sweeney appear to have one mind."[15] Personally, I would rest easier if I knew the military were full of such educated, reflective individuals, but I remain unconvinced.

A number of critics felt the film was not so much a new vision of the army as a dress-up of older genre vehicles. Several mentioned Victor McLaglen as a prototype for the good-hearted sergeant always ready for a barroom brawl. However, although there is a scene in which the three soldiers go to a bar, get involved in a fight, and come home drunk, Coppola cuts away from the fight itself. A scene that plays longer is the dinner party with the two sergeants and their girlfriends. Coppola spends more time on the character's cooking virtuosity than on prowess with fisticuffs.

It results in a very low-key performance from Caan. Characteristically, the film does not show when Caan receives the news of Jackie's death. We'd expect a tight close-up and an eruption. Instead, other characters learn of the death and then go to see Caan already in progress with a rage in which he destroys furniture. The restrained soft-voiced Caan is more in the vein of *The Rain People* or *Hide in Plain Sight* than *The Godfather* or *Thief.* Probably the most interesting performance of the film is James Earl Jones, who steals every scene he's in with an imperial, scathing mirth about the absurdity of existence. D. B. Sweeney as Willow is uncharismatic and hollow, and Angelica Houston's part is trimmed too violently from the novel. The ensemble as a whole does not seem to sparkle the way it did with *Peggy Sue Got Married.*

*Gardens of Stone*'s problems at the box office and critically were more of its own making than the coincidence of its release against *Platoon*, which along with the subsequent *Full Metal Jacket* were turning the nation's mind back toward Vietnam. Both *Garden of Stone* and *Peggy Sue Got Married* suggest Coppola in a holding period, waiting for his financial troubles to abate so that he would again initiate his own projects and exert the care and consideration more characteristic of his earlier productions.

As a final note on the "auteurship" of *Gardens of Stone*, it seems the military exerted considerable influence with the film, even as they gave key production support, including locations and extras. Columnist Jack Anderson reported that prior to script approval, the Army made more than forty complaints about the acceptability and veracity of the story. A negotiating session was arranged and: "The moviemakers agreed to rewrite 'the funeral and interment scenes with drunken widow,' and were asked to make 31 other concessions to the Army censors. Three weeks later, the Army approved the revised script. Three months later, Coppola was made an honorary member of the Old Guard."[16] Certainly Coppola has been forced to make larger compromises in his long, distinguished career. The latest example only serves to remind us of the inescapability of such considerations in the medium of Hollywood film and the care with which we should judge one individual's impact on that medium.

## NOTES

1. Rita Kempley, "Francis Coppola and the Creative Bond," *Washington Post*, May 8, 1987, pp. D1, D9.

2. Gene Siskel, "Celluloid Godfather," *Chicago Tribune*, October 5, 1986, Section 12, p. 4.

3. Ron Rosenbaum, "All-American Dream-girl," *Mademoiselle*, December 9, 1986, pp. 193, 232.

4. Joseph Gelmis, "*Peggy Sue* May Help Put Coppola Back on the Top," *Times-Picayune*, October 12, 1986, p. N1.

5. During early 1985, Coppola was involved with post-production on *The Cotton Club*, which premiered in December of 1985. *Peggy Sue* was shot in early fall 1985.

6. On this subject, see Marc Cooper, "Up in Smoke," *American Film* 12, no. 5 (March 1987), 53–56.

7. Roberta Pearson, "Peggy Sue Got Married," *Cineaste*, 15, no. 3, (1987), 47.

8. Bob Bartosch, "And Invited Charlie to Dinner," *Jump Cut*, 32 (April 1987), 4.

9. Ibid.

10. Susan Dworkin, "Back to the Future for Grown-ups," *Ms.*, November 1986, p. 17.

11. Siskel, p. 5.

12. J. Hoberman, "Apocalypse Then," *Village Voice*, May 19, 1987, p. 58.

13. Rita Kempley, "Francis Coppola and the Creative Bond," *Washington Post*, May 8, 1987, p. D1, D9.

14. Nicholas Proffitt, *Gardens of Stone* (New York: Carroll and Graf, 1983).

15. J. Hoberman, p. 58.

16. Jack Anderson, "Coppola Bows to the Army," *San Francisco Chronicle*, July 15, 1987, p. 47.

# 11

## *Conclusion*

The real truth is that I've always wanted to be a writer who wrote original material for the screen and it takes a year at least, certainly eight months to write original material. So I never had a chance to do that and was always forced to go with projects that already had scripts. So from that standpoint, I did not get to do my aspiration. But maybe now that I no longer have that debt I can go more in the direction that I want to do.[1]

I would like to pass on to another job classification. I would like to be a kind of—I don't have a name for it, so I can only toss out some funny names for it—but I would like to be like a chromakey novelist.. . . . I want to basically pick up not with the great filmmakers but with the great thinkers and novelists who were my brother's interests: Joyce, Thomas Mann, etc. And to try to write a novel. But instead of it being a novel on the written page, it would be written in cinema.[2]

In discussing Francis Coppola as a "Hollywood auteur," I am aware of the irony such a signification connotes. As suggested in the introduction to this study, the auteur theory has fallen into critical disfavor and polemical dead-ends. While the mass media have created an unprecedented hagiography of director celebrities, academic film study has swung away from auteur studies more toward cine-structuralism. That orientation in its many guises posits film as a sociopsychological construct in need of deconstruction to understand the viewer's complex interaction with the images that dominate our culture. Focus on the originator of the text in the auteur tradition is now seen as overly Romantic in its deification and mystification of the creative individual, which comes at the expense of understanding the larger nexus of systemic influences and constraints that govern the artistic text.

This book comes as a full-length examination of the viability of the auteur theory when subjected to the scrutiny of an auteur versus the original sources of films, the many collaborators, the commercial influences, the expectations of the system, and the personal limitations of the auteur. Perhaps to the point of redundancy I have emphasized factors that mitigate the myth of overriding personal vision in a Hollywood film, with Coppola's career as a case in point. At one point I was told that this project might offend the very people that would be naturally attracted to it. The myth of the auteur dies hard. Yet while this may be read as a fullscale debunking of the possibility of a Hollywood auteur, at the end I find myself experiencing something like a Kirkegaardian leap of faith in a new appreciation of the value of the auteur theory.

If we can look at one man or woman's career and as honestly as possible eliminate our own need for heroes, villains, father figures, or whatever, can we not reach some sort of truth about the system that governs that career? Perhaps in the courage and cowardice, the triumph and the defeat, we find in any individual's encounter with an omnipresent system, we finally arrive at a humanistic understanding of both ourselves and the art that gives us such enduring pleasure, in this case Hollywood film.

In the final analysis, I feel a great deal of compassion for this man I do not personally know, Francis Coppola. His public myth has evolved from an angry student revolutionary determined to change an ossified system to a middle-aged artist, wiser for his defeats, but still nurturing utopian dreams of a more uncompromised personal cinema, even within the strictures of Hollywood commercialism. That interpretation excludes others—for example, that Coppola has become what he initially rebelled against—but this study has not turned a blind eye to those interpretations. Perhaps celebrities and historical personages are finally constructs of their biographers, of which Coppola will have many. But it seems the most useful material we will take from this particular auteur is both tragic and optimistic.

As we examine Coppola's career at this writing, he has finally reconciled his enormous personal debt, said at one time to have reached $50 million. With the completion of *Tucker*, he has announced that he will take an indefinite leave of absence from filmmaking to gather his thoughts. *Variety* termed it a "sabbatical," perhaps appropriately for the filmmaker who once personified the college-trained filmmaker gone Hollywood.

The conception of *Tucker* as reported by Coppola in the news media already seems a compromise of the film Coppola intended to make in the 1970s. Coppola had initially conceptualized the piece as a Capraesque musical, celebrating ambition and entrepreneurship as it was revealed in a historical auto designer, Preston Tucker, who was ultimately crushed by the corporate system in Detroit in the late 1940s. Because of Coppola's inability to devote time to the project, as explained in the above quotation, he instead went to a period drama about Tucker, written by Arnold Schulman. In moving from the artifice of a musical to the realism of a period drama, it would seem that the vision of *Tucker* will be much darker, perhaps more reflective of Coppola of the 1980s than Coppola of the more optimistic 1970s.

In the time ahead Coppola seems determined to alter the course of his career, to pull out of the director-for-hire status of his films since *Rumble Fish*. In the second above quotation, he again reveals a dissatisfaction with the limitations of his current career, and it seems bound up in a frustration with the lack of seriousness and import in the popular culture with which his films are most closely associated. Rather than be a "movie brat," Coppola longs to travel in a circle of European intellectual artists—Joyce, Gide, Thomas Mann, and so on. His screenplay, *Megalopolis*, which he will work on following *Tucker*, will tell the tale of 24 hours in New York City with Catiline Rome as a backdrop, just as Joyce's *Ulysses* used Homer against modern Dublin. His theme will be utopia, an ambitious task in our cynical age.[3]

David Thomson spoke of *Apocalypse Now* as exhibiting the classic struggle of American art films, the struggle to be both "popular and profound."[4] *Megalopolis* will escape that requirement only if Coppola can reach his dream of films shot on non-prohibitive budgets as a result of state-of-the-art technology, or some fundamental changes occur in the American audience's taste for unconventional film. If Hollywood and its American audience has changed from 1967, when *You're A Big Boy Now* appeared, to the present, Francis Coppola has not stood by idly. It remains to be seen whether the unfulfilled dreams of the first half of his career are resolved in the new climate of the second half of his career.

## NOTES

1. Francis Coppola, radio interview for National Public Radio, August 29, 1987.
2. David Thomson and Lucy Gray, "Idols of the King," *Film Comment* (Sept./Oct. 1983), 270–271.
3. Thomson's interview gives more details of these plans.
4. David Thomson, *Overexposures* (New York: William Morrow, 1981), 290.

# Selected Bibliography

## Books

Adair, Gilbert. *Vietnam on Film*. New York: Proteus, 1981.

Alpert, Hollis, and Andrew Sarris, eds. *Film 67/68*. New York: Simon and Schuster, 1969.

Andrew, Dudley. *Concepts in Film Theory*. New York: Oxford, 1984.

Bach, Steven. *Final Cut*. New York: William Morrow, 1985.

Baker, Fred, and Ross Firestone, eds. *Movie People*. New York: Douglas, 1972.

Baxter, John. *Hollywood in the Sixties*. New York: Barnes, 1972.

Benedictus, David. *You're a Big Boy Now*. New York: E. P. Dutton, 1964.

Bluestone, George. *Novel into Film*. Berkeley: University of California Press, 1973.

Brady, John. *The Craft of the Screenwriter*. New York: Simon and Schuster, 1981.

Caughie, John. *Studies in Authorship*. Boston: Routledge and Kegan Paul, 1981.

Coates, Paul. *The Story of Lost Reflection*. London: Verso, 1985.

Cohen, Keith. *Film and Fiction: The Dynamics of Exchange*. New Haven: Yale Press, 1979.

Conrad, Joseph. *Heart of Darkness*. New York: Signet, 1950.

Coppola, Eleanor. *Notes*. New York: Simon and Schuster, 1979.

Eisenstein, Sergei. *Film Essays and a Lecture*. Winnifred Ray, trans. New York: Praeger, 1970.

————. *Film Form*. New York: Harcourt, 1949.

Ewen, David. *The Story of American Musical Theater*. Philadelphia: Chilton, 1961.

Farber, Stephen, and Marc Green. *Hollywood Dynasties*. New York: Fawcett, 1984.

Field, Syd. *Screenplay*. New York: Delta, 1981.

Frazer, James George. *The Golden Bough*. New York: Macmillan, 1951.

Gelmis, Joseph. *The Film Director as Superstar*. Garden City, NY. Anchor Press, 1970.

Greene, Stanley. *The World of Musical Comedy*. London: Barnes, 1974.

Herr, Michael. *Dispatches*. New York: Avon, 1978.

Hinton, S. E., *The Outsiders*. New York: Dell, 1970.

———. *Rumble Fish*. New York: Dell, 1975.

Hougan, Jim. *Spooks*. New York: William Morrow, 1978.

Jacobs, Diane. *Hollywood Renaissance*. New York: Delta, 1977.

Jacobs, Lewis, ed. *Introduction to the Art of Movies*. New York: Noonday Press, 1970.

Johnson, Robert. *Francis Ford Coppola*. Boston: Twayne, 1977.

Kael, Pauline. *Deeper into Movies*. New York: Bantam, 1973.

———. *Reeling*. Boston: Atlantic Monthly Press Book, 1976.

———. *When the Lights Go Down*. New York: Holt, Rinehart, and Winston, 1980.

Kauffmann, Stanley. *Before My Eyes*. New York:Harper and Row, 1980.

Kobal, John. *Gotta Sing Gotta Dance*. New York: Hamlyn, 1970.

Kolker, Robert. *A Cinema of Loneliness*. New York: Oxford University Press, 1980.

Kracauer, Siegfried. *Theory of Film*. New York: Oxford University Press, 1980.

Loeb, Anthony. *Filmmakers in Conversation*. Chicago: Columbia College, 1982.

Luhr, William, and Peter Lehman. *Authorship and Narrative in the Cinema*. New York: G. P. Putnam's Sons, 1977.

Madsen, Axel. *The New Hollywood*. New York: Crowell, 1975.

Mast, Gerald, and Marshall Cohen, eds. *Film Theory and Criticism*. New York: Oxford University Press, 1970.

Monaco, James. *American Film Now*. New York: Oxford University Press, 1979.

Munsterberg, Hugo. *The Film: A Psychological Study*. New York: Dover, 1970.

Nichols, Bill, ed. *Movies and Methods*. Berkeley: University of California Press, 1976.

Nicoll, Allardyce. *Film and Theater*. New York: Crowell, 1936.

Puzo, Mario. *The Godfather*. New York: G. P. Putnam's Sons, 1969.

———. *The Godfather Papers*. Greenwich: Fawcett, 1972.

Pye, Michael, and Lynda Myles. *The Movie Brats*. New York: Holt, 1979.

Ruppert, Peter, ed. *Ideas of Order in Literature and Film*. Tallahassee: Florida State University Press, 1980.

Sarris, Andrew. *The American Cinema*. New York: E. P. Dutton, 1968.

Schatz, Thomas. *Old Hollywood/New Hollywood*. Ann Arbor: UMI Research Press, 1983.

Smith, Cecil. *Musical Comedy in America*. New York: Theater Art Books, 1950.

Solomon, Stanley. *Beyond Formula*. New York: Harcourt, Brace, Jovanovich, 1976.

Suid, Lawrence. *Guts and Glory*. Reading, Mass.: Addison Wesley, 1978.

Thomas, Bob. *Marlon*. New York: Random House, 1973.

Thomson, David. *Overexposures: The Crisis in American Filmmaking*. New York: Morrow, 1981.

Wollen, Peter. *Signs and Meanings in the Cinema*. Bloomington: Indiana University Press, 1972.

Zuker, Joel. *Francis Ford Coppola: A Guide to the References and Resources*. Boston: G. K. Hall, 1984.

## Articles

Ablow, Gail. "Coppola's Ultimate Fairy Tale." *Videography*, April 1985, pp. 40–41.

Aigner, Hal, and Michael Goodwin. "The Bearded Immigrant from Tinsel Town." *City Magazine* (San Francisco), March 12–25, 1974, pp. 30–41.

Ambrogio, Anthony. " 'The Godfather, I and II' Patterns of Corruption." *Film Criticism*, 3, no. 1 (Fall 1978): 35–44.

Ames, Katrine, with William J. Cook. "Godfather III." *Newsweek*, July 21, 1975, p. 34.

Anonymous. "The Final Act of a Family Epic." *Time*, December 16, 1974, pp. 70–74.

———. "The Making of *The Godfather*." *Time*, March 13, 1972, pp. 57–58 +.

Baer, Randy C., and Christopher Baffer. "Grooming *The Godfather*." *Sight and Sound*, 44, no. 2 (Spring 1975): 83.

Blake, Richard. "Apocalypse Within." *America*, 141 (September 8, 1979): 96.

Bliss, Tony. "*Apocalypse Now*: Bonanza or Bomb?" *Soldier of Fortune*, 5 no. 2 (February 1980): 56–60.

Bock, Audie. "Zoetrope and *Apocalypse Now*." *American Film*, 4, no. 10 (September 1979): 55–60.

Braudy, Susan. "Francis Ford Coppola: A Profile." *Atlantic*, August 1976, pp. 66–73.

Buckley, Tom. "Getting a Bigger Bang at End of *Apocalypse*." *New York Times*, October 12, 1979, p. C6.

Bygrave, Michael, and Joan Goodman. "Meet Me in Las Vegas." *American Film*, 7, no. 1 (October 1981): 38–43 +.

Canby, Vincent. "The Heart of *Apocalypse* Is 'Extremely Misty.' " *New York Times*, August 19, 1979, pp. 2, 15B.

———. "*The Godfather Pt. II*: One *Godfather* Too Many." *New York Times*, December 22, 1974, pp. 11, 19.

Caughie, John. "Teaching Through Authorship." *Screen Education*, 17 (Winter 1975/76): 3–10.

Clark, Michael. "Dynamite, But It Never Hits Full Force." *Detroit Free Press*, October 12, 1979, p. 1B.

Coppola, Francis Ford. "Case Histories of Business Management: Hollywood Artistic Division." *Esquire*, November 1977, pp. 190–196.

———. "The Director on Content Versus Technology." *Washington Post*, August 29, 1982, p. 30.

———. "*Godfather, Part Two* (Nothing is a Sure Thing)." *City Magazine* (San Francisco), December 11–24, 1974, pp. 35–39.

Coppola, Francis, and Gay Talese. "The Conversation." *Esquire*, July 1981, pp. 78–87.

Cott, Jonathan. "Francis Coppola: The 'Rolling Stone' Interview." *Rolling Stone*, March 18, 1982, pp. 20–25.

Corliss, Richard. "Using Darkness to Bring Light to Cannes." *MacLeans*, June 11, 1979, pp. 47–48.

Cowie, Peter. "*The Godfather*." *Focus on Film*, 11 (Autumn 1972): 5–7.

Crawley, Tony. "Apocalypse Then, Now and Forever," in *Cinema 80*, David Castell, ed. London: Colibri, 1980.

Daly, Michael. "The Making of *The Cotton Club*." *New York*, May 7, 1984, pp. 40–62.

Dempsey, Michael. "*Apocalypse Now.*" *Sight and Sound*, 49, no. 1 (Winter 1979/80): 5–9.

Denby, David. "*8 1/2 Now*: Coppola's Apocalypse." *New York*, May 28, 1979, pp. 101–106.

———. "Hollow Movie." *New York*, August 27, 1979, pp. 87–89.

———. "The Two Godfathers." *The Partisan Review*, 43, no. 1 (1976): 113–118.

De Palma, Brian. "The Making of *The Conversation.*" *Filmmakers Newsletter*, May 1974, pp. 30–33.

Eagle, Herbert. "Film Genre/Genre film: Mutual Implications," in *Film: Historical–Theoretical Speculations*, Ben Lawton and Jaent Staiger, eds., pp. 29–32. Pleasantville, NY: Redgrave, 1977.

Edelman, Rob. "Viet Vets Talk About Nam Films." *Films in Review*, 30, no. 9 (November 1979): 539–542.

English, Deirdre. "The Dark Heart of *Apocalypse Now*: Telling It Like It Wasn't." *Mother Jones*, Sept./Oct. 1979, pp. 34–39.

Farber, Stephen. "Coppola and *The Godfather.*" *Sight and Sound*, 41 (Autumn 1972): 217–223.

———. "End of the Road?" *Film Quarterly*, Winter 1969, pp. 3–16.

———. "L.A. Journal." *Film Comment*, March/April 1975, pp. 2, 60, 62.

Gallagher, John. "John Milius." *Films in Review*, 32, no. 6 (June/July 1982): 357–361.

Geng, Veronica. "Mistah Kurtz—He Dead." *The New Yorker*, September 3, 1979, pp. 70–72.

Gomery, Douglas. "Review: *The Movie Brats.*" *Screen*, 21, no. 1 (Spring 1980): 15–17.

Goodwin, James. "Literature and Film: A Review of Criticism." *Quarterly Review of Film Studies*, 4, no. 2 (Spring 1979): 227–245.

Green, Marc. "Coppola Unleashes a Numbing *Apocalypse Now.*" *Books and Arts*, September 14, 1979, pp. 20–21.

Grobel, Lawrence. "*Playboy* Interview: Al Pacino." *Playboy*, December 1979, pp. 99+.

Hagen, William. "Review: *The Movie Brats.*" *Cineaste*, 11, no. 4 (1982): 54–55.

Haller, Scott. "Francis Coppola's Biggest Gamble." *Saturday Review*, July 1981, pp. 20–28.

Hartung, Phillip. "The Screen." *Commonweal*, November 1, 1968, p. 160.

Highham, Charles. "Director's Guild Winner: Francis Ford Coppola." *Action*, May/June 1973, pp. 8–11.

Hunter, Tim. "The Making of *Hammett.*" *New West*, September 22, 1980, pp. 31–46.

Jameson, Richard T. "Journals." *Film Comment*, May/June 1981, pp. 2–4.

———. "It Is, Too, Good." *Film Comment*, March/April 1985, pp. 51–53.

Just, Ward. "Vietnam: The Camera Lies." *Atlantic*, December 1979, pp. 63–65.

Kael, Pauline. "Fathers and Sons." *The New Yorker*, December 23, 1974, pp. 63–66.

Kauffmann, Stanley. "Coppola's War." *The New Republic*, September 15, 1979, pp. 24–25.

———. "*The Godfather Pt. II.*" *The New Republic*, January 18, 1975, p. 22.

Kennedy, William. "*Cotton Club* Stomp." *Vanity Fair*, November 1984, pp. 42–48+.

Kerr, Paul. "The Vietnam Subtext." *Screen*, 21, no. 2 (Summer 1980): 67–72.

Kinder, Marsha. "The Power of Adaptation in *Apocalypse Now*." *Film Quarterly*, 33, no. 2 (Winter 1979/80): 12–20.

Koszarski, Richard. "The Youth of Francis Ford Coppola." *Films in Review*, 19, no. 9 (November 1968): 529–536.

Latham, Aaron. "Francis Ford Coppola: The Movie Man Who Plays God." *Life*, August 1981, pp. 61–74.

LaValley, Albert J. "Loneliness: The Search for a Center in Recent American Film." *Quarterly Review of Film Studies*, 6, no. 2 (Spring 1981): 229–236.

Leonard, Terry. "The Major Stunts of *Apocalypse Now*." *Filmmakers Monthly*, 12, no. 10 (August 1979): 16–20.

Lindsey, Robert. "The New Wave of Filmmakers." *New York Times Magazine*, May 28, 1978, pp. 11–17+.

Macksey, Richard. "The Glitter of the Infernal Stream." *Bennington Review*, 15 (Summer 1983): 2–16.

Marcus, Greil. "Journey up the River: An Interview with Francis Coppola." *Rolling Stone*, November 1, 1979, pp. 51–57.

MacBride, Joseph. "Coppola Inc." *American Film*, November 1975, pp. 14–18.

McCormick, Ruth. "*Apocalypse Now*." *Cineaste*, 9, no. 4 (Fall 1979): 51–53.

McInerney, Peter. "Apocalypse Then: Hollywood Looks Back at Vietnam." *Film Quarterly*, Winter 1979/80, pp. 21–32.

McVay, Douglas. "*The Godfather Part Two*." *Film*, 28 (July 1975): 22.

Michener, Charles. "Finally, *Apocalypse Now*." *Newsweek*, May 28, 1979, pp. 100–110.

Milne, Tom. "*Finian's Rainbow*." *Sight and Sound*, 38, no. 1 (Winter 1968/69): 43–44.

Morgenstern, Joseph. "A National Anthem." *Newsweek*, February 20, 1967, pp. 96, 98.

———. "Paradise Lost." *Newsweek*, October 21, 1968, p. 88.

Mottley, Bob. "Two *Godfathers* Are Better Than One?" *New Times*, 2 (May 3, 1974): 54–57.

Murray, William. "*Playboy* Interview: Francis Ford Coppola." *Playboy* July 1974, pp. 53–68+.

Myles, Lynda. "The Zoetrope Saga." *Sight and Sound*, 51, no. 2 (Spring 1982): 91–93.

O'Brien, Tim. "The Violent Vet." *Esquire*, December 1979, pp. 96–104.

O'Toole, Lawrence. "Descent into Hell." *MacLeans*, August 27, 1979, pp. 34–38.

Onosko, Tim. "Media Madness." *Village Voice*, April 21, 1980, pp. 28–29.

Orth, Maureen. "Godfather of the Movies." *Newsweek*, November 14, 1974, pp. 74–76, 80.

———. "Watching the Apocalypse." *Newsweek*, June 13, 1977, pp. 57–64.

Palmer, William J. "*The Movie Brats*." *Film Library Quarterly*, 13, no. 4 (1980): pp. 5–13.

Peer, Elizabeth, with William Cook. "City Slickers." *Newsweek*, September 1, 1975, p. 42.

Pollock, Dale. "An Archival Detailing of UA's *Apocalypse Now* Since 1967 Start." *Variety*, May 23, 1979, p. 3+.

———. "Coppola the Artist: 'I Think I'm a Threat.' " *L.A. Calendar*, December 23, 1984, pp. 25–26.

Puzo, Mario. "Dialogue on Film." *American Film*, 4, no. 7 (May 1979): 33–44.

Pym, John. "*Apocalypse Now*: An Errand Boy's Journey." *Sight and Sound*, 49, no. 1 (Winter 1979/80): 9–11.

Reveaux, Anthony. "Stephen H. Burum, ASC, and *Rumble Fish*." *American Cinematographer*, 65 (May 1984): 52–56.

Rickey, Carrie. "Let Yourself Go." *Film Comment*, March/April 1982, pp. 43–47.

Rockwell, John. "My Own Little City, My Own Little Opera." *Saturday Review*, December 2, 1979, pp. 56–58.

Rosenbaum, Jonathan. "*The Godfather Part II*." *Sight and Sound*, 44, no. 3 (Summer 1975): 187–188.

Rosen, Marjorie. "Francis Ford Coppola." *Film Comment*, July/August 1974, pp. 43–49.

Ross, Lillian. "Some Figures on a Fantasy." *The New Yorker*, November 8, 1982, pp. 48–50+.

Sarris, Andrew. "The First Assault on *Apocalypse Now*." *Village Voice*, May 28, 1979, pp. 1, 47, 73.

———. "Heart of Coldness." *Village Voice*, August 27, 1979, p. 45.

Scheuer, Philip K. "On the Road with *The Rain People*." *Action*, January/February 1969, pp. 4–6.

Schelsinger, Arthur, Jr. "Coppola's Self-Appointed Epic." *Saturday Review*, January 5, 1980, p. 44.

Sharrett, Christopher. "Operation Mind Control: *Apocalypse Now* and the Search for Clarity." *Journal of Popular Film and Television*, August 1, 1980, pp. 34–43.

Siskel, Gene. "Coppola: America's Tilt-a-Whirl Director." *Chicago Tribune*, December 16, 1984, Section 13, pp. 7–12.

———. "Celluloid Godfather." *Chicago Tribune*, October 5, 1986, Section 13, pp. 4–5.

Stark, Susan. "Talia." *Detroit News*, May 28, 1982, p. 1D, 3D.

Suid, Lawrence. "Hollywood and Vietnam." *Film Comment*, October 1979, pp. 20–25.

Taylor, John Russell. "Francis Ford Coppola." *Sight and Sound*, 38, no. 1 (Winter 1968/69): 21.

Tessitore, John. "The Literary roots of *Apocalypse Now*." *New York Times*, October 21, 1979, p. 21D.

Thomson, David. "The Discreet Charm of *The Godfather*." *Sight and Sound*, 47, no. 2 (Spring 1978): 76–80.

———. "The Missing Auteur." *Film Comment*, July/August 1982, pp. 34–39.

Thomson, David, and Lucy Gray. "Idols of the King." *Film Comment*, September/October 1983, pp. 64–75.

Turner, Dennis. "The Subject of *The Conversation*." *Cinema Journal*, 24, no. 4 (Summer 1985): 4–22.

Valley, Jean. "Martin Sheen: Heart of Darkness, Heart of Gold." *Rolling Stone*, November 1, 1979, pp. 47–50.

Vogelsang, Judith. "Motifs of Image and Sound in *The Godfather*." *Journal of Popular Film*, 2, no. 2 (Spring 1973): 115–135.

Walters, Tim. "The Private Apocalypse of Francis Coppola." *Life*, June 1979, pp. 111–120.

Wells, Jeffrey. "Francis Ford Coppola/Part Two." *Film Journal*, 85, no. 1 (September 21, 1981): pp. 8–10.

Williams, Christian. "Coppola's New Terrain," *Washington Post*, August 29, 1982, p. 1D.

Yacowar, Maurice. "The Carpet-Baggers' Progress." *The Canadian Review of American Studies*, 10, no. 3 (Winter 1979): 379–386.

Yates, John. "*Godfather* Saga: The Death of the Family." *Journal of Popular Film*, 4, no. 2 (1975): 157–163.

Yurrick, Sol. "*Apocalypse Now*/Capital Flow." *Cineaste*, 10, no. 1 (Winter 1979/80): 21–23.

Zablotny, Elaine. "American Insanity: *Apocalypse Now*." *Film/Psychology Review*, 4, no. 1 (Winter/Spring 1980): 95–103.

Zimmerman, Paul. "*Godfather*: Triumph for Brando." *Newsweek*, March 13, 1972, p. 57.

————. "Godfathers and Sons." *Newsweek*, December 23, 1974, pp. 63–64.

Zurawik, David. "John Milius: The Writer as Warrior." *Detroit Free Press*, October 12, 1979, p. 1B.

Zewin, Mike. "On Set with *The Godfather*: Crime and Nostalgia." *Rolling Stone*, January 20, 1972, pp. 1, 6, 7.

# Index

## About the Author

JEFFREY CHOWN is an associate professor in the Communication Studies Department of Northern Illinois University. His courses include: Film Theory and Criticism, Narrative Screenwriting, and The Documentary Tradition, as well as seminars in Theories of Popular Culture and The Business of Film. He holds a Master's Degree in English Literature from the University of Oklahoma and a Ph.D. in American Studies from the University of Michigan. He has also written two full-length original screenplays.